Reshaping Social Life

Caught up in current social changes, we do not fully understand the reshaping of social life. In sociological analyses there is a conceptual gap between subjectivities and social structural processes, and we face real difficulties in understanding social change and diversity. Through analysis of key areas of social life, this book develops a new and exciting resource for better understanding our changing social world.

Reshaping Social Life breaks with conventional approaches and reconnects the subjective and objective. It develops a new conceptual and analytic perspective with social relationality, interdependence and social context at its heart. The new perspective is developed through grounded analyses of empirical evidence, and draws on new data. The book explores and analyses:

- Significant changes in family forms, fertility, gender relations and commitments to employment, children and care now, with comparisons with developments at the start of the twentieth century. The book develops new analyses of the meshing of norms and social relations in contexts of change.
- Diverse values, norms and perceptions of fairness. These are analysed with respect to diversity over the life course, and in respect of gender, ethnicity and social class. Through analysis of context, the book offers new insights, and tackles puzzles of explanation.

Reshaping Social Life offers a fascinating and innovative way of slicing into and reinterrogating our changing social world. It will become a landmark resource for students, scholars and researchers.

Sarah Irwin is Senior Lecturer in Sociology at the University of Leeds. Her research interests include family change, gender, employment, social difference and diversity and inequality and she has published extensively in these areas. Her last book, *Rights of Passage: Social change and the transition from youth to adulthood* (UCL Press), won the 1995 Philip Abrams Memorial Prize.

Reshaping Social Life

Sarah Irwin

LONDON AND NEW YORK

First published 2005
by Routledge
2 Park Square, Milton Park, Abingdon, Oxon OX14 4RN

Simultaneously published in the USA and Canada
by Routledge
270 Madison Ave, New York, NY 10016

Routledge is an imprint of the Taylor & Francis Group

Typeset in Sabon by
Keystroke, Jacaranda Lodge, Wolverhampton
Printed and bound in Great Britain by
TJ International Ltd, Padstow, Cornwall

British Library Cataloguing in Publication Data
A catalogue record for this book is available from the British Library

Library of Congress Cataloging in Publication Data
A catalog record for this book has been requested

ISBN 0–415–33937–5 (hbk)
ISBN 0–415–33938–3 (pbk)

To Emma and Beth

Contents

Tables

Acknowledgements

I am most grateful to all who have offered me support and encouragement in writing this book. A number of colleagues and friends have read and commented on draft chapters or related written work and I would like to thank Katrina Honeyman, Lorraine Harding, Malcolm Harrison, Kirk Mann, Jennifer Mason and Simon Duncan for their valuable comments and input. To Katrina also very special thanks for diversions and general moral sustenance. I am grateful to colleagues within the ESRC Research Group for the Study of Care, Values and the Future of Welfare. It has been a pleasure collaborating with them over recent years. Particular thanks to Jennifer Mason, Carol Smart and Simon Duncan for sharing data, and to Yasmin Hussain and Lise Saugeres who, as Research Fellows in CAVA, conducted interviews on which I draw in the book. Physical distance, fortunately, does not necessarily diminish social distance nor the exchange of ideas. Without Wendy Bottero this book would be all the poorer. She has helped me develop and shape my ideas and probably gave me the better ones in the first place. She read the entire manuscript and I thank her too for her valuable comments. Finally but importantly a very special thanks to Ian Jones for his enduring support and to our children, Emma and Beth. The book is dedicated to you.

1 Introduction

Recent theories of society and social change have become caught in a dilemma. A renewed focus on individual agency, on beliefs and values and on cultural processes falls short of any adequate specification of social structural process. Sociological researchers have often made a leap of faith between agency and structure, and between norms and concrete social relations. This book explores a range of areas, including the changing shape of gender, work and family, life course processes, ethnicity and class-related hierarchy. Within the literatures across all these areas there are problems of analysis due to a conceptual gap between normative processes and social structural processes. We need to reconnect the normative and social structural. This book tackles these analytic problems by treating evidence of a gap between norms and social relations as a puzzle of explanation, rather than as a feature of social systems. To move forward we need to renew our understanding of the nature of social structure, and construe it as a dynamic process in which norms play an integral part.

The latter decades of the twentieth century onwards have been characterised by marked changes across most domains of social life. There have been significant developments in family organisation and in the fabric of family life, and in ties of intimacy, interdependence, care and commitment more widely. There have been important changes in patterns of fertility, increasing childlessness, significant increases in divorce, a growing proportion of single parent households, cohabiting partnerships and independent living. There have been very marked increases in women's employment participation rates, particularly amongst those who have in modern times been least represented in employment: mothers of very young children. This trend is linked to a shift in the organisation of social reproduction, an erosion of breadwinner divisions of labour and a repositioning of women and men alongside changing assumptions about women's and men's proper roles. The period has seen a growing age exclusiveness of employment, an extension of the partial dependence of youth and a rocketing of educational participation rates, and increases in longevity and the time spent in retirement. The latter third of the twentieth century has also seen a significant growth in recognition claims and politics. There has been a growth in social movements and claims around gender, 'race' and ethnicity, sexuality and disability as dimensions of social inequality. There is a sense that status inequalities and related claims are more important in the current era than class-related claims. Although socio-economic inequalities in Britain increased through the 1980s and 1990s many have noted a demise of class-based solidarities and claims through the last quarter of the twentieth century and a seeming eclipse of the politics of redistribution by the politics of recognition. Questions of change lie at the heart of much current sociological research and theory. Many social scientists have sought to better understand contemporary experience and the processes underpinning and shaping social change. As we will see serious difficulties of explanation have ensued.

Materialist, structural analyses which held sway in the 1960s and 1970s came to be seen as static, deterministic and monolithic. Analysts were seen to make too many assumptions about the consequences of social position for determining consciousness and action, and further to read off individuals' and groups' interests from their social position. There has been a shift away from such analyses in part due to a sense of their narrow and exclusionary partiality and in part through an increased interest in the cultural bases of oppression and inequalities of recognition as well as material inequalities. Unease with the shortcomings of structuralist explanations led to new and important disciplinary departures, including what is commonly termed the 'cultural turn' in social sciences, and a newly important emphasis on norms, values, agency, diversity and difference (e.g. Hall 2000; Williams 1999; Roseneil 1995; Young 1990). The linked recent focus on agency, specificity and moral processes, and on issues of diversity and recognition, seemed to offer a more enabling route to exploring new forms of diversity, uncovering people's experience of that diversity, and to be in tune with newly significant expressions of misrecognition and cultural devaluation. Additionally, from a methodological perspective, an expansion of the use of qualitative methods contributed to the kinds of research questions being asked, as well as the ways in which they were asked, with a consequential focus on individual experience and proximate context. These developments allowed researchers not only to explore the texture of human experiences in a much more extensive way, but also to challenge some of the orthodoxies about the nature of those experiences.

Research into cultural processes has reaffirmed their central importance in social life. It is no longer possible to meaningfully discuss a material base and a cultural and normative superstructure. The 'stories we tell ourselves about ourselves' do not just circulate in people's heads, but make us who we are. For example, ideas about the nature of gender or age or ethnic identifications, and linked notions of social difference and competencies, shape social life in important ways. However, we are left with some significant problems of understanding and explanation. Why? Because new accounts face difficulties in specifying the social grounding and consequences of normative and cultural processes. For critics, the turn to agency has generated difficulties in locating action as *social* action (Walby 1992, 2001; Maynard 1994; Bradley 1996). This is a major gap in sociological understanding. What is required is an approach capable of capturing the central importance of normative processes, but doing so as part of a new theorisation of social structure, so the normative is not 'free floating' of the social contexts which give it meaning, but analysed as an integral part of such contexts. This would facilitate a more processual and dynamic account of structure.

In recent analyses there are a range of emphases and assumptions. In some, structure and norms do not tally, such as in individualisation theory, where norms appear to have become separated from any cohesive structural grounding. For other theorists structural analysis is out of favour since it is seen still to carry deterministic overtones, and researchers simply orient themselves away from structural issues. Elsewhere researchers still operate with a theoretical idea of social structure, arguing it is newly complex and diverse, and using it as a frame for empirical research, yet the focus on the particular is often not matched by an equivalent focus on general processes, so the light shed on structure is weak.

The absence of frameworks for analysing the articulation of value and social contexts has encouraged some new emphases. Recent research and writing has highlighted the importance of local cultural contexts, broader social contexts, and networks and their links to values and identities (e.g. Duncan *et al.* 2003; Duncan and Edwards 1999; Himmelweit 2002; Crompton and Harris 1998, on identifications and values relating to parenthood, commitments to work and care of children; Brubaker 2002; Jenkins 1997; Back 1996 on 'race' and ethnicity; Reay 1998a, b, c and Ball 2003 on class, dispositions and educational inequalities). Other writers have explored how values are 'grounded', worked out in practical engagements and social interactions (e.g. Williams 2004; Mason 2004; Smart *et al.* 2001; Finch and Mason 1993). This move to analysing the ways values are embedded in specific contexts, and relate to people's immersion in diverse reference groups and social practices, is a welcome and productive direction for research (e.g. Duncan *et al.* 2003; Walby 2001). Research which has followed this direction has generated a rich and detailed picture of complexity and diversity. There is, however, an important gap in research. We have no *general* understanding of the nature and patterning of values and of moral judgements. This cannot be furnished within current frameworks.

Part of the problem is that where structure is conceived as important it is typically presented in terms of the material grounds of social structural inequalities, and linked variation in the distribution of choice and constraint. However, this is a partial lens on social structural process. To advance our understanding it has become crucial to rethink structure.

There has been a growing interest in 'relationality' as an alternative metaphor which takes us beyond the stasis of older structural interpretations but also helps to *locate* social differences and agency. This is increasingly seen as a key area for development but has been theoretically under-developed.

It has become quite usual to hear sociological discussions of how social actors should be seen not as atomised or individualised, autonomous agents, but rather as embedded in social relationships, often in specific, proximate, contexts. This is not new as a sociological insight, indeed it is a core part of a sociological understanding and has been since its inception. However, relationality and context have been newly emphasised, perhaps, as a reaction against the perceived ascendance of individualising modes of explanation. It is crucial now to move beyond general statements about the importance of relationality and context, to develop concepts for analysing how social relations are configured. We need not just an expression of the importance of diverse contexts, but an ability to 'scale up', and make connections between the specificity of lived experience and the nature of social structural processes. We need to move between different levels of analysis with a sufficiently robust conceptualisation of how the particular and the general mesh. Recent research has been important in providing a nuanced picture of complexity and diversity. However, we need *new ways of describing and analysing the shaping (and reshaping) of complexity and diversity.*

The conceptual perspective developed here is built through a grounded analysis of empirical evidence. Components of the new conceptual approach are discussed in the latter part of Chapter 2. These components are operationalised and developed through analyses of diverse social domains in Chapters 3 to 8. One of the core themes which runs throughout is how to best analyse links between micro-level experience and perception and broader social processes. Frequently theorists make an analytic leap of faith between structure and agency. It is the under-researched 'middle', the social contexts of action within a differentiated social structure which require further analysis. The effective analysis of empirical evidence requires an adequate conception of how it fits within a bigger picture. The shape and salience of 'contexts' of social action is both an empirical and conceptual question. We need a more adequate specification of how individuals are located within the social structure and how their subjective experiences, perceptions and views provide core evidence, a lens on diverse parts of the system and not, necessarily, on the system as a whole. *The new perspective developed in the book is not intended as a definitive account of structure, but rather it offers a particular way of slicing into, and reinterrogating, our social world.* The perspective provides a new lens on social patterns, process and change. The first part of the book focuses on issues relating to social change, and the ways in which normative processes are integral to change in social structural relations. It does so through a focus on issues of gendered difference and interdependencies, and patterns of family, work and care, at the turn of the twentieth and of the twenty-first centuries. The processes are examined through evidence on the shaping of difference and interdependence across gender, and generational, groupings and its importance in transforming family relations and social and work identities. I also analyse new data, at the level of the individual, to further illuminate the mutuality of disposition, and position, in the current context of change. Questions of social change tend to crystallise explanatory difficulties, revealing them more clearly. The issues are tackled through analysis of diverse contexts of social action and of the reconfiguring of such contexts. The latter part of the book focuses on other dimensions of social differentiation: specifically age and the life course, 'race' and ethnicity and class-related hierarchy. Again, we find problems of explanation and unresolved difficulties arising from a gap between empirical evidence and researchers' analytic categories. In the chapters on life course, ethnicity and class I develop new analyses of how individual level perceptions and beliefs mesh with general social structural processes, and use empirical data to explore and analyse the salience of proximate social contexts as an important component of explanation. The overall argument offers a renewal of structural explanation, with cultural process and social relationality and interconnection at its heart. I detail the contents of each chapter below.

In Chapter 2 I argue that current conceptual developments in sociology have led to an impasse. A fascination with contemporary patterns of social change has not been matched by conceptual and analytic tools for its deciphering. I critically review two influential areas of debate, of individualisation and social difference, since they raise important issues and reveal problems of explanation which are tackled in the book. I then go on to outline a series of conceptual pointers, grouped under the heading social configuration, to develop an alternative perspective and help inform the development of the more grounded analyses of social life which lie at the heart of the book. Changing patterns of social difference and interconnection, and the ways in which they link with norms and subjective beliefs, and social contexts are core conceptual and analytical issues. The perspective breaks with the common separation between the structural and the cultural, and sees each as implicated in the other, mutually made and necessarily central to analysis of social diversity and social change. As such it provides an alternative to accounts of fragmentation of our social world, and analyses current social change as a complicated, but coherent, round of social transition.

In Chapter 3 I explore some important past historical developments in changing family life, and in the reshaping of gendered relations to work and care. These form a particularly interesting counterpoint to contemporary shifts in family life and employment. We can draw important lessons from the historical analysis of the dramatic transformations in fertility, family life and gendered divisions of labour at the end of the nineteenth century and early decades of the twentieth century. We can clearly see these transformations as part of a coherent round of restructuring. This is an important point since there is a tendency by analysts to interpret current transformations, which in some ways are less dramatic, as chaotic and not amenable to a conventional analysis. A sufficient understanding of past transformations reveals clearly the mutuality of subjective processes and altered conditions.

The contexts of social action changed and so too, then, motivations and choices. I explore explanations of the first fertility decline, and the importance there of a reconfiguring of difference and interdependence across gender and generation. In addition I explore the changing position of women and men, the link between gendered claims and emerging new social identities, and the tightening of gendered divisions of labour and linked norms about appropriate roles for women and men. The evidence reveals the mutual significance of norms and the social positioning of women and men in a time of change. This provides not just historical context but also insights of value for analysing current changes in gender, family and work

In Chapter 4 I explore recent, late twentieth-century changes in aspects of family life, including fertility decline, and changes in gendered relations to employment. Clearly the context is vastly changed from that which obtained a century earlier. Many interpret women's recent 'move' to increased rates of employment participation as being linked to marketisation. For theorists of individualisation the developments generate tensions in family affairs and shape demographic change. There are parallels with neoclassical theories of individual decision-making. However, rather than intepret changes in terms of marketisation and individualisation we can better understand them as components of a shift in the relative position of women and men, a restructuring of gendered relations and interdependencies. Altered motivations, choices and behaviours are inseparable from their contexts. Analysing changing patterns of difference and interdependence, and their links with changing values and motivational bases, provides insights into shifts in fertility and parenting decisions and patterns. As well as developing an analysis of important developments in family formation and decisions and actions around parenting, I explore changes in gendered, and especially women's, relations to paid work. Influential market models which imply women are now finding their 'true level' in employment, less hindered by cultural constraints, neglect the still socially embedded position of women and men. Indeed evidence shows that market processes exacerbate socially biased assumptions about labour force groups, and patterns of discrimination. Individualisation theorists get short shrift in feminist debates about change in gendered relations to work. Yet whilst there is a wealth of empirical evidence here, there is a shortage of general conceptual models through which to analyse change. I consider the changed context of women's employment through the post-war decades and recent debates which have evolved from a concern about gender inequality to a broader consideration of diversity and complexity. I argue that we are witnessing a pattern of gender re-differentiation, in part manifest through the erosion of the family wage system, and with different causes and consequences at the top and bottom of the income hierarchy. There has been a repositioning of gender and a shift in gendered patterns of interdependence. The altered context is partly made by, and partly itself makes, altered norms and expectations regarding gender, and a new diversity in the salience of gender.

Chapter 5 develops an analysis of change in gendered relations to work and care, and the changing place of work in women's, and men's, experiences and outlooks. It incorporates a micro level perspective and analyses the links between diverse social positions and dispositions, with reference to commitments to care and work amongst parents of young children. In it I look at these developments through the lens of attitudinal data, drawn from the British Social Attitudes survey, and with reference to new survey and qualitative data collected by the ESRC Research Group for the study of Care, Values and Future of Welfare (CAVA). The analyses challenge recent arguments of a discrepancy between values and subjective beliefs and social circumstances. Such conclusions follow from a mis-specification of social structural diversity. Discrepancies between social position and disposition tend to disappear when we have a more sufficient definition of position, indeed then we can see a very clear pattern of consistency between both. This is especially noteworthy in the context of ongoing social change in women's and men's patterns of employment, and of childcare. Dispositions and attitudes have not broken off from structural conditions, but rather reveal a pattern of coherence even in the midst of change. As well as coherence we see evidence of new kinds of expression of social identity amongst women, in which work identities are a more central part of many women's experiences even where they are parents of very young children. Drawing on the evidence of Chapters 4 and 5, we can say that whilst this is not general, it is increasingly widespread, and normalised.

Chapter 6 explores aspects of the life course, specifically youth and later life. A criticism of life course analysis is that it fails, paradoxically enough, to engage sufficiently with social change. This has been particularly a difficulty for studies of life course stages, and transitions between them, which tend to get separated out from broader social relations of interconnection and interdependence. Additionally some writers recently posit a disembedding of identities and perceptions from their social contexts. However, the evidence reveals a pattern of coherence between perceptions and social positioning, a pattern which is core to understanding social change. In much sociological literature on later life we see a clear emphasis on life course difference, as many seek to better locate later life and its disadvantaging. I argue that many writers here reinforce a notion of social difference as a consequence of their analytic categories. This pattern is evidenced in general descriptions of the positioning of later life, and also in recent discussions of older people's identities. Often metaphors and categories lead to a picture of older people on the margins of social structure. This reification of life course difference is unhelpful. It treats later life as homogeneous, exaggerates life course differentiation and works with an inappropriate metaphor of older people 'looking back' on the social structure. A presumed dissonance between perception and positioning is a feature, also, of some recent literature on youth. For some writers recent changes have exaggerated the gap between subjective perceptions and objective circumstances. A more sufficient theorisation of social change would locate subjectivities as part of a highly differentiated set of positions in the social structure. Recognising this coherence between perception and position allows a more convincing analysis of social change. Youth as a life course stage, of partial dependence and growing autonomy, has been significantly restructured over recent decades, a development bound in part up with changing patterns of interdependence across gender and generation in the reproduction of social life. Change in life course trajectories is a part of change in social relations more broadly.

Chapter 7 explores some key aspects of ethnicity and racism. There has been much interest recently in the discursive construction of difference, both in claims for recognition and in racist beliefs. There has been a good deal of emphasis on 'difference', and less on social differentiation, that is the processes which render difference salient, and shape it, or conversely, undermine such constructions. Part of the difficulty in developing such an analysis is the way in which theorists tend to assume the salience of categories of ethnic difference rather than seek to better understand how and why their salience varies across diverse contexts. Recently some writers have stressed the need to better understand the articulation of cultural constructions and extant social relations. Chapter 7 draws on new data and some key studies in seeking to advance understanding of this articulation. The chapter examines data on perceptions of belonging and difference, and identity, across different empirical studies focusing on the experience of Asian and African-Caribbean minority groups. The data provides different lenses on the salience of social contexts in shaping people's perceptions. Through the evidence we can see a central importance of concrete social relations as well as cultural belief, indeed the two are mutually made. Locating beliefs and attitudes about difference within contexts, including contexts of association and interaction, enables a much more nuanced picture of ethnicity and racism than do generalised accounts of difference and discursive constructions of imagined communities of difference. The sociological task is to understand when such imaginings hold purchase, and why.

Chapter 8 focuses on analyses of the link between perceptions and attitudes at the level of the individual and the general social order, with specific reference to socio-economic hierarchy, and perceptions of distributive justice and class. There is a long tradition of research into how and why people come to act on the basis of their social experience and position, and how this contributes to reproducing, or challenging, the social order. Failures of predictions based on presumed interests (say given by position in the class order) are part of the background to the recent growth of research into cultural difference and experiences of disrespect. For example, how are people positioned as different by more powerful others, and how is disrespect internalised or resisted? This emphasis on positioning and moral othering is significant in debates on cultural difference and recognition claims and recently this cultural interpretation has been accorded to class inequalities, with writers exploring how cultural disrespect and misrecognition is bound up with class. Whilst this is a welcome development in some respects there is a tendency for all evidence to be read in terms of moral evaluation. One of the difficulties of such approaches is that they operate with a sociologically depleted conception of the bases of perceived injustice, which are wider than experiences of disrespect. Further they operate with an inadequate conception of how individual experiences are embedded within particular social contexts. Runciman's conception of reference groups and social comparison processes offers a more helpful point of departure, helping conceptualise social contexts as the domain of relevance in people's experiences and outlooks. A consideration of empirical data on perceptions of distributive justice reveals ways in which 'what ought to be' is embedded in 'what is', or at least in perceptions of 'what is'. This is the case in perceptions of the overall system. It is also important in more proximate social interactions and meaningful reference points against which people tend to adjudge their own circumstances. To understand better how people see themselves and explore perceptions of fairness we need to conceptualise the social contexts, or social spaces, in which people make such judgements.

In Chapter 9 I review the core arguments presented through the book. It is often the case that theories of contemporary social life operate with a gap between norms and social relations. In recent theories this gap has come to be seen not as a difficulty of explanation but as a chronic feature of the system, and described in terms of fragmentation, or 'effaced' by ideologies of individualisation and responsibilisation, or acts of resistance. However, the gap is not a feature of the social system, but a product of deficient explanation. A more resourceful explanation lies in better conceptualising and analysing the mutuality of normative and social process. Such a move will allow us to better understand the shape, and reshaping, of social life.

2 Envisioning social landscapes of interconnection

2.1 Introduction

Remarkably perhaps, recent conceptual developments in sociology have drawn us away from a sufficient understanding of the social. Renewed interest in studies of cultural processes and social agency, and theoretical emphases, have frequently engendered difficulties in connecting new insights with older understandings of the importance of social structure in shaping human lives and experience. Thus values and norms appear often at least partly free-floating of the social. Within older understandings too, norms often appear as a distinct layer, separable from a material, structural 'base'. What is required is a reworking, so we can analyse the mutuality of the cultural and the social. This study presents an argument for conceptual development and does so through grounded, empirical social analysis.

Chapter 1 provided an overview of directions and dilemmas in sociology as they are relevant to the substantive areas I will be addressing throughout. I now discuss two influential developments in sociological theorising: theses of individualisation, and debates about social difference. These have a core relevance to the study, because of their influence within substantive areas of research to be addressed later. Theses of individualisation have been applied to explanations of shifts in family form and relationships as well as other significant changes in ties of intimacy, care and commitment. Further, individualisation theses have made influential claims about significant developments in gender relations particularly women's social position, employment patterns and linked changes in the organisation of social reproduction. However, the concept of 'individualisation' provides only a partial perspective on social change, and is unproductive as a general acount of change. In diagnosing and building into theory a presumed separation of norms and social arrangements the individualisation thesis actually fails to gain purchase on the dynamics of social change. Debates about social difference have emerged in part due to recognition of the importance of issues of status and inequality around gender, ethnicity, sexuality and disability, and paralleled a seeming erosion of class identifications and solidarities. Whilst often quite separate from theses of individualisation, in an echo of them, debates about social difference also reveal a gap between norms and cultural process on the one hand and social arrangements on the other, although this is more by default than by design. I discuss the dilemmas and questions generated by these debates, and introduce a series of wider questions relating to how we conceptualise social life. In the latter part of the chapter I will introduce a series of concepts which will be key throughout the study. These are described under the heading social configuration. This refers to the composition of social relations, differentiation and interdependencies, and linked norms and values. This provides the conceptual grounds on which to build a more sufficient analysis of social continuity and change, of the shape and reshaping of social life.

2.2 Individualisation

Individualisation and other, linked, 'trend' theses of change in social reproduction do not provide a sufficient account of social change. The term individualisation is generally used to signify a diminution in the strength and permanence of social ties and obligations which previously bound people into groups, networks and allegiances which were crucial to their social experiences, beliefs and ways of acting in the world, in short, to their social identities. People are seen to be less securely tied into social networks of actual and felt obligation and duty. No single interpretation has been placed on these developments. In popular discourse questions of selfishness and individualism are raised in debates about working mothers and child-rearing, divorce and so on. In academic debate recent social developments have been described in terms of an increased autonomy at the level of the individual, and construed as new forms of social control (Beck 1992; Bauman 1995; Rose 1999).

For example, in a concrete area of research to be explored in some detail in Chapter 4, many have argued that emergent trends in family demography, and new forms of diversity in family arrangements, can be understood in terms of a change in the nature of the social, or moral ties that bind individuals and groups in contemporary society (e.g. Aries 1980; Lesthaeghe 1995; Beck 1992; MacInnes 1998; and cf. McRae 1999; Strohmeier and Kuijsten 1997). Demographic changes (fertility decline, and divorce for example) are seen here to stem from cultural shifts which allow greater agency and self determination by individuals (Lesthaeghe 1998; Lesthaeghe and Surkyn 1988). These alter the motivations to create and maintain intimate relationships. In this perspective, values now are shaped less by one's ties and obligations to others and more through a duty to oneself.

The individualisation thesis of Beck (1992) and Beck and Beck-Gernsheim (2002) posits that people are not so much free, as *forced to choose* in conditions of late, or 'second' modernity, and they are simultaneously caught in a web of social structural contradictions and imperatives (Beck and Beck-Gernsheim 2002). The argument again is that there has been an erosion of older cultural constraints and ties. This does not allow a 'freedom' of individuals in so far as they are forced to make choices within a system which generates contradictions for how they live their lives. People have greater autonomy, but they are forced to 'become themselves' (Bauman 2002). Elsewhere Bauman identifies an apparent loosening of people's identity from its social moorings (Bauman 1995). In the individualisation thesis, it falls more and more to the individual to resolve the dilemmas thrown up by the system:

> [C]ertainties have fragmented into questions which are now spinning around in people's heads. But it is more than that. Social action needs routines in which to be enacted. One can even say that our actions are shaped, at the deepest level, by something of which we are hardly or not at all aware . . . It is precisely this level of pre-conscious 'collective habitualizations', of matters taken for granted, that is breaking down into a cloud of possibilities to be thought about and negotiated.
>
> (Beck and Beck-Gernsheim 2002: 6)

Individuals are less 'fixed' in their social position and identity, and values, in 'second modernity' so they hold new kinds of autonomy. They are 'disembedded': 'Individuals become actors, builders, jugglers, stage managers of their own biographies and identities and also of their social links and networks' (ibid.: 23).

Beck's notion of disembedding works with a particular metaphor of individual and society, positing a new kind of articulation between the two. The individual is deemed to become the reproduction 'unit' of the life world (Beck 1992; Beck and Beck-Gernsheim 2002). The seminal example of individualisation is the commodification of women's labour and the ensuing individualisation of gender relations. In this view the asymmetrical gender division of labour, which accommodated family demands, has been undermined, bringing new stresses and tensions to family life; and rendering family relationships increasingly contingent (Beck 1992; Beck and Beck-Gernsheim 2002). Taken to its logical conclusion the trend towards a market family, where individuals are rewarded solely for their labour and are thus unable to resource the claims of any dependents, is predicated on its own demise: 'the ultimate market society is a childless society – unless the children grow up with mobile, single fathers and mothers' (Beck 1992: 116). Beck is pointing to what he sees as a tendency inherent in capitalist social relations, a dynamic which generates a growing contradiction between reproduction and production. Forms of social disintegration appear to follow on from the deepened pressures of systemic contradictions, for some an upshot of the commodification of female labour and the marketisation of family relations (Beck 1992; Beck and Beck-Gernsheim 2002). As women have become further drawn into the realm of paid employment the tensions are increasingly overt and consequential. In the absence of institutional solutions there is a growing pressure on the family and within individuals' lives. It is within these trends that Beck locates the modern 'negotiated' family, where marital partnerships are increasingly subject to recall.

Ultimately then Beck discerns not autonomy, but its absence, as a late modern correlate of individualism, and maintains that there has been an increase in social control. Individuals are forced to make decisions, yet more subject to forms of control, through increased dependence on the market and on institutions of various kinds (Beck 1992). There are parallels between this perspective and Rose's description of modern governance as a double movement of autonomisation and responsibilisation. Rose argues that increasingly people are made responsible for their own destiny, and that understandings (and fabrications) of 'the social' are in retreat from the political imagination and state practices. Governance increasingly is about self-governance (Rose 1999). Various writers have engaged with this notion that people feel that 'the political is personal', and carry the practical and psychological burdens of social troubles as if they were responsible for their own fate (Rose 1999; Arnot 2002; Walkerdine *et al.* 2001). This pattern, however, is not new. Writers emphasise its significance and find it especially current in political rhetoric and in policy. But one could equally point to a society of litigation and blaming the other. Neither generalisation holds immediate purchase on the why of value and belief.

Another picture of an unfolding logic, of rationalisation, is offered by MacInnes in his account of how modernity ultimately undermines patriarchal processes. MacInnes describes the era of modernity, from enlightenment to present, as a transitional society, with modern material and ideological forces existing in tension with an older, but ongoing, patriarchal ideology. Modernity embodies a logic of rationalisation, importantly promoting formal equality between individuals:

> One of the most profound but unanticipated and unintended consequences of the spread of market relations is the rise in modern societies of a formal commitment to the equality of all human beings in principle, and material and social pressures which sustain this: what could be called universalism. We might think of the era we are living through as the collapse of patriarchy.
>
> (MacInnes 1998: 238)

The greater lifetime commitments of women to paid employment and, more broadly, claims to equality of status are interpreted as a culmination of an Enlightenment logic. It will be argued that it is premature to suppose that cultural processes have delivered a universal rationalism. Processes of distribution and attributions of value remain socially embedded.

Many of the trends which Beck and Beck-Gernsheim highlight, such as the growing importance to women of education, employment and 'a claim of their own on life' are well rehearsed, and are not in dispute. More broadly too it seems that we can plausibly say that people have more room for manoeuvre than in the past and that they (and more of them) are more able to be agents of their lives than were their forebears. However there are problems which emerge from the characterisation of change in terms of individualisation (e.g. Irwin and Bottero 2000; Duncan *et al.* 2003). Because 'value' cannot be read off from 'structure' as it could in the past, we are told, we are confronting a new social departure, in which individuals are 'disembedded': part of a new articulation of individual and society. We need be cautious of the metaphor of disembedding, in which individuals are thrown upon themselves in finding their own solutions. *What the perspective appears to do is to 'dislocate' individuals, values and identifications from the contexts of which they are a part.*

Accounts of social change which emphasise individualisation, marketisation and rationalisation capture vital aspects of human experience in contemporary society: the importance of reflexivity; the enlarged scope for autonomous action, the forcing of choices in 'knowledge society', and the importance of claims that all persons are of equal moral worth. It seems plausible that recent decades have seen a growth of the social spaces in which people can contest status quo arrangements, and challenge various givens, although it is important not to overstate the extent of reflexivity and the extent to which it is a new phenomenon. Theses of individualisation have been influential in recent sociological explanations although many writers develop and work with some critically revised version of it (e.g. Savage 2000; Phillipson 1998; Smart 1997; Furlong and Cartmel 1997). Certainly as it stands the concept of individualisation offers a rather particular interpretation of the changing social relations which are influencing contemporary transformations. I outline three main lines of critique:

(a) The notion of a linear historical logic to social change is questionable and so too is the presumption of an unfolding logic of economic change.
(b) Theories of individualisation carry an implicit but implausible assumption of an erosion of culture.
(c) Arguments of individualisation do not give an adequate basis for analysing the links between subjective aspects of human experience and extant social relations, making a leap of analytic faith between agency and structure.

The first criticism is that accounts of individualisation and rationalisation represent economic and cultural processes in terms of an unfolding logic. In consequence, history is reconstructed in a linear fashion, in terms of how we arrived at the present. For example, the 'logic' of capitalist development is accompanied by a 'logic' of demographic transition, within which prior social, familial ties break down under the pressures of an individualising tendency, engendered by economic change and, in some versions, by a partly autonomous cultural process of rationalisation (Beck 1992; MacInnes 1998; and cf. Van Krieken 1997). The '*longue durée*' view seems to imply an unfolding logic or working out of some historical contradiction. History is analysed from the perspective of 'where it has got us'. This may turn out to be a retrospective mythologising of historical tendencies. We should not be too taken with the *longue durée* view with its tendency to bulldoze historical complexity and diversity (Szreter 1996; Levine 1987). The alternative perspective to be developed will locate change in terms of a reconfiguring of contexts of social action and belief.

Within arguments of equalisation (MacInnes 1997; cf. Phillips 1999) is another construction of historical 'progress': an imperative embedded within the social system. Here the importance of identity-based social movements in the late twentieth century and the significance of rights- and recognition-based claims reveal a 'working through' of the Enlightenment ideal of the equal moral worth of persons. The argument runs that this unfolding logic has been important to the historical emergence and strengthening of such claims by women, ethnic minorities, disabled people's groups, and gay and lesbian groups. However, an argument of a trend within modernity towards equality ideals is not wholly accurate as an interpretation of historical change. Whilst identity-based movements found a renewed, if not new, voice and momentum in the latter part of the twentieth century this does not necessarily reveal a trend to equalisation. What we are witnessing is a newly perceived salience of particular, (group) recognition, claims. The notion that history proceeds in the form of linear change is merely a metaphor which has been found wanting in many contexts. We need an account capable of exploring and locating historical specificity.

The second critique of theories of individualisation is that they appear to run a risk of absenting culture from explanation, and of insufficiently exploring and analysing contemporary belief systems. For example, it has been argued that the notion of a diminution of 'traditional' economic and status constraints echoes neoclassical economic assumptions of a socially unencumbered 'rational' individual decision-maker. In both perspectives people appear to be individualised decision-making units, a view which tends to absent culture from accounts of contemporary social action (e.g. Irwin 1995; Irwin and Bottero 2000; Gardiner 1996; Duncan and Edwards 1999. See also Oppenheimer 1994; Block 1990; van Krieken 1997).

Block describes as the economistic fallacy the view that, unlike primitive or premodern societies, capitalist societies do not have cultures:

> This, in fact, has been one of the central conceits of modernity; our institutions are supposed to be shaped by the dictates of practical reason rather than by the kinds of deeply held, but unexamined, collective beliefs that are known to dominate in less enlightened societies. But when we recognize that the pursuit of economic self interest is itself a cultural creation, then it is apparent that we, too, are ruled by deeply held, but unexamined, collective beliefs.
>
> (Block 1990: 27)

Others too stress how we need to locate 'economic' processes as predicated on social and cultural bases (e.g. Sayer 2004; Di Maggio 1990; Friedland and Robertson 1990; Rubery 1996). It is with this argument, of the centrality of the cultural, that an account of current changes needs to (re)commence. In Chapter 3 I explore how culturally based claims and assumptions which were forged in the nineteenth century, and at the turn of the twentieth century, shaped gender asymmetries in the labour market through much of that latter century. In Chapter 4 I explore the reconfiguring of gendered positions over recent decades and argue that it does not reveal individualisation but a reconstruction of gendered difference and cultural claims about gender, and about the nature of economic processes. Whilst there has been an expansion of the scope, and tightening of the grasp, of marketised relations over recent decades such relationships are not inevitable 'trends' but rather mark the ascendance of a particular set of claims and a shift in contexts, such that particular economic trends appear more or less inevitable. There has been political recognition of the social consequences of economic processes particularly through the 1990s and after in Britain. However, it often appears, wrongly, that the processes themselves occur outside social contexts. It will be argued that women's and men's changing relations to employment are not adequately described by marketisation, and they remain socially embedded. Employment patterns still relate to gendered positions, and to norms and culturally based claims.

The third critique of individualisation theories is that they provide an insufficient conceptualisation of the relationship between subjective and objective: between norms, perceptions, values and dispositions on the one hand and the structure of social relations and diverse social positions on the other. Beck for example, argues that a radical shift in regard of gender equality claims has occurred in people's consciousness and yet not in conditions and behaviours: 'Consciousness has rushed ahead of conditions' (Beck 1992: 104). People are not solidly embedded within social bonds and networks since:

> Individualization liberates people from traditional roles and constraints . . . [and] . . . At the same time as this liberation or 'disembedding' occurs, new forms of reintegration and control are created ('re-embedding'). With the decline of class and status groups the individual must become the agent of his or her own identity making and livelihood. The individual . . . becomes the unit for the reproduction of the social in his or her own lifeworld.
>
> (Beck and Beck-Gernsheim 2002: 202–3)

In a highly differentiated society people play many diverse roles and hold many diverse facets to their identities, interacting with others across diverse domains. However, it is doubtful that this should be construed as a lack of integration. Such a perspective operates with a particular metaphor of structure in which people can be disembedded and re-embedded. It is unclear that the metaphor can be operationalised at an analytic level. It operates as an explanatory *deus ex machina*, necessitated by a theoretical gap between individual and society. A more enabling perspective would analyse individual agency as an integral and necessary part of social structure, and of social change.

The analyses of substantive areas in this book make it clear that the general picture is one of coherence between subjectivities and diverse dispositions on the one hand, and people's positioning within a differentiated social structure on the other. Even in contexts of significant social transformation, such as demographic transition and family change at end of the nineteenth and end of the twentieth centuries, or in contemporary gender relations, we observe a mutuality of subjectivities and social relations at the heart of social change. If these are analysed as facets of a coherent pattern of restructuring we do not require metaphors of disembedding and re-embedding of the individual in society. Theories of individualisation have too loose a grip on social relations and interconnection and their link with subjectivities. These concepts are very much to the fore in recent debates about difference. As we will see, however, again there is a risk that beliefs and values get separated out from the social contexts of which they are a part.

2.3 Deconstructing and reconstructing 'difference'

Having identified difficulties inherent in theses of individualisation I turn to another area which has seen a major growth of sociological interest: that of difference and diversity. Culture and belief systems are central to accounts here, but again there is a need to better understand the articulation of subjectivities and the contexts which shape them. Difference is an interesting and useful concept, but a partial one. Nevertheless, engaging with the debates here also helps move us closer to framing the questions to be addressed in this study.

Difference, social diversity and social agency are important concepts within current accounts of social life. Increasingly writers and researchers have focused on new status-related identities and divisions as they cleave around gender, sexuality, 'race', dis/ability, and age and generation. Seemingly these divisions have eclipsed the emphasis on class so central to the sociological project at least in the 1960s and 1970s, although if class temporarily became the poor relation of the sociological imaginary, and of the political imaginary, it is being written back in in various ways (e.g. Savage 2000; Reay 1998a; Phillips 1999).

'Difference' as a concept is used across a diverse literature with quite distinct agendas. However there are some key themes which we may discern which are of interest to the current discussion. A useful point of departure is the couching of difference in terms of imagined communities (Anderson 1983). Communities are imagined in the sense that in modern, large-scale societies people cannot ever expect to come into direct contact with more than a vanishingly small proportion of their 'fellow' countrymen and women. Yet people tend to hold a notion of national identity, a shared idea of nation. In short the very notion of community here on such a large scale is more a way of organising thought than a necessary reflection of reality. *It is about a construction of similarity and difference.*

There has been a growing interest in imagined communities of difference, but not just with the emphasis on nation but also on 'minority/majority' formations in the shaping of difference by gender, sexuality, ethnicity, age and disability (e.g. Maynard 1994; Brah 1992; Fraser 1995; Young 1990; Jenkins 1997; Hockey and James 1993; Priestley 2000; Bottero and Irwin 2003). Many writers have addressed the ways in which perceptions of social difference shape inequalities: both material inequalities and inequalities of recognition. The critique of biological essentialism is well established in social scientific thinking and to a large degree sociology has focused on the social construction of difference. A key point of departure is the consideration that difference is not an objective reflection of the content of two or more groups' values, or behaviours but rather it is about the relationship in which the 'groups' stand to one another. The anthropologist Barth for example insisted on the significance of how boundaries between groups are maintained. It is this boundary maintenance which defines group differentiation rather than the other way around (Barth, cited in Jenkins 1996). Construction of 'the other' is central to perceptions of 'we'. Jenkins talks of internal group definitions and external categorisations where some impose their definitions on others. Internal definitions cannot ultimately be separated from external impositions (Jenkins 1996). Thus boundaries of difference are formed by internal definitions, beliefs and a sense of belonging and by the imposition of notions of difference from without. Group formation and maintenance is part of a process, of differentiation and social positioning.

In seeking to locate difference there has been a growing emphasis on its relational underpinnings (e.g. Young 1990, 1997a; Jenkins 1996; Burkitt 1998; Anthias 1998). Young (1997a), for example, says:

> Groups should be understood in relational terms rather than as self-identical substantial entities with essential attributes. A social group is a collective of persons differentiated from others by cultural forms, practices, special needs or capacities, structures of power or prestige . . . In a relational conceptualization, what constitutes a social group is not internal to the attributes and self understanding of its members. Rather, what makes the group a group is the relation in which it stands to others.
>
> (Young 1997a: 389)

This is interesting in the clarity of its emphasis on relationality. The definition however begs the question 'when is a group a group?', one which parallels concerns that descriptions of 'group' difference may themselves become essentialising, or normalising. Where perspectives are seen to 'fix' difference, even where it is acknowledged to be socially constructed, they put themselves at risk of charges of social essentialism, that is with inadvertently policing socially constructed, oppressive and normalising boundaries (e.g. Butler 1990; Smith 2002).

There is a risk that binary oppositions reify the taken for granted nature of difference. This is a critique made by Epstein (1988) who argued that the tendency to think in binary categories reinforces, perhaps creates, our perceptions of the world in terms of difference. Epstein's focus is on gender and she argues:

> Gender distinctions are basic to the social order in all societies. Like age, gender orders society and is ordered by it. Only by some social arrangement (ordering) between the sexes can societies reproduce, and certainly a concern for reproduction constrains the way in which social groups regard the sexes . . . All societies provide an explanation for the distinctions between the sexes, and because biologically based sexual dimorphism is a simple, visible basis of differentiation, it tends to be used as a major rationale . . . We must ask why men and women are classified in the social order in ways unrelated to their biological differences and biological functioning – that is, by their intellectual, moral and emotional makeup. We should also identify the ways in which only the female sex is identified in terms of biology while members of the male sex are regarded as social beings.
>
> (Epstein 1988: 6)

The title of Epstein's book, *Deceptive Distinctions*, refers to the way in which presumptions of gender difference are essentialised in social practices. In fact gender differences in outlooks tend to be superficial. They are typically situation specific, and they are linked to power differentials. The two-culture approach, Epstein argues, is constraining and normalising. We tend to see characterisations of behaviours or qualities as 'masculine' and 'feminine' extensively in popular culture, although sociologists too are not innocent of assigning such labels. In the postmodernist view the very act of categorisation risks perpetuating a pattern of power and regulation: Butler for example argues that unthinking use of the category 'woman' is essentialising and risks reinforcing a notion of fixed differences between women and men (Butler 1990). However it is not peculiar to postmodernist critiques to argue that diverse values and ethics are human, and not the singular domain of women or men.

Young herself sought to tackle the problem that specifying boundaries separating one group from another seems both essentialist and static as a mode of analysis. She seeks therefore to describe the social positioning of women in a way which avoids strong statements about groupness, acknowledging concerns that 'group' is just as likely as 'difference' to risk both fixity (ahistorical analysis) and imposition (ignoring salient diversity within, and being normalising and exclusionary) (Young 1997b). Part of her concern is to ensure that the term 'woman' should not imply a common identity nor a common set of attributes. The problem as she states it is that: 'We want and need to describe women as a group, yet it appears that we cannot do so without being normalizing and essentialist' (Young 1997b: 22).

Drawing on Sartre, she develops an argument that we treat women in terms of a 'series'. Women do not necessarily identify with one another, nor do they share a common situation or attributes, other than that they are unified passively by 'the objects their actions are oriented around' (ibid.). They are 'connected' not by something 'held' or by an identification but by an orientation. That is, we might say they can be classified as women by their social location, rather than by their membership of a group as such. This is an important argument. However, it is worth noting that in Young's account women still appear to be positioned in much the same way as they were within patriarchy theory. In the examples given by Young the 'series' women are constituted through enforced heterosexuality and the sexual division of labour (ibid.). Women's position in society seems quite static and the notion of 'series' does not seem to move us beyond a general statement that women and men have a different structural location in society. We have no sense of the dynamics of social relations which might reposition women and men in relation to each other, or alter the salience of gender across contexts, for example. The concept of social positioning is to the fore. To give the concept empirical purchase we need to engage in concrete ways with the shape-shifting of gender, including its variable salience and its articulation with other social arrangements.

Anthias (1998, 2001) also stresses the importance of relations and social 'positionality' in shaping difference and inequality. Her objective is to integrate gender, ethnicity and class into sociological theory, through theorising difference, and intersectionality, or how the relations of gender, ethnicity/'race' and class interconnect in specific contexts. She rightly notes that categories of difference, such as ethnicity and gender, are sometimes treated as causal rather than as *outcomes* of social processes (Anthias 1998, 2001). For example, it is frequently the case that gender divisions, ethnic divisions, and divisions of age and generation are treated as a starting point of analysis. This can serve useful practical purposes since not every empirical study can go back to first principles and since status divisions serve a useful probabilistic function (they are 'indicators', rather than measures). However, not infrequently assumptions that these social divisions are primary and causal become embedded in theory. In consequence they hide as much as they reveal (Brubaker 2002; Siltanen 1994; Jenson 1986). It is problematic to accept gender or other dimensions of social difference as categorical: we must orient to the processes which shape them and give them salience. The concept of difference holds value in targeting the socially and historically made nature of diversity and hierarchy. *The point is not to start from difference but to analyse its making.* To do so would provide a clearer understanding of the social nature of cultural and normative beliefs.

We can consider two distinct lenses on the making of difference. One is to recognise that difference is, in many of the contexts in which it is used, a social, political or intellectual claim or set of assumptions – about 'being different', about different outlooks, cultures, and/or competencies, for example. The other lens reveals social differentiation as a process which often entails no overt constructions of difference. Diverse positionings and perceptions are reproduced in no small part by routinised behaviours and modes of conduct. Therefore we need to recognise the limits to difference as a concept. Crucially we need to locate difference as a partial statement of social differentiation. Social processes position individuals and groups differently, yet do not solely reflect attributions of difference. For example, sexism, racism, homophobia, ageism and disablism are extremely important but they are partial as descriptions of processes shaping linked inequalities.

Some express concern that a focus on difference means that analysts focus on the difference of 'the other' – the difference 'of' women, ethnic minorities and disabled people for example (e.g. Maynard 1994). However an adequate analysis of the processes shaping difference necessarily requires analysis of mainstream, normalising assumptions and how they engender difference and inequalities. In short we need concepts which account for difference but are not captured by it. Debates about difference are of value in giving insights into the shape of diversity, and in seeking to theorise the meshing of normative patterns and social relations. However, in the focus on difference, we are left with an inappropriately narrow basis for such a theorisation. We need to step back, to the broader concept of differentiation. In the next section I outline components of a conceptualisation that can be operationalised, moving us beyond abstractions towards developing analytical tools, and ones which are sociologically grounded (cf. Walby 2001).

Theses of individualisation operate with a gap between individual level processes and general social arrangements. Debates about difference are more oriented to 'middle level' processes of social positioning and group identifications. However, writers often assume too much about the cultural making of diversity so that status dimensions of difference, such as gender and ethnicity, take on a fixity and are not related to the social contexts in which they are given shape and meaning. In the next sections I develop some concepts as part of an alternative approach to analysing social life. I refer to *social configuration* to designate the configuration of social interconnections, and the linked normative assumptions about the proper place and role of different social groups. The approach draws on a conception of historical transitions in terms of a reconfiguring of contexts of social action. It allows us to explore both values, and the relations which bind and differentiate social groups, within the same analytical framework. The perspective provides a new lens on contemporary developments.

2.4 Social configuration – some conceptual pointers

2.4.1 Introduction

Social interconnections count. Social relationality has seen a widening interest. In part it is offered as a counter to assumptions of atomised, seemingly autonomous and unconnected individuals, evidenced in some policy formulations and in some social science paradigms. However, despite this interest in relationality and its use in signalling the ongoing importance of social relationships and ties, it has been underdeveloped as an analytic tool. Relationality itself is a very broad concept and can contain rather different meanings. The broad discussion here will give way to more precise concepts which are operationalised, as analytic tools, throughout the book.

Social configuration refers to an historically specific configuration of social relations, interconnections and hierarchy, and values, identifications and claims which are linked, in contingent ways. This definition operates with a particular metaphor of society. Diverse groups occupy and comprise spaces within a broader social space. Differently positioned they reveal patterns of difference and hierarchy, which result from historically specific processes. Subjective identifications link to the specific contexts in which they are forged. To systematise the notion of social configuration, which will serve as a series of concepts and directions for analysis, rather than a rigid 'framework', we can say that it refers to:

- The configuring of social relations in a multi-dimensional space which includes gender, generation, age, class, and 'race' and ethnicity (and could encompass other key dimensions of difference). For example, with respect to contemporary developments in gender relations we can talk of a changing social space of gender. It is not just gender positions which change but they may be constituted differently.
- Social relations include patterns of mutuality, interdependence and hierarchy. These are not separable from the values and norms which position groups differently in social space and which also and simultaneously shape social groups as meaningful collectivities.
- Specific configurations are themselves shaped, and reproduced, through historical and social processes which include routinised social actions, implicit assumptions and overt claims.
- Specific patterns of diversity and inequality are perceived and constructed as meaningful in particular ways. These perceptions and constructions may mean that difference and hierarchy is naturalised; it may be seen as socially made but immutable; or it may be contested; these different perspectives may result in different kinds of action which shape and reshape social relations and institutions.
- Specific configurations are comprised of a diverse positioning of people and groupings in particular contexts and sets of social relations. The

> proximate relations and contexts in which people interact and act are a crucial linking concept and layer through which to analyse the meshing of the subjective and evaluative on the one hand and the more general configuring of social relations on the other.

The articulation of configuring of social relations on the one hand, and evaluations and subjective perceptions on the other, is historically contingent: a matter for empirical recovery. Below I explore in more detail the key concepts.

2.4.2 *On the configuration of social relations*

The notion of a configuration of social relations operates with a metaphor of society as a multi-dimensional space in which individuals and groups acquire different positions in respect of each other. Group differences reveal no essential characteristics or propensities, but they do reveal a relational underpinning to attributions of difference (cf. Young 1997a; Maynard 1994; Friedman 2000; Friedman 1995). The focus on social relations has, in different contexts, seen a widening interest, not least since it seems to move beyond debates about essentialism. I have argued that whilst most sociologists would challenge biological essentialism as a frame for interpreting social differences, there is a risk that a form of social essentialism enters into analysis. Some arguments about gender and difference have valorised aspects of 'woman's nature' whilst seeing this (relational, empathetic, morally complex) nature to be socially made (e.g. Gilligan 1993). However, it is not appropriate to assign certain human values as feminine and other human values as masculine. Social relations shape social positions and identities and behaviours which are coded as masculine and feminine, but it is clearly inappropriate to accept a singular picture of women and men. A focus on relations giving rise to different subject positions and identities allows us to better locate the importance of gender in shaping and differentiating life chances, and allows for the variable importance of gender across different contexts. Jenson asks how, in any particular social formation, gender difference is given meaning:

> It is possible to constitute it as a maximal or a minimal difference. Sexual difference could be permitted to cross all other relationships, or, such a process of differentiation could be effaced through the political actions of resistance.
>
> (Jenson 1986: 26)

That is, gender difference and its salience is not given but socially, historically and politically made. Importantly, too, gender differentiation will often be implicit in social processes. In short we can treat gender as neither biologically nor socially essentialist, but as embedded in a broader set of social relations in which the saliences of gender may vary. A parallel argument can be made in respect of ethnicity, class and life course stages.

The focus on social relations also moves us away from a notion of underlying structures which shape interests and patterns of behaviour, yet it retains a sense of structured action and valuations. Relations position people differently in social space, with diverse material and citizenship-related opportunities and constraints. Interpretation of these diverse 'positions' requires analysis of how difference is constituted culturally as well as materially. It entails consideration of attributions of difference, and linked evaluations of cultural worth, as well as differential economic life chances.

Social relations of difference are also crucial to theorising the social ordering of interdependence across social groups or those in different social locations. These relations of interdependence often do not mark an exchange between equals, but one which is imbued with hierarchy and inequalities. Additionally such relational ties can contribute to the naturalisation of particular roles, and an asymmetry of risks, responsibilities and rights. Key examples which I explore in Chapters 3 and 4 are patterns of interdependence and constructions of difference between women and men, and between adults and children. The differential positioning of groups across social space, and cultural evaluations and attributions of differential competencies are important in the shaping of social identities.

2.4.3 Subjectivities and social identities

One of the difficulties which emerged from contemporary materialist accounts of oppression (of class, 'race', dis/ability, gender) is connecting subjectivities, and people's perceptions of their own experience, with a general account of an oppressive and exploitative system. For example, in neo-Marxist analyses of class various writers made an analytic leap of faith between the general account of social structure and presumed perceptions and motivations on the part of social actors. Honneth notes how in such accounts actors' interests are read off from 'structural' position (Honneth 1995). Honneth seeks to analyse the dynamics of social recognition, and emphasises the connection between the emergence of social movements and the moral experience of disrespect. He argues that sociological analyses of protest movements have often taken interests to be 'given' by objective inequalities. For Honneth these interests are rarely analysed as elements of the 'everyday web of moral feelings'. He argues that moral feelings of indignation should be the starting point for theorising social conflict (Honneth 1995; Fraser and Honneth 2003). Whether or not such feelings should be taken as a starting point is doubtful, and is a point taken up in Chapter 8. Nevertheless the general point Honneth makes is important: we need to better connect subjective experience and objective social relations in analysis.

Social identities are closely tied to people's social position. Identities relate in part to how we locate ourselves in society and how we see others as locating us (Bradley 1996). We need an ability to explore different articulations of social location, identity and action. Aspects of identity deemed important in current academic and policy discourse centre on key aspects of social diversity: gender, ethnicity, sexuality and disability. Clearly these will have variable salience, but *the context* in which aspects of identity take on salience are of crucial importance to thinking about the correspondences between social location and forms of reflexive action. In part the salience of identity, or the construction of experiences into a particular sense of identity, will relate to people's experience of their social location, and their interactions with others. For example, it may be that people's sense of themselves and their aspiration are out of line with the presumptions or impositions of others, potentially engendering a sense of misrecognition. It may be that a misrecognised facet of felt identity becomes politicised, and becomes a more salient aspect of a person's overall identity. In contrast, people are often not particularly reflexive about aspects of their social location, and operate as practitioners in their social behaviours and interactions, rather than theorists. Precisely how diverse interpretations relate to people's social position is a particularly interesting question.

To sufficiently understand the links between general social relations and the identifications, perceptions and evaluations of individual social actors we need to be able to move between levels of analysis which relate directly to the processes under consideration. Consequently then I move now to a consideration of social context and proximate social relations, since these will be often most influential in shaping people's perceptions of their experience. The next section considers the central importance of social contexts, or milieux, as a middle layer, largely underplayed in contemporary research. Diverse contexts shape perceptions and link to social behaviours and action.

2.4.4 *Social contexts*

The retreat from 'structuralist' explanations, in which interests ostensibly are given as part of a system imperative, left a series of questions: who holds particular values and why, when do some values or visions gain momentum, how are some claims naturalised and others subject to overt contestation and so on. In part this may be because such questions are deemed empirical ones, so generalising answers would be inappropriate. However, there is less research than we might expect on the array of social contexts of diverse values and dispositions. We are short of analytic tools through which to locate diverse strands in Honneth's (1995) 'web of moral feelings'. Additionally, where researchers do examine the diverse strands there are conceptual and methodological difficulties in 'scaling up' to a picture of the entire web.

Earlier I critiqued individualisation theories, and structuralist theories, for making a leap of faith between analysis of what is happening at the level of individual experience and macro level processes. In theories of difference and diversity there is a clear need for more detailed elaboration of the processes shaping cultural attributions of difference and differential worth. In Chapter 1 I indicated recent research into values and agency across domains in family and care, and noted that the emphasis on contextual specificity and contingency and the *fact* of social diversity is often not matched by illumination of the *shape* of social diversity. *Analysis of social context is a crucial 'missing link' in theorising social diversity and rethinking the individual society puzzles described above.* Such a statement seems almost a truism. However, to take the statement seriously is to point to some significant gaps in contemporary sociological research. Additionally it requires that we attend to some fairly complicated, conceptual, issues. It is not simply a case of saying that a perception, disposition or action occurred in a particular social locale or setting (although obviously this will be important). It is also a case of how we conceptualise the issues under examination. Many arguments which allude to the connection between structure and agency, or between individual and society, often fail to sufficiently address social context. So, for example, various writers have argued that people generally may not be critical of oppressive and unequal social relations, and do not realise their position, since recent developments have undermined critical awareness of structural inequalities (Arnot 2002; Rose 1999; Beck 1992; Furlong and Cartmel 1997). However, an enduring argument about the nature of hierarchy is that it teaches people to know their place, and not be reflexive about structural inequalities (cf. Runciman 1966). It may be the case that people do not criticise the overall system, not because they cannot see its contours so much as because it is generally experienced as an abstraction from their daily lives. For whom it is an abstraction and for whom it holds political immediacy is itself a sociological question. The point is that, in general, people are social practitioners, not theorists, and have no necessary interest in an overview of social structure. Their views of their social position are more likely formed through the contexts of association and interaction in which they are embedded. The issue is explored through Chapters 5 to 7, and taken up in detail in Chapter 8, where I look at how these patterns function in shaping perceptions of fairness and inequality. *The emphasis on social contexts or milieux, then, will lead beyond analysis of physical spaces (neighbourhoods, workplaces and so on) to a more inclusive consideration of social spaces, of meaningful reference points and social interaction.*

But how do we get from the proximate contexts and milieux in which people make sense of their lives and society, to a general statement of social arrangements, and indeed to change in such arrangements? It is not simply a case of 'scaling up'. Rather we need to understand how 'context' is part of a wider structure of social arrangements. This is a conceptual question as much as a substantive question. We need to access both the specific and the general, the micro and the macro and understand their mutuality. This is one of the central purposes of this book.

2.4.5 Social claiming

A better theorisation of social context will provide insights into important social processes relating to orientations to care and work, perceptions of class and inequality, and life course difference, and expressions of belonging and ethnicity amongst other things. Much of the discussion in the book will link to routinised actions and 'standard' social processes. These operate in contexts in which various claims and values may have become embedded and naturalised. Indeed part of our concern is with the naturalisation of social arrangements. However, overt and politicised claims have some relevance to this study, and will be highlighted accordingly.

Claiming as an analytical concept allows us to better locate values and ideologies. Wendell, in the context of disability debates, points to the philosophical arbitrariness of ideas concerning which of us is independent (Wendell 1996). However, whilst expectations may have a philosophical arbitrariness they do not have a social or historical arbitrariness about them. Rather they tend to reflect 'normal processes', and the power of different groups in pressing various claims, which then become embedded in systems of distribution and recognition. Patterns of social difference are frequently also social hierarchies. The concept of claiming allows us to explore such hierarchies in relation not to presumed interests, as given by say the requirements of capitalist, or patriarchal, social relations, but in relation to the ways in which normalising processes empower certain groups, and to the differential ability of groups, and alliances, at different historical junctures, to press claims more or less effectively.

The emphasis on claims as a useful concept for helping explore social reproduction should not be taken as offering a consensual model. The current diversity of claims and argument regarding recognition and distribution issues belies any argument that we are participants in a shared moral universe. Peattie and Rein define claims in terms of ideas about rights, entitlements and just deserts (Peattie and Rein 1983). The shape of such entitlements and deserts are not necessarily arrived at through consensus but through forms of social action in which people press their bids for resources. As claims are institutionalised they become embedded in social roles and expectations and may appear as part of a natural order (ibid.). The process is never complete, and the processes which shape how claims are advanced and how they are translated – or not – into new social practices are complex. As well as the inappropriateness of seeing a consensus in social evaluations, it would be an error to see claims as being free of unanticipated consequences. The context of claims and the ways in which they are contested may lead to radically different outcomes (Pedersen 1993; Baldwin 1990[1]).

The concept of social claiming contributes to locating values and to interrogating their articulation with the configuring of social relations. For example, the concept of claiming helps us reflect on how certain gendered assumptions became entrenched in twentieth-century divisions of labour and assumptions about fit work for women, and men, and how then 'implicit' values were challenged and reshaped as part of the contemporary restructuring of gender relations. Additionally we can usefully reflect on the articulation of overt claims about class, ethnicity and life course difference, and their link to extant social relations.

2.5 Conclusion

In this chapter I have explored in some detail individualisation and related trend theses of social change, and debates about social difference and its making. Writing in these domains helps provide bearings, if by counterpoint, to the directions taken in this study. One of the core difficulties confronted by the debates described lies in specifying how the normative meshes with the social. Individualisation theses do not attempt this, seeing a chronic separation between social conditions and consciousness as a feature of the late modern condition. However, such a division fails to convince, and it hinders analysis of social process and dynamism. Debates on difference take us forward with their emphasis on relationality and interdependence. However, within the debate there is another kind of division made between the cultural and the social. Here, cultural dimensions of difference are often not related to the social contexts in which they are shaped. An emphasis on difference leaves us with a partial lens on social diversity and its reproduction. An account which can shed light on change and underlying process needs to focus directly on the shaping of difference.

I have argued that a more adequate understanding requires analysis of social differentiation and linked relations of social difference and interdependence. The process of social change is partly comprised of relational changes and linked normative change. So, in the substantive domains examined in Chapters 3 to 5, we can analyse significant developments in gendered and generational difference and interdependencies, and see the material working through of these changes as inseparable from norms about gendered and age-based social roles and duties. These changes reveal a general shift in the relative positioning of different groupings or identities, and the mutuality of social order and norms. *Social change in these domains is better construed not as an unfolding logic, but as a reconfiguring of interdependence, difference and linked norms and assumptions.* The articulation of social relations on the one hand, and norms and claims on the other, is historically contingent: a matter for empirical recovery. It is the exploration of this articulation which is at heart of the book. The concepts discussed do not simply provide 'framing devices' for empirical analyses. Rather it is intended that the empirical analyses will serve to operationalise these concepts as analytic tools. In so doing they expand our resources for understanding and explaining social process.

An important part of the argument is that the social order and norms are closely linked. These material and cultural domains are not isomorphic, but nor are they separable from one another. To understand the articulation of social order and norms entails analysis of how norms and values get embedded in the social order, in institutional assumptions and so on. But it also demands that we pay attention to context: to the immediate environments, patterns of association and interaction, and proximate milieux and close personal relations which form the core of most people's lives. In contrast to presumptions about a chronic separation of norms and values from social contexts, data presented throughout the book reveals clearly continuities and coherence between individuals' dispositions and their social positions, and between values and context. However, a stress on context by itself is important, but also limited. Crucially we must make connections between the immediate, lived contexts in which people experience and interpret the world, and act in it, and the general social landscape. To do so effectively provides crucial resources for understanding and analysing society and social change.

Sometimes historical reconstruction can help reveal social processes more clearly than the apparent chaos of which we are a part. In the next chapter I explore the radical reconfiguring of social relations in the latter decades of the nineteenth century and the early decades of the twentieth century. I explore linked shifts in evaluations, identifications and claims in respect of family, care, work and welfare. The developments provide both fascinating historical background to current developments and enable analytic insights we can very productively use for exploring contemporary social change.

3 Reshaping difference and interdependence

The transformation of family life and divisions of labour into the twentieth century

3.1 Introduction: history and social configurations

What lessons might history hold for analysis of current transformations? Social transformations in the realms of gender, generation, family and work at the turn of the twentieth century provide a fascinating comparison with current changes. Their analysis, too, provides valuable insights into the shaping of social change. In this chapter I focus on changes in gender and generational relations in the decades at the end of the nineteenth and beginning of the twentieth centuries. The social positioning and identities of gender and generation groupings altered in especially interesting ways in this time. The period from the 1870s to the 1930s was marked by the 'first fertility decline': the historically unprecedented and rapid decline in fertility, and by the entrenchment of the connected, and ascendant, discourse of gendered difference and distinct roles across separate work and family 'spheres'. The chapter explores how gender and generation, and linked patterns of differentiation and interdependence, are central to understanding the first fertility decline, and to interpreting broader shifts in the organisation of social reproduction. It explores links between changing social relations, and changing identities and values, and it considers the changing efficacy of various social claims.

Broadly, it is organised into three parts. The first focuses on changing gendered roles, claims and identities through the nineteenth century, since this is crucial historical context for interpreting subsequent developments. It also exemplifies how particular values and claims came to be embedded in new, material, social arrangements. Notably, new claims around masculine identity and breadwinning gathered momentum and recognition, within a changing economic context, and fed into an entrenchment of gendered divisions of labour around separate, domestic and employment, spheres. The second part focuses on explanations of fertility decline as integral to changing gender and generational relations. Here change in the relative positioning of children within households, and within society more generally, was integral to dramatic shifts in reproductive motivations and behaviours. We can see clearly how radically new kinds of choices, indeed the emergence of reproductive choice itself as meaningful, are inseparable from a change in the social order. It is of especial interest given the influence of theories stating that a current expansion of choices means that people are more autonomous of social structural conditions. In the historical example it is very clear that new choices were an integral part of social structural transformation, part of a reconfiguring of contexts of social action. The third part of the chapter focuses on the cultural and institutional embedding of gendered divisions of labour and linked social identities, and the linked narrowing of diversity and undermining of claims by women to social and economic independence. Women had fewer opportunities to work and were increasingly marginalised from employment, and there were linked shifts in assumptions and norms about the proper roles and identities of women and men as gender asymmetry seemed inevitable, indeed natural, to many. Again the links between changing social conditions, norms and social identifications are not just of historical interest but will be part of the subsequent analysis of contemporary social change.

As elaborated in the last chapter, the notion of social configuration is intended to explore social relational differentiation and its articulation with norms and values. These are not simply 'sides' of an equation, since values, claims and imaginings are inscribed in relational configurations, just as the latter shape the former. The term reconfiguring is intended to denote the (re)making of patterns and perceptions of difference. The focus of this chapter is with historical developments in the reconfiguring of gender and generation relations, and in claims and values regarding gender and generational difference. The reconfiguring of differences, and of linked interdependencies and social identities, offers valuable insights into the nature of social change.

3.2 Nineteenth-century change in gender and generational differences and interdependencies

Amongst its many transformations the nineteenth century reveals significant changes in the positioning of women and men in social reproduction and economic production. These changes were bound up with a long-run shift from a family economy to a family wage economy in which the need for cash income rather than labourers shaped family and household composition and organisation (Tilly and Scott 1989). Evidence suggests a growing significance, through the nineteenth century, of the perceived propriety of a family wage system, of male 'providers' and female homemakers. This was a practice for some and an ideal for many. It was also an important claim in Chartist campaigning, and in the Trade Union movement in the last decades of the nineteenth century (McClelland 2000). Trade union strategies of excluding women from employment were driven in part by a logic of excluding low-paid workers who might undermine wage rates, but were also bound up with identity claims (Rose 1992; McClelland 2000). In the first part of the nineteenth century masculine identity was expressed principally through skill and through family headship and economic independence, but the latter meant freedom from poor relief. Masculine identity was to become increasingly associated with sole provider status requiring therefore, as its complement, female domesticity (Rose 1992; Davidoff *et al.* 1999; Honeyman 2000). The fact that a man's wife was seen not to work was visible proof that the family was not pauperised, a sign of manly independence (Hobsbawm 1987). Through the nineteenth century, then, the family wage ideal appears increasingly important to masculine identity.

This 'current' was present early on according to Taylor, so even before mid century, for some groups: 'The wage earning wife, once seen as the norm in every working class household, had become a symptom and symbol of masculine degradation' (Taylor 1983: 111). Broadhurst, the leader of the TUC in 1877 said it was a duty of male unionists:

> As men and husbands to use their utmost efforts to bring about a condition of things where wives and daughters would be in their proper sphere at home, instead of being dragged into competition for livelihood against the great and strong men of the world.
>
> (cited in Seccombe 1993: 114)

It is inappropriate to suppose that such beliefs were simply imposed on women, rather than integral to a widely held pattern of an accepted order of things. Gertrude Tuckwell, secretary of the Women's Trade Union League, and later to be its president, was in favour of: 'the gradual extension of labour protection to the point where mothers will be prohibited from working until their children have reached an age at which they can care for themselves' (cited in Lewis 1991: 79).

The notion of separate and gendered spheres of work and domesticity, then, was a component of a newly dominating discourse of distinct roles for women and men. This discourse appears to have been important to the shaping of social identities through the nineteenth century and beyond, and important in creating a new vision of family life (Rose 1992).

Culturally embedded notions of masculinity became important in the shaping of union claims for a family wage, and the exclusion of women, notably in the newly important heavy industries where unions were strong. The collective bargaining strategies of trades unions stressed a definition of independence as the ability to maintain a family (McClelland 2000). The claim for a family wage was acceptable to many employers, since it was consistent with both middle-class values regarding proper female (domestic) roles and with the emergent pattern of labour utilisation: a shift from an extensive to an intensive consumption of labour. In the former pattern, characteristic of early industrialisation, 'worn-out' labour was replaced by 'new' rural to urban migrant labour. In the middle decades of the nineteenth century employers supported a more intensive investment in labour and its reproduction, and so claims for improved wages and reduced working hours were accommodated, indeed required, by employers increasingly reliant on the survival, health, competencies and value of labour (Seccombe 1993; Hobsbawm 1969). Technological breakthroughs in manufacturing meant that labour turnover became increasingly costly to firms as their training costs increased. Employers came to favour restrictions on child labour and on the length of the working day, and to support the schooling of children, seeing in this an investment in the future, thus accommodating demands for breadwinner wages, which were consistent with their own concerns (Seccombe 1993).

The male breadwinner 'norm' was a reflection of arrangements in specific areas but not in others. The breadwinner claim was strengthened through the latter part of the nineteenth century and into the twentieth century by the shift in industrial significance away from textiles and towards heavy industry. Newly expanding heavy industries, broadly, excluded women from employment and provided relatively well-paid jobs, for example, in engineering, iron and steel, shipbuilding and mining. In contrast the old industries, such as textiles, clothes manufacture and lighter metal goods production, had a significant female workforce already established before the 1850s, and before the mobilisation of the male breadwinner wages claim (Szreter 1996; Walby 1986). There was great diversity in the composition of household income and in its gendered provenance. Women did not relax into a state of domestic ease furnished by their breadwinning husbands. Only the most skilled workers achieved wages sufficient to support their families and this was an experience not of the majority, although it became more prevalent amongst skilled working-class households in the early decades of the twentieth century. However, through the nineteenth century women were less routinely employed in the formal economy (Honeyman 2000). Developments through the final decades of the nineteenth century and into the twentieth served to marginalise women's work in many areas of the formal economy. Additionally, even where male earnings were sufficient to support their households at least through parts of the family life course, the family wage economy remained extremely precarious in a context of low wages for many, ill health and still high mortality rates (Tilly and Scott 1989).

The marginalisation of women's paid employment meant not the absence of paid work for many women but rather an increased burden of combining domestic and paid activities where the latter were to be found or made in the informal economy, or at the fringes of the formal economy in often vulnerable positions, in sweated labour and homeworking for example (Szreter 1996; Honeyman 2000). Szreter argues that through the latter half of the nineteenth century most working-class men were still able to secure only low and irregular earnings, despite the rhetoric and campaigns surrounding family wages. Most households still required the economic contributions of all members to survive; and yet the capacity for earning amongst women and children was minimalised by the exclusionary arguments and policies of employers and trade unions (Szreter 1996). Szreter describes this situation as putting women and men in a predicament of 'competitive interdependence' (ibid.). The existing wage structure required intensive working by women, but in a context where women were denied a work identity, and where formal employment opportunities were often limited (Honeyman 2000).

In short a range of processes combined to shape the emerging configuration of gendered differences and interdependencies, manifest in the increasing asymmetry of access to employment opportunities amongst women and men. These included the shifting industrial composition, the strengthening of collective bargaining in expanding sectors of the economy and constructions of working-class respectability which were mobilised strategically to converge with middle-class and governing notions of moral propriety and thereby strengthen the claims to a family wage. Changing gendered relations were clearly contingent in part on changing claims and the legitimacy accorded to them. It would be mistaken to make any general statement on shifting gendered identities given the very diverse experience, and different norms, across geographical areas and occupational sectors, and the far from total dominance of the family wage pattern. Nevertheless, as we shall see, the reconfiguring of gendered relations had a crucial, if mediating, role in the shaping of fertility decline. Most central is the shift in the social positioning of children. It is to nineteenth century changes in generational relations that I now turn.

The turn of the twentieth century is sometimes characterised as encapsulating a transformation in childhood, with a transition from a 'factory child' to a 'schooled' child (Hendrick 1990). The 'transformation' was longer in the making than implied by such notions of a systemic switch following the introduction of compulsory education. As with gender relations, change was composed of a diverse and differentiated transition, in which children came to be positioned as dependents over a lengthening part of their early life course.

The nineteenth century was characterised by an overall trend away from children as producers, contributing to the family economy from quite a young age, to children as dependent, a net cost, and as 'future' producers. In the predominantly rural economy of early industrial England, children were integral players in the family economy. Very young children were likely to work in arduous conditions, in domestic and agricultural tasks, and in production tasks in small-scale cottage industry (Levine 1987). As industrialisation progressed and the factory system became more extensive children's labour remained important, now within the new context of a family wage economy. Thompson highlights the transformatory consequences for human experience of the shift from a primarily rural economy based on cyclical time, to the time discipline of the factory (Thompson 1991). Factory and mill machinery dictated the pace of things, and workers – adults and children alike, came within its grip. In so doing they 'inherited the worst features of the domestic system [of production] in a context which had none of the domestic compensations' (ibid.: 370).

Critical of arguments that a humanitarian awakening rendered child labour unacceptable, Thompson describes the complacency and opposition to campaigns for reform of child labour between the 1820s and 1840s. To move forward required a shift in cultural terrain: 'We forget how long abuses can continue "unknown" until they are articulated: how people can look at misery and not notice it, until misery itself rebels' (ibid.: 377). With various Factory Acts and legislation restricting child labour, and with a shift to a more intensive mode of labour consumption by employers, with greater mechanisation reducing the demand for child labour, and with improved standards of living generally, children became less extensively engaged in economic activity. Diversity and differentiated change is again significant, there is no 'singular account' of change in child labour and its significance. Hunt (1981) estimated that in 1851, 30 per cent of children aged 10–15 were at work, compared to 11 per cent in 1911 (cited in Hopkins 1994). A substantial proportion of children were attending school in advance of the Education Acts. Ross estimates that 40 per cent of children under 10 were attending school before the 1870 Act (Ross 1993). Evidence from Birmingham reveals that in 1861, amongst those aged 5–8, around 40 per cent were at school, and of those aged 9–10 around 34 per cent were at school (Heward 1992, cited in Stephens 1998). However, few children under 10 were in employment, most were 'at home' according to the census. In some contexts however, child labour increased , with rising numbers in the textile factories and in agriculture (Stephens 1998). Whilst formal work was, by the 1871 census, fairly minimal for children under 10, amongst 10–14 year olds 32 per cent of boys and 21 per cent of girls, nationally, were in work. The averages hide great diversity in geographical and sectoral experience (ibid.).

The combination of campaigning for reduced working hours, the factory reform movement and increasing concern about children's education were all important to the introduction of legislation limiting the extent of child labour: the minimum age and the number of hours permissable. The Factory Acts passed from the 1830s on, which initially applied to textiles only, restricted the hours and conditions of employment for children and women. In restricting hours to ten and a half, the 1853 Factory Act by extension also restricted male hours. By 1878 a ten-hour day was the new maximum across all workplaces with over 50 employees. Additionally the 1878 Factory and Workshops Act raised the minimum age for part-time employment to 10, and the minimum age for full time employment to 14 (Szreter 1996). The Education Act of 1876 made elementary school attendance compulsory between the ages of 5 and 10, with the school-leaving age raised to 12 in 1899, and 14 by 1918 (Tilly and Scott 1989). The introduction and extension of compulsory education consolidated the exclusion of children from formal employment, although evidence attests to the ongoing significance of children's paid, and especially unpaid, work amongst poorer working-class households well into the 1900s, with children often employed in home-working and attending school intermittently (Levine 1987), or employed in casual labour out of school hours (Szreter 1996).

Different sets of interests were entailed in the passing of legislation for compulsory schooling of children. Williams highlights the significance of the rise of an organised working class which was making demands for an adequate education for its children, and employers' requirements in the context of industrial and economic restructuring. The interests of various parties converged in instituting mass education, including humanists, industrialists and the working classes (Williams 1961). Williams argues that the pervasiveness of the industrialists' case 'led to the definition of education in terms of future adult work, with the parallel clause of teaching the required social character – habits of regularity, "self-discipline", obedience, and trained effort' (ibid.: 141). The result of the combined restrictions on child labour and the extension of compulsory education, along with changes in the family economy and rising living standards for those in work, served to place children very differently in the social division of labour, and in the cultural imagination. In respect of the latter, Zelizer speaks of turn of century developments as amounting to a sacralisation of childhood: a shift from children being seen as an economic asset to an economic cost, but a priceless emotional asset (Zelizer 1985).[2]

In summary, developments through the nineteenth century culminated in a reconfiguring of the relations between children and their parents, at the level of the household, and children and adults more generally at the societal level. In respect of the latter, children came to be positioned with reference to the future, both as a metaphor for, and an investment in, the future, whether industrial, imperial or moral. With the reconfiguring of generational relations, then, came a shift both in the positioning of children relative to adults, and in values and claims regarding the proper rights and responsibilities of both. The social position of children was changing, bound up with altered patterns of interdependence across generations of parents and children. The extension of childhood dependence is crucial to analyses of change in the perceived costs of children. In conjunction with the reconfiguring of gender relations, these changes are at the heart of explanations of the first fertility decline. It is to these I now turn.

3.3 The first fertility decline

The European fertility revolution is widely cited as occurring between the 1870s and the 1930s. This period saw a remarkably rapid, and Europe-wide, decline in fertility rates. Within the UK the marriage cohort of 1860–1869 had an average of 6.16 children, those who were married between 1890 and 1899 had an average of 4.13 children and those who were married between 1920 and 1924 had an average of 2.31 children (Levine 1987). Of the 1870s marriage cohort 51.6 per cent had six or more children, yet of the 1925 marriage cohort only 6.7 per cent had six or more children (Anderson 1998). This was a remarkable and dramatic change in the space of just two generations, with birth rates falling to unprecedented lows. An historical first, too, was that 'stopping' had become a key strategy of family limitation. Historically fertility regulation had been achieved through late marriage, principally, and through the spacing of births. Gillis and his colleagues suggest that:

> Beginning in the 1870s . . . women were starting to stop before the end of their fertile years signalling not only a fundamental strategic change in patterns of family limitation but new attitudes towards fertility itself.
> (Gillis *et al.* 1992: 2)

Of course birth control techniques remained haphazard, and spacing remained an important component of fertility patterns. The emergence of new attitudes was a gradual and highly differentiated process (Szreter 1996).

Interestingly, changing attitudes towards having children are suggested not only by the aggregate declines in family size, but by novel family size distributions across the population. Anderson notes how most accounts of the European fertility decline have offered analyses of 'aggregated behaviour', paying remarkably little attention to emergent distributions. In fact the decline in large families of six or more children was accompanied by an increasing incidence of very small families. Some figures illustrate the marked nature of the change. In the UK, of those who married in the 1870s 8.3 per cent remained childless, of those who married between 1900 and 1909 11.3 per cent remained childless, and of those who married in 1925 16 per cent remained childless. Amongst the same three successive marriage cohorts, those who had a single child rose from 5.3 per cent to 14.8 per cent to 25.2 per cent. Thus families with one child or no children increased from 13.6 per cent for the 1870s marriage cohort to 41.3 per cent amongst the 1925 marriage cohort (Anderson 1998; also Hobcraft 1996).

How has the first fertility decline been interpreted? Amongst some historical demographers the main (and most general) dimensions of change to be identified lie in shifting economic and social relationships which altered the material and normative bases of fertility behaviours and related values and expectations. Amongst the social transformations of the period, as we have seen, were changes in patterns of interdependence between generational and gender groups. These changes contributed to altering the perceived costs of children, and the nature of costs and benefits which accrued to having (or not having) children. Broadly, the extension of legislation restricting child labour and the introduction of compulsory education raised the perceived relative costs of children (cf. Szreter 1996). Improved living standards became a real possibility for many working-class households if they had fewer children (Tilly and Scott 1989). Change in gender relations and ties between family members are crucial to theorising changes in the perceived costs of children, mediating the consequences of children's altered position (Seccombe 1993). Whilst more salient to consolidating, rather than initiating, fertility decline a number of other factors appear crucial. Declines in child mortality raised the likelihood that children, newly dependent for longer, would survive. A growing ideology of childhood which will be explored later celebrated 'good mothering' and emphasised the duties and obligations of women as mothers of the race. More reliable methods of birth control may have had significance in consolidating fertility decline yet widespread education and access to birth control technologies came relatively late in the demographic transition (e.g. Brookes 1986).

In the following I briefly review arguments which offer insights into cultural changes, as these altered the bases of rational action amongst women and men, and ushered in a quiet revolution in reproductive behaviours (cf. Gillis *et al.* 1992). The nature of cultural change is explored at different levels of generalisation – from the macro level of changing institutional arrangements, to the micro level of spousal relationships. The evidence reveals that the reshaping of interdependence between women and men and across generations, along with shifts in the relative positioning of women and men, children and parents, are a crucial part of the changing cultural context of fertility decline.

Modernisation theories of the demographic transition have offered a highly generalised account of change in subjectivities: a broad description of a 'modernizing of mentalities' according to Levine (1987). That is, such theories were abstracted accounts of a shift in motivations consistent with the transition from traditional to modern industrial society. Caldwell, in contrast, offered an influential account based on a more grounded conception of changing mentalities (Caldwell 1980). He placed the moral economy of the family at the centre of analysis, locating economically rational fertility-limiting behaviour within a newly altered cultural context. A key determinant of fertility behaviour is seen by Caldwell as the direction of intergenerational wealth flows. The fertility transition was induced by the introduction of mass, compulsory education (ibid.). For Caldwell, mass education led to a restructuring of family relations and altered the direction of wealth flow across generations. High fertility had been rational in the early industrial period, and before, when household survival depended largely on labour inputs. The introduction and extension of mass education from the 1870s meant that rather than wealth flowing 'up' generations, from children to parents, through the formers' contribution to household resourcing from a young age, wealth now flowed 'down' from parents to children, in support of their new and prolonged economic dependence. Consequently incentives for reproducing were radically altered, and birth rates declined rapidly (ibid.).

Handwerker argues that in Caldwell's model the link between wealth flow and behaviour is blurred. What is needed is additional specification of how changes in material factors alter values and behaviour by altering the means by which people create and stabilise income flows (Handwerker 1986). For him the period in the latter part of the nineteenth century saw a shift in lines of access to strategic resources – away from kinship and other personal relations and towards formal education and skill training. He argues that fertility transition did not straightforwardly follow the onset of mass education but followed from its conjunction with changes in the opportunity structure that increasingly rewarded educationally acquired skills and perspectives (ibid.).

In some ways this echoes Banks' analysis of fertility decline amongst the Victorian middle classes (Banks 1954). Banks stressed the importance of middle-class aspirations for their children's futures, and the growing attainability, for sons, of access to 'gentlemanly' jobs in the professions. In a context of very rapid growth in commerce and with a formalising of entry criteria to some of the professions, middle-class parents invested more in their children's futures, and expenditure on prolonged education became more customary. Despite a context of economic recession in the 1870s middle-class parents were determined to maintain the prospects of their children. The growing relative costs of children provided a significant disincentive to having large families (ibid.). Banks emphasised consumption aspirations amongst the middle classes, and the ability to attain the 'paraphernalia of gentility' (ibid.). Szreter also stresses status aspiration as important in shaping middle-class fertility decline. In the latter decades of the nineteenth century, young middle-class men were struggling to establish themselves, and sexual abstinence and small families became integral to successful middle-class careers and lifestyles (Szreter 1996).

Mackinnon rightly notes the relative absence of feminist research in the area of fertility decline (Mackinnon 1997). She explores, in part as a concomitant, the absence of research into the position and motivations of middle-class women in fertility decline. There is as we will see a more extensive body of work on working-class women and fertility decline. It was, however, middle-class couples who were the first to delimit family size, with declines being recorded from the 1860s. Mackinnon stresses the importance of the extension of higher education amongst young middle-class women. This contributed to an alteration of these women's sense of self, and of their possibilities as individuals. Thus more women gained the resources, both economic and cultural, to refuse to wholly give up their autonomy to men (ibid.). Mackinnon suggests a linked significance of the feminist movement, the diffusion of whose ideas, especially those questioning male conjugal rights, allowed women the space for increased control over their bodies, and their reproduction (ibid.; see also Seccombe 1993).

Notions of a 'trickle down' impact of middle-class ideas and practices have long been widely rejected and a body of research has grown to address the specific experiences and context of fertility decline amongst the working class. I explore this below. Crucial to this work has been the stress on disaggregation: recognition of complexity and diversity as key to adequate explanation. This disaggregation has entailed analyses of spousal relations and the potentially divergent interests and identities of wives and husbands rather than treating as a unit of analysis the 'reproductive couple'. Another crucial emphasis has been diversity across occupational and industrial sectors. Research here takes as central shifts in the perceived costs of children. In these interpretations economic rationality must be interpreted within its cultural contexts. A body of work, then, focuses on change in the perceived costs of having children, and its variation across socio-economic groups, and its mediation by gendered relations, and puts these at the heart of processes shaping fertility decline (e.g. Gittins 1982; Levine 1987; Seccombe 1993; Szreter 1996). Shifts in material circumstances and in gender and generational relations altered the pattern of motivations which shaped reproductive behaviour (indeed made family limitation fall within the realm of conscious choice). These in turn entailed profound shifts in practices of birth control.

In an early contribution in the area Gittins (1982) addressed diverse working-class patterns of fertility decline, with reference to gendered positions within the economy and to marital role relationships. In a context where sexual abstinence and coitus interruptus were major techniques of birth control clearly issues of communication and shared responsibility between sexual partners were crucial, the only realistic alternative for many being abortion, with its attendant risks (ibid.). Various developments increased the perceived costs of children, and Gittins both documents these developments and explores variability in patterns of fertility decline, and gendered experiences, through census data and oral history evidence. A rough correlation between women's employment participation and levels and fertility levels obtains, but it is not a general pattern. Gittins argues that a more adequate description and a more complete explanation requires us to consider a range of factors including occupational experience before as well as after marriage, the extent to which work and domestic 'spheres' were separated, and linked marital role and power relationships, and patterns of knowledge, outlook and communication and sharing of responsibility in reproduction and birth control, exemplified by the 'extreme' cases of locales dominated by textiles and mining occupations, and their respective patterns of low and high fertility.

Like Gittins, Seccombe too is concerned to work at both macro and household levels of analysis in developing an interpretation of general change which also addresses the level of individual motivation, 'reproductive consciousness', and power relations between spouses. Seccombe stresses the importance of childhood dependence, and the reversal of wealth flows between children and parents, as radically altering incentives to bear (many) children. The greater chances of children surviving, and the delay, and dissipation, of children's contributions to the family economy, meant a new economic 'squeeze' on working-class households. In this context there was an enhanced economic incentive to reduce family size, and so male breadwinners came to share in a longer-standing female interest in reducing family size. The latter is not fully explained by Seccombe, but arguably revealed in evidence of significant rates of abortion. With the switch in children's social position, and cost, male and female interests converged in limitation, a shift in reproductive consiousness amounting to a cultural revolution (Seccombe 1993). Contingent factors entrenched new norms and the altered 'meaning of things'. For example, Seccombe argues, an altered, medicalised discourse of pregnancy in the early decades of the twentieth century allowed women the possibility of some control, at least removing multiple childbearing from the realm of the natural and inevitable (ibid.; see also Gittins 1982). In this way, Seccombe argues, working-class families brought fertility in line with the new production regime. The intensive mode of production characteristic of the period (and outlined in section 3.2) was, then, paralleled by an intensive mode of reproduction, with an intensified investment of time, energy and resources devoted to each child (Seccombe 1993).

Seccombe seeks also to analyse the historical mutuality of modes of reproduction and production, and offers valuable insights regarding the linked nature of generational and gender relations in shaping fertility decline (ibid.). Whilst Szreter is critical of the notion of a graded class hierarchy on which Seccombe draws, he offers some parallel insights regarding the changing cultural and motivational context of fertility decline (Szreter 1996). He does so through a detailed and comprehensive engagement with diversity and differentiated fertility change, critiquing notions of a singular fertility decline and replacing it with a frame of multiple fertility declines, in diverse local cultural and occupational contexts. The research identifies the general social, economic and cultural transformations of the period, deemed to have restructured the motivational bases of fertility behaviour, and Szreter explores their particular negotiations in diverse contexts. The general changes altered the perceived costs of children, yet for this 'framework' to have purchase, Szreter argues, it is crucial to know how different social groups and communities defined childrearing costs and benefits within their diverse cultural contexts.

Szreter argues that the embedding of nineteenth-century gendered ideologies of familial and working roles were a necessary condition for the declines in fertility, since such ideologies altered men's involvement in childrearing. With policy interventions through the latter part of the century in particular serving to extend childhood dependency, incentives for childbearing and rearing were being significantly restructured. In parallel with Seccombe, Szreter highlights how the breadwinning pattern was conducive to family size becoming a more singularly economic assessment. Like the others, Szreter stresses too the intensity and pressure of state and voluntary intervention in the lives and affairs of working-class households, and the accompanying ideology of the primacy of maternal responsibility in children's welfare. The internalisation by women of this ideology of individual responsibility for what were effectively communal failings, Szreter argues, was an enormous motivator, raising the perceived costs of children and discouraging large families (Szreter 1996). The infant and maternal welfare movement appears to have consolidated changes in reproductive consciousness and patterns of fertility decline.

In respect of variation in patterns of fertility and decline, Szreter argues that the most important single factor was the way in which local labour markets were age- and gender-structured. He explores the two 'extreme' cases of textiles and mining occupations, since they serve to exemplify key processes present, but in more mixed form, in other contexts. They are 'extreme' in respect of the availability of work strategies realistically available to members of working-class households. Fertility declines began amongst textiles workers in the 1860s and 1870s and ended with the mining communities in the 1920s and 1930s. In textiles areas there was wide availability of female employment and of low-paid, but regular, juvenile employment, for both sexes. Often women in textiles were married to men in the same sector, or in casual, low-paid and low-skilled jobs such as labouring. In this context there was a clear logic to women remaining in work, at least until children were old enough to earn reasonable wages in their teenage years. Childbearing and rearing would impose severe financial difficulties in this context. The textiles sector had employed women and children quite extensively from its early industrialisation. Since mothers' and children's labour was often substituted, education and factory legislation reinforced the pattern of female-labour use, and amplified its key effects through raising perceived costs of childrearing (ibid.). In contrast in mining areas there were few earnings opportunities available to women, and relatively high earnings and job security available to adult men (ibid.). Iron and steel, and heavy engineering, shared some features with mining, and were also characterised by relatively high fertility rates well into the twentieth century. Miners had relatively high wages from quite a young age, a factor encouraging earlier marriage and higher fertility. Families were dominated by the unionised male breadwinner, and married women were socially segregated and had few or no economic opportunities or roles outside the home. The incentive structure, and patterns of reproductive consciousness, looked very different across these communities (ibid.). The extension of childhood dependence had negligible impact on the opportunity costs of childbearing, since there were few opportunities for women's employment.

Within the above perspectives on the fertility decline, the reconfiguring of difference and ties of interdependence between generation and gender groups is central to the shaping of fertility decline and its diverse patterning. In particular there were important changes in the family economy and the relative positioning of women and men, and of children and parents, within that family economy. These groups acquired a novel positioning within the organisation of social reproduction. Generation and gender relations do not define, nor explain, trends in fertility decline, yet they give crucial insights into radical change in reproductive behaviours through the period. The reconfiguring of generational and gendered social positions and interdependencies is crucial to understanding a radical shift in fertility behaviours and the first fertility decline. Choice and decision-making came to be newly meaningful to people within this altered context. We will see later that interpretations of current change assume that because new kinds of choices are available to people, at the end of the twentieth century, they provide new explanatory purchase on current change. It is particularly pertinent then to recognise that radically new kinds of choices became meaningful to people at the end of the nineteenth century, and yet it is not appropriate to look back and imagine that such scope meant people were more autonomous, more freed from social conditions. On the contrary new kinds of choices were inseparable from changing social conditions. Later in the book I will argue that in parallel, although to a lesser degree, late twentieth-century changes in fertility can be interpreted as part of a reconfiguring of gender and generational relations. And in parallel new kinds of choices and values are integral to changing social relations, not separable from them.

In the next section I refocus on changing gender relations and identities in consideration of work, family and welfare policy in the early twentieth century. Here we can see how particular claims and values regarding gender roles and identities 'play through' and feed into a hardening asymmetry around sexual divisions of labour in the first decades of the twentieth century.

3.4 Gendered relations and claims in the early twentieth century

3.4.1 Introduction: the embedding of the family wage ideal

The first decades of the twentieth century revealed a new dominance or scope of the breadwinner/carer ideology (Gittins 1982; Lewis 1980). Such a pattern attained a new breadth of coverage and came into its own as the 'proper' aspiration for working households. A quite clear-cut division of labour by gender, between paid work and domestic labour, certainly appears to have been the model of respectability for better-off working-class families (e.g. Roberts 1986). Evidence suggests a consolidation of these divisions and a quite widespread consensus around the appropriate division of labour. The social and subjective identities of women as domestic managers and carers and men as breadwinners were shaped in a context in which gender-differentiated roles and responsibilities became more tighly drawn (Pedersen 1993; Lewis 1986; Jenson 1986).

By 1914 it seems fewer married women worked, and spent less of their lifetimes working, than had 50 years previously (Tilly and Scott 1987). Between 1911 and 1931 approximately 10 per cent of married women were employed in the formal labour market, that is paying insurance contributions and therefore enumerated in the census. Employment was the norm amongst single women, around 70 per cent of whom were working. Being married entailed presumptions of women's dependence, and the general expectation was that married women would not work. The cultural context was unfavourable to married women's employment; the available employment was badly paid relative to men's, and the very extensive labour entailed in household work along with childcare meant that many women would not aspire to work in the formal labour market if they could afford not to. We can point to a number of bases for the contraction of married women's employment opportunities and the cultural marginalisation of such employment. Increased living standards had allowed better diets, and health and life expectancies had improved. The incidence of illness and mortality amongst working-age men declined. Consequently there was less of a need for improvised wage-earning, which had been such a significant factor for women's employment through the nineteenth century (ibid.). Additionally, men's real wages had improved across the period from 1880 to 1910, yet the differential between the sexes remained. The family wage was a reality for better-off working-class households (ibid.), amongst many of which declines in family size had reduced financial necessity. For Roberts, households with a skilled main earner exemplified the breadwinner-homemaker ideal, yet as an ideal it was much wider spread, an aspiration even amongst those who could not realise it. Many women it seems saw liberation as lying in the move away from paid employment and into domesticity (Roberts 1986; Harris 1993), a move facilitated by the rise in living standards amongst households with a skilled worker. For the first time, economic scarcity was no longer the driver of working household strategies for survival and reproduction, allowing new kinds of independence from the dictates of economic need (cf. Harris 1993). However, as women's livelihoods were funnelled through the hands of men, their claims to independence were more narrowly delimited (Honeyman 2000).

The realisation of the male breadwinner wage claim in strongly unionised sectors and the linked marginalisation of women in the formal labour market meant there were few openings for the employment of married women. There was still diversity, yet by the inter-war period even in some textiles sectors women would find themselves increasingly discriminated against (Walby 1986). The marginalisation of married women's employment continued through the inter-war period. As we will see, the increase in women's employment in the First World War was framed as temporary. We may sidestep the question as to whether, after the war, women left jobs willingly or were pushed (both were true), and focus on how women's and men's options and social identities were framed.

The context, then, is one of a sharpened difference of roles and responsibilities, and a linked asymmetry in the interdependence of women and men. How does this pattern of difference articulate with norms and expressed values regarding gendered roles, and with the variable success of related claims? Jenson discusses the inter-war construction of gender roles and identities in terms of a narrowing of the 'universe of political discourse' (Jenson 1986). She suggests there was a closing down of space in which alternative ideologies, identities and patterns of living could be constructed and expressed. There was a social embedding of particular assumptions and notions of what was right and proper. This is not to say that everyone simply 'bought into' an ideology of separate spheres and proper roles for women and men. However, the pattern did attain an unprecedented currency and dominance (ibid.). It shaped people's experiences and aspirations, and it influenced the perceived legitimacy and scope of oppositional voices. Jenson's 'universe of political discourse' is a macro level statement of claims and values which hold cultural currency. For Jenson, the 'notion of the universe of political discourse leads to an analysis which concentrates less on the bases of difference than on the way difference is constituted in any social formation' (ibid.: 26).

Her analysis is of value since it reminds us that gender difference and its salience is socially and historically made, and its contours, therefore, changeable with context. I address here the issue of how gendered difference was constituted in the early twentieth century. Further, the analysis exemplifies the ways in which claims and values contribute to shaping extant material relations. I consider in turn: issues in the infant and maternal welfare movement; employment patterns and practices during and after the First World War; feminist campaigning around family allowances; and unemployment policies and their interpretations. These all help reveal the cultural and material shaping of gendered difference.

3.4.2 Good mothering

The decline in family size both facilitated and was reinforced by an intensified investment of time, energy and resources devoted to each child, and an ideology of 'good mothering'. This was especially influential in the early decades of the twentieth century, and buttressed the ideal of separate, domestic and work, spheres. Strengthening claims in this domain served to further entrench the pattern of gender differentiation and separate roles. Idealised visions of maternity grew in part from the eugenics movement, with its concern for the quantity and quality of the population, and in part from broader welfarist concerns regarding infant and maternal mortality and health. Fears about population decline, infant mortality and the health of the working class, and the position of Britain as an imperial and commercial power are widely cited as important to a strengthening ideology of 'good mothering' by the beginning of the twentieth century. The declining birth rate was well known by this point and anxieties about the nation's future were compounded by evidence of working-class ill-health and by a high and recently increasing rate of infant mortality, at over 150/1000 at the turn of the century (Davin 1978). Recruitment of soldiers to fight in the Boer War revealed very low levels of health amongst working-class recruits, many of whom were unfit to serve, and is widely cited as galvanising opinion and policy-makers in the domains of public health and child welfare. The stress on the future of the race and the role of mothers in raising children as befitted their role as 'the future of the country and the Empire' (Earl Beauchamp 1902, cited in Davin 1978: 10) was part of a context in the early part of the century where the survival of infants and the health and welfare of children was a national priority (Lewis 1986). Several writers point to the growing emphasis on both child health and maternal duties within public discourse and guiding policies (e.g. Davin 1978; Lewis 1980, 1986; Roberts 1986; Ross 1993). Whilst there was clearly some recognition that 'environmental' factors were significant in shaping disease and mortality, much discourse and policy revealed a much more individualised notion of responsibility: if maternal ignorance could be blamed then so it could also (at relatively little cost) be countered (Davin 1978; see also Lewis 1986; Jones 2000).

A host of measures were put in place to improve both material conditions and to promote public health. For example, in the early 1900s midwives were newly required to have training, local authorities were empowered to provide meals for poor children, and medical inspection in schools was established (Davin 1978; Lewis 1980). There was a rapid growth in the number and activities of voluntary societies dedicated to promoting public health and hygiene. Despite some recognition of the social factors behind infant mortality, a good deal of stress was placed on the proper education of potential and current mothers. Most local education authorities included classes in mothercraft in their school syllabuses. Voluntary agencies ran 'schools for mothers'. By the end of the First World War local authorities were administering an extensive network of infant welfare centres across the country (Lewis 1980). These schools and centres provided advice and classes in the areas of infant health and in cooking, sewing and so on. A health visiting system was established and administered by local authorities, absorbing a significant amount of the available grant for maternal and infant welfare work. Evidence suggests unsurprisingly a preference amongst working-class women for drop-in centres, rather than the impositional visits of health visitors who were often seen as patronising and out of touch with the realities of working-class life (ibid.).

As noted, Szreter suggests that the ideology of good mothering, the expanded sense of responsibility which working-class women came to have for their children's health, was internalised and may itself have consolidated fertility decline through raising the costs of material and emotional investment in children (Szreter 1996; Ross 1993). Other evidence suggests that working-class women took on such ideals so far as they suited their own ends. Nevertheless, the writers discussed here imply that contemporary ideals of good mothering both derived from and contributed to a broader context of rhetoric, campaigning and policies which consolidated a particular pattern of gender difference and interdependence.

3.4.3 Gender and work across the First World War

The early decades of the twentieth century saw the seismic shift of world war. This concerns us here in respect of its consequences for gendered claims to work and welfare. In brief, the apparently radical restructuring of women's roles in social reproduction was framed within a pattern of continuity of norms and policies regarding their proper roles. Women significantly increased their level of employment participation during the war but the increase was temporary. The labour unions had a very strong hand in setting the conditions for the cooperation of their working class-members in the prosecution of war (Pedersen 1993). The strength of the unions, the inability to conscript recruits in the early stages of the war, and the importance of wartime manufacturing production allowed the unions some power in the making of a contract between labour and government. Unions agreed to give up customary trade practices, for wartime only, for a guarantee that the pay and positions of unionised workers would not be undermined (ibid.). Between 1914 and 1918 women's employment participation rate increased from 31 per cent to 37 per cent, and they significantly increased their participation in better-paid jobs in industry as well as in the service sector. By the end of the war a significant number of women worked in munitions and engineering. Women's employment conditions and earnings levels improved. General data on married women's employment is not available, but the increase appears to have been marked (ibid.). Pedersen describes how, despite forecasts that women's radically altered position in employment would be maintained after the war, the war ultimately confirmed pre-war patterns. Although there was a marked increase in female trade union membership, formal policy such as advanced by the National Federation of Women Workers (NFWW) followed a 'working-class', family wage strategy rather than an explicitly feminist strategy, with women being advised to demand equal pay on behalf not of themselves but of the men who would return to the jobs. The general context remained one of a family wage strategy, with mothers' work constructed as a temporary wartime expedient, by the women unionists in much the same way as by male unionists (ibid.).

Separation allowances were granted to soldiers' wives throughout the war, worth around half the wage of skilled workers, and classed as entitlements. These helped to raise living standards, and Pedersen notes the value to women of a source of income which was independent and reliable, with evidence of improved health of women and children in receipt of such allowances. Although women may have experienced the allowance as a wage, the logic of the allowances was one which buttressed the breadwinner /dependent ideal, with women's entitlement derived not from her citizenship status but from the fact of her marriage to a soldier, with the state simply taking over temporarily the duty to maintain (ibid.).

The 'ejection' of women from employment after the war and subsequent social policy are, then, continuous with aspects of policy through the war years, and suggest important continuities in the social positioning of married women. At the end of the war the government was faced with the problem of managing demobilised soldiers seeking work, and the unemployment of women who would lose their jobs. The Restoration of Prewar Practices Act restricted women's employment, and many women were simply dismissed from their jobs and men recruited. As it became less acceptable to employ women in 'men's jobs', women were displaced by demobilised soldiers and by men who had never served (Braybon and Summerfield 1987). Whilst in a brief postwar period of relative economic prosperity some women retained employment in engineering and other factory jobs, the economic slump of 1920 led to mass unemployment. A sharp decline in the number of women registered as unemployed reflected new requirements for eligibility. For example, women were required to have been paying contributions before the war, and to accept low-paid domestic or service work if offered, or lose their right to benefits (unlike unemployed men who could only be offered jobs in their trade) (ibid.). The context was clearly one of the inappropriateness of women 'taking jobs' from men, and the media and, reportedly, public opinion turned very much against working women (ibid.). The leaders of women's unions did not campaign on behalf of women to keep their wartime jobs. Mary Macarthur, leader of the NFWW, said that women should give up their jobs to returning men. This may have been a compromise born out of the relative lack of resources of women's organisations who could not afford to alienate men's trades unions (Walby 1986). As Pedersen argues, female unionists were locked into a framework where women's interests were defined by their position as dependents, in a context of claims for the male family wage (Pedersen 1993).

Reactions to leaving paid employment by women must have been mixed, according to Braybon and Summerfield characterised more by regret than by bitterness, but also by a new sense of self-worth amongst women (Braybon and Summerfield 1987). Certainly for many women their self-worth was constructed in terms of their role as household managers. Maternal and infant welfare concerns continued, with ideals of good mothering still important in rhetoric, policy and practice. This was a period of enforced exclusion of women from much employment, with semi-formal marriage bars on women working in the civil service and in teaching, and exclusion of female labour from unionised trades in much of industry. If the 'average' pattern was one of exclusion this hides great diversity, with some sectors and areas where married women's employment was the norm. This was most evidently the case in the North West textiles areas, and amongst expanding new industries in the South East (Glucksmann 1990). Additionally, many married women worked quite routinely in casual and temporary jobs which would not be enumerated in the census, and which significantly understates the extent of women's paid labour (ibid.; Roberts 1986). From 1921 onwards there was a limited increase in the percentage of married women in insured jobs, but the aggregate change was slight, with married women's participations rates lying at 9.6 per cent, 8.7 per cent and 10.0 per cent in 1911, 1921 and 1931 respectively (Gittins 1982, after Halsey 1972).

The breadwinner model did not furnish a neat fit between economic needs and asymmetrical family roles. Married women were restricted in their employment opportunities regardless of household need and of their interests as potential workers. Many such women engaged in casual and temporary jobs, or in informal economic activity. Nevertheless, the breadwinner pattern was clearly more prevalent than it had been and held significant force in policy interventions. It reflected power differentials in society and the mobilisation of resources by certain groups in pressing their particular vision of social organisation. The linked pattern of separate spheres seemed inevitable, if not natural, to many. Yet within this construction of gendered differences there was still scope for different visions of interdependence, and space for claims to equality, a space which was effectively closed off, as we see below.

3.4.4 Gender and social policies: difference, claims and social identities

To speak of a set of cultural 'ideals' is in part to acknowledge the power of certain claims, and certain voices, in propagating their vision of society. As we have seen, the norm of separate spheres had attained a particular currency by the early decades of the twentieth century. Certain values were embodied effectively in claims which were translated into policies and practices, and which marginalised and undermined other voices and arguments. As Abrams said:

> [M]en act on the basis of ideas but the ideas they have at any particular time, and still more the influence of these ideas, is not just an intellectual matter. Many good ideas never get a hearing; many bad ideas flourish for generations.
>
> (Abrams 1982: 11–12)

We have noted the apparent cultural force of the family wage pattern – as an ideal for some and, perhaps, best bet under the circumstances for others. However, the pattern clearly entailed a fundamental gender inequality. The story of how this was challenged and with what consequence is of interest since it further reveals then current ideas about gendered positions and interdependencies. The campaign for the endowment of motherhood presented a significant challenge to the family wage system, albeit a challenge contained within broad acceptance of separate spheres of work and family, and linked male and female roles shaped in part by an acceptance of women's natural maternal responsibilities (Lewis 1991; Thane 1991; Pedersen 1989, 1993). The aim of the campaign was to achieve cash income paid directly to mothers by the state: an argument for equality through difference, and a challenge to a system in which women's livelihoods were dependent upon men. With the passing of legislation to secure women's pensions, Pedersen suggests that women's claims were undermined and reshaped, in the hands of trades unions, the Labour Party and government, into policies which in fact encoded women's dependence on men (Pedersen 1993).

Before the First World War many feminists had advocated an egalitarianism in which women should enter work and politics on the same terms as men (Lewis 1991; Pedersen 1989). Claims for mothers' endowment were also being voiced before the war. The fate of such claims in some ways echoes the sentiments of Ramsay MacDonald, leader of the Labour Party, who referred to the claim to maintenance of women by the state rather than through the family, as 'an insane outburst of individualism' (MacDonald 1909, quoted by Land 1980: 70). War may have temporarily unsettled gender relations, but it appeared also to open up an opportunity for campaigning and policy intervention to reorder gender relations and revalue women's claims to independent income. In the event various factors stalled and redirected the momentum of the family allowance claim. Pedersen notes the role of reactionary civil servants in drafting policy (Pedersen 1993), and Jones the reluctance of government to be drawn into avoidable public expenditure commitments (Jones 2000). According to Pedersen, research on which parliamentarians drew in their debates claimed that women were rarely responsible for resourcing dependents, reasserting the match between the breadwinner system and family needs, a claim based on an assumption rather than on empirical evidence (Pedersen 1993). And perhaps most importantly, the family allowance claim was effectively sidelined within the labour movement. A Labour Party and TUC Joint Committee on Motherhood and Child Endowment reported in 1922, rejected proposals for cash endowments for mothers, and instead pressed the case for universal services: health, education, provisioning of milk and school meals. A concern here was that benefits for women would lead to cuts in men's wages (Pedersen 1993). Again though we need to recognise not simply an economic argument, but one embedded in cultural constructions of masculine identity. The critique by feminists of this stance and the rift between them and the Labour Party served to further marginalise women's voice in policy formulation. Social policy, Pedersen argues, like labour market policies, came to tighten the assumption of women's dependence on men. Claims for the state endowment of motherhood were transmuted into the Widow's Pension Act of 1925: this was a reflection not of 'the belief that a women should be endowed because she is a mother, but rather when and because she is the trustee of her dead husband's family' (Davies 1923, cited in Pedersen 1989).

Evidence regarding reactions to unemployment benefits policies suggests that the assumption of proper gendered roles and responsibilities ran deep in the popular imagination. Two examples suggest widespread acceptance of female dependency on male breadwinner wage, and the unacceptability of undermining men's 'independent' status as breadwinners. In a context of rising unemployment and fiscal crisis, the Labour government of 1931 passed the Unemployment Insurance Act 1931: more commonly known as the Anomalies Act. This restricted receipt of unemployment benefits by some classes of worker, particularly married women. The new law made it very difficult for any married woman worker to collect insurance benefits if she became unemployed. It specified that in order to receive unemployment benefit, women needed to be unemployed *and* able to prove that they had a good chance of finding work. Women faced discrimination in finding work – but the very fact of discrimination meant that benefits could be denied to women as well (Pedersen 1993). When a woman became married she was effectively giving up her right to any insurance cover, despite having paid insurance contributions. The regulations were used indiscriminately so most married women were blocked from receipt of benefit. The regulations clearly reflected, and strengthened, the breadwinner norm:

> [The] bland tolerance of the marriage bar was possible only because of the assumption, so pervasive as to be almost unspoken, that married women did not – and should not – normally earn wages. The relevant fact considered in determining whether the woman was 'genuinely seeking work' and deserving of benefit became not whether she was looking for work, had worked, and had paid her contributions, but whether there was a man in the house.
>
> (Pedersen 1993: 306)

There appears to have been little popular sympathy for employment amongst married women, a group construed as more properly fulfilling their domestic and childrearing duties full time. The employment of men was seen as a right, whilst married women's employment was seen as inappropriate and even, by many, as selfish. Pedersen notes that the Anomalies regulations evoked relatively little response or opposition. In contrast the household means test, which undermined men's claims to independence and family headship status, aroused much greater protest, amongst women as well as men. The National Government of 1931 introduced the Household Means Test in which those who had exhausted contributed benefits would receive a new 'transitional benefit' after a household means test (the 'dole'). The household means test meant that men were expected to live off the income of others in the household, in full or in part, after exhausting their insurance benefits. As the ability to earn a family wage had become a kind of litmus test of masculinity, many saw this as an assault on male identity. The means test was widely protested. Labour Party's women's sections gave greater protest to this than to 'feminist' causes (Pedersen 1993). A resolution of the TUC (1933) calling for abolition of both Anomalies regulations and the means test aroused opposition from many who did not want to link the issues. The male breadwinner ideal was sufficiently pervasive by 1930 as to make the regulations seem reasonable and only the household means test an 'injustice'. It was the undermining of men's position as earner and breadwinner which aroused so much opposition, not the further undermining of married women's claims to 'independent' income (Pedersen 1992). Through these changing constructions we can see a change in norms regarding the appropriate roles and duties of women and men, consistent with a hardening asymmetry in women's and men's social positions.

A situation of some relative flexibility in women's and men's roles, governed in part by pragmatics, contingency and economic necessity gave way increasingly to a more rigid pattern of asymmetry, gender division and separate spheres, and male economic independence and female economic dependence. Although there were protests and no general consensus there is evidence that gender divisions became more entrenched both as a material social ordering and as a norm to which many adhered and, indeed, saw as proper and just.

3.5 Conclusion

This chapter has explored the reconfiguring of gendered and generational relations through the latter part of the nineteenth century and the early decades of the twentieth century. This reconfiguring entailed a repositioning of gender and generational groups and a linked recomposing of gender, and of child/adult, difference. The reconfiguring of gender and of generational difference refers to both change in groups' positions in society and the linked cultural constructions of difference. The basis of group differentiation lies as much in value, claims and imaginings as in harder 'facts' of difference revealed through gender and generational divisions of labour, employment policies, legal rights and so forth.

Change in generational and gendered relations is crucial to an adequate understanding of the shaping of fertility decline, a social revolution alongside the more widely acknowledged economic and political transformations at the birth of the twentieth century. The altered social location of children and revised social identities of childhood and parenthood are absolutely central to understanding the marked declines in family size, and shifts in the family as a social form, and altered constructions of the nature of childhood and the role of child, and parent, in society. The chapter explored the reconfiguring of gender relations through the family wage 'apogee' in the early decades of the twentieth century, with the embedding of a particular set of assumptions and notions of gendered moral propriety in respect of family, work and welfare rights and duties. Altered social identities and norms were all part of a set of developments leading to a narrowing of the 'universe of political discourse', and therefore of the scope of perceived alternatives, and the voice achieved by their advocates. The patterns of gender difference, and the evaluations which shaped such difference, were not hegemonic, and there was protest and variability. They did, though, come to hold a particular, and dominant, cultural currency. Change in the social ordering of gender relations, as well as change in the positioning of children, was linked to changing norms and cultural constructions of moral propriety.

The evidence and analysis described here offers insights for the analysis of recent, late twentieth-century social changes. Clearly what is happening now is no repetition of what went before: in its substance it is obviously historically unique. However, in its *form*, social change now holds some parallels with former historical change. Then, as now, a reconfiguring of social relations and linked values and claims reveals insights into the nature of social change. For example, change in the relative positioning of women and men, and of generational groups, and linked shifts in interdependence are again relevant to understanding recent patterns of fertility decline. Changes in the position of women and men in employment and social reproduction is again linked to changing gendered identities and assumptions about morally appropriate roles for women and men. Of course the content of such changes now is very different. However, we need not see contemporary society as generating a pattern of transformation which is uniquely difficult to interpret: rather we can use the same kinds of analytic tools to interrogate current change as another historically situated, coherent, round of social transition. These themes are taken up in the next chapter.

4 Contemporary transformations in gender, work and family

4.1 Introduction

The last decades of the twentieth century have seen a recomposing of social relations and values, and the emergence of new patterns of diversity and inequality. In this chapter I focus on the reshaping of gendered difference, interdependencies, and relations to family and to work. The chapter is divided into two linked parts. The first of these focuses on family change, and the second on women's and men's relations to employment. These issues are very closely linked but are considered separately in order to draw out some key issues which relate most directly to one or the other. In respect of family change, there are parallels between developments in the latter part of the twentieth century (called by some the second demographic transition) and the first fertility decline around the turn of the twentieth century. We will see that various writers explain recent developments in family demography through theses of individualisation. Such an analysis is misplaced. A very valuable lesson for interpreting recent developments in family forms, and the social relations reshaping them, lies in analyses of the first demographic transition. As we saw in Chapter 3 radical transformation in fertility patterns in the late nineteenth and early twentieth centuries are best understood with reference to a shift in the relative position of gender and generational groupings, and linked changes in assumptions of appropriate social roles for women and men, child and adult. These developments were linked to broader social changes. So, too, we can analyse recent changes in family form and relations. In contrast to theses of individualisation, often invoked in explanations of current demographic change, we can better interpret recent developments as part of a reconfiguring of patterns of difference and interdependence, and a change in contexts of social action. Furthermore, like the first fertility decline recent demographic changes reveal a mutuality of norms and social relations. I develop the argument through a focus on issues of fertility, patterns of parenthood and childlessness.

The second part of the chapter explores contemporary transformations in gender relations. I explore recent debates surrounding continuity and change in women's and men's relations to paid employment and social reproduction.

Emphasis on gender inequalities, and the expansion in women's employment opportunities have been important issues framing much debate in the area since the 1980s (e.g. Arber and Ginn 1995; Glover and Arber 1995; Joshi and Hinde 1993). Continuity of women's disadvantage relative to men has been a watchword of much of this research. Recently there has been a growing emphasis on complexity and diversity, and recognition that the question of continuity or change in the gender inequality gap is a narrow basis on which to research a more general question about gender restructuring. Thus there has been a growing interest in changing gender relations and recognition of diversity, complexity and the unevenness of gendered changes (Humphries and Rubery 1992; Walby 1997; Bottero 2000). Another important theme in research on gender change and employment has been recognition of an erosion of the breadwinner claim and the emergence of a new, and as yet somewhat indeterminate, set of gender arrangements. I explore these arguments and what they reveal about the recent reconfiguring of gendered differences and interdependencies. A core argument is that we are witnessing a reshaping of gender: specifically change in the social position of women and men relative to each other, and in changing assumptions and expectations regarding gender difference. These developments have been brought about in part by gendered processes, for example, through change in the demographic availability of women to work in the labour market, through changes in women's claims and expectations, and through changes in their relative attractiveness to employers in the newly extensive service economy. Gendered developments in employment patterns have also been shaped by other processes in which gender is more incidental: the expanded significance of market models of economic organisation, and linked patterns of deregulation. In short we can see important shifts in the ordering of gender difference and interdependencies, and a reshaping of the relative social positioning of women and men and of norms and assumptions about proper gendered roles.

Throughout the chapter I develop an argument about changing patterns of interdependence and change in the social positioning of women and men, and argue also that gender, as a dimension of difference, has variable salience. In some contexts we see a reproduction of older patterns of gender difference and inequalities, in other contexts we see a pattern of de-differentiation where gender is less relevant than it was to people's life chances or social roles. This chapter focuses on restructuring with a lens on the macro level, the next chapter explores the meshing of norms and social relations and moves between micro and macro levels of analysis

4.2 Demographic change and issues of explanation

4.2.1 Individualisation theories of demographic change

The long-run trend from the latter part of the nineteenth century to the present has been, broadly, one of fertility decline, although there was an important counter-trend in the early post war decades. Through the 1930s and early 1940s fertility declines were, as previously, accompanied by state-level anxieties about a shrinking nation, about security and prosperity (e.g. Thane 1999). Mass Observation data collected in 1944 reveals the extent of women's preferences for a reduced family size (ibid.). Still many working-class women, particularly in some local labour market contexts, had very large families in the early decades of the twentieth century, and their daughters interviewed as part of the Mass Observation research overwhelmingly expressed their desire for smaller families, a decent living standard and education for their children (ibid.). Thane suggests this was indicative of new conceptions of social selfhood, in the context of it being possible and meaningful to control family size, although as shown in Chapter 3 this pattern was already well established for many working-class groups. The post-war period saw an increase in the birth rate following demobilisation. It then stabilised before manifesting a more sustained increase from the mid 1950s to a peak in 1964: the baby boom. Alongside the high fertility rates from the mid 1940s to mid 1960s a range of indicators reflect what is often seen as a heyday of family stability, with low rates of divorce, little cohabitation and few births outside marriage (McRae 1999a).

The last quarter of the twentieth century saw a series of significant demographic developments which, for some commentators, reveal a transformation in patterns of relational and reproductive behaviour. There have been some marked alterations in the organisation of household living arrangements and family ties, a shift in the texture of lived experience indicated in a now very familiar list of headings. There has been a growth in cohabitation, a decline in marriage rates and increases in the proportion of births outside marriage; significant increases in divorce rates, particularly marked in Britain at least until the early 1990s, and a significant increase in the proportion of families headed by a lone parent (e.g. McRae 1999b; Kiernan *et al.* 1998; Haskey 1996; Murphy and Berrington 1993). Rates of fertility declined and stabilised at below replacement levels in Britain, as across many European countries. Patterns of deferral in the timing of parenthood and increased rates of childlessness have contributed to changing fertility patterns, and changing family size distributions (Pearce *et al.* 1999).

In addressing changes in the latter decades of the twentieth century it is pertinent to be reminded of the evidence that longer-run comparisons are often important. Recent historical changes may be seen as revealing the particularity of family-related living arrangements in the 1950s and 1960s: it is the stable and relatively homogeneous family forms of that period which were the historical novelty, not late twentieth-century diversity (e.g. McRae 1999a).

Developments from the late 1960s onwards are described by some authors as a second demographic transition, to compare with the first demographic transition, and its fertility decline, at the turn of the twentieth century. A model of individualisation has been an important component in some explanations of current demographic change. For example, Lesthaeghe has argued, influentially, that ideational change is important to understanding the second demographic transition, with a growing value placed on individual rights and autonomy in the latter part of the twentieth century (Lesthaeghe 1998; Lesthaeghe and Surkyn 1988). In other words the motivations of demographic behaviour are deemed to have changed in recent decades. Lesthaeghe concludes that the 'second demographic transition', a series of developments including declining fertility, increasing cohabitation and increasing divorce rates, can be located within cultural traditions which promote individual autonomy and self-fulfilment (Lesthaeghe 1995). Beck and Beck-Gernsheim (2002) identify a greater fragility to familial bonds as chosen forms of cooperation displace imposed duties of obligation. To describe contemporary trends in terms of fragmentation and individualisation is to overstate the notion of breakdown. Individualisation, of course, does not necessarily imply more selfish behaviour, but an altered relationship between individual and society is implied. So for example some researchers see fertility decline (and the second demographic transition more widely) as an outcome of cultural shifts which allow greater agency and self-determination by individuals (Lesthaeghe 1995). Other arguments of growing individualism have been invoked also in explanations of fertility decline. Aries for example, argues that the first fertility decline was a consequence of a surge in emotional and financial investments in children. In contrast, he suggests, late twentieth-century declines in fertility are due to the emergence of a more individualist and adult-centred orientation (Aries 1980). Children are less pivotal in young adults' future plans, but '[fit] into them as one of the various components that make it possible for adults to bloom as individuals' (ibid.: 650). That is, an individualistic and more self-centred outlook means that the decision to have children is both freely chosen, and about individual self-fulfilment, whereas in the past it was less likely to be freely chosen, and less subject to reflexivity. In a parallel vein Sporton argues that a shift from altruism to individualism has caused fertility decline (Sporton 1993, cited in Crompton 1999). Interestingly Cliquet notes that changing demographic behaviours during the first demographic transition, when it was men who had new opportunities for self-fulfilment, have been characterised in terms of altruistic behaviour. Now, when it is mainly women who are achieving greater emancipation and scope for self-development, characterisations of altered demographic behaviours are in terms not of altruism but of individualism, egocentricity and selfishness (Cliquet 1991).

Oppenheimer draws attention to a paradox which emerges from the growing emphasis on cultural explanations of change in family behaviour. In such cultural explanations modernisation is seen to have underlain a growth of individualism:

> [T]here is a general erosion of family norms with the result that marriage and family behaviour is becoming more discretionary and less important

> in people's lives. This perspective takes us beyond the economist's narrow individualistic decision making concern with the gain to marriage and into the sociological realm of norms and values; but, in a sense, the cultural argument is that the self interested man (or woman) of traditional micro-economics is what has been emerging from the more tradition bound conformist of the past.
>
> (Oppenheimer 1994: 309)

As I argued in Chapter 2 this is part of a more general problem of theses of individualisation. Within them, people appear less encumbered in the content of their choices and decisions, although more encumbered in the compulsion to make them. However, we are left without meaningful ways of understanding the links between such choices and decisions and the social contexts in which they are made. With Oppenheimer, we may welcome the revived interest in norms and values but, as she indicates, there is no way of locating them within the conceptual frameworks described.

The role ascribed to forces of individualisation and marketisation is a clearly circumscribed one. These terms capture interesting and crucial facets of contemporary social developments but it is far from clear that we can accept them as general descriptions of historical trends. They are historically situated, and particular processes. We may better locate them as particular facets of the late twentieth-century cultural context, a context in which the frames of reference for social action were being reshaped. It is important to locate the specificity of 'market forces', and 'individualisation', and recognise that they are every bit as 'cultural' as other sets of socially structured preferences. Theses of individualisation from within both demographic and sociological theorising offer a partial take on recent social changes and do not properly capture the social nature of processes shaping recent demographic developments. Notions of an historical logic, say of modernisation or rationalisation, which drive demographic change in a certain direction, are flawed not only by virtue of problems of empirical 'fit', but also through overstating the continuities between very different historical cultural contexts. In Chapter 3 I discussed the first fertility transition at the turn of the twentieth century, elaborating how fertility decline was inextricably bound up with a reconfiguring of social relations across generations, and between women and men. A parallel, but new and more modest, reconfiguring of social relations across gender and generation since the 1960s will be elaborated here as integral to recent changes in components of aggregate fertility, specifically the timing of family formation and the incidence of childlessness. As with the first fertility decline, recent trends in fertility are best understood as an integral component of changes in the shaping of difference and interdependence across gender and generation groupings. We can productively interrogate changes in fertility patterns, and broader demographic changes, through a consideration of a reconfiguring of relations between social groups: the changing social location and identity of gender, life course stage and generation, and the reworking of linked patterns of interdependence. It is within this broader account that individualism and claims to independence and autonomy are most suitably located.

4.2.2 Reconfiguring gender and generation and fertility change in the late twentieth century

The post-war period has seen a significant rise in fertility followed by a sustained decline: the so-called baby boom and baby bust. The general pattern is Europe-wide, although with important national variations. In the following discussion and analyses I focus on UK patterns and trends. In the UK the Total Period Fertility Rate (TPFR)[3] has been quite stable at around 1.8 since 1980.[4] Following the Second World War there was a sharp peak in fertility rates (at 2.75) and then the TPFR remained close to 2.1 (the population replacement rate) until the mid 1950s. For the next ten years there was a rapid increase in fertility rates to a peak, of 2.95, in 1964. This then fell to 1.69 in 1977. The fertility rate stabilised at approximately 1.8 thereafter and has since declined to 1.66 in 2000 (ONS 2002b). The two major components of downward fertility trends are change in family size and change in the timing of parenthood. In respect of the fertility decline, it was the dimininishing likelihood of having large families which initiated the decline in the 1960s, and the pattern of delay in the timing of parenthood which entrenched the decline in the 1970s (Hobcraft 1996).

In aggregate there has been a shift to later ages at first birth. Between 1989 and 1994 there was a crossover in the relative birth rates amongst women in their early twenties and women in their early thirties. Births to those aged 30 to 34 came to exceed births to those aged 20 to 24 (Pearce *et al.* 1999). In 1964, when fertility rates were at a peak, the average age of women at their first birth was 23.9 years. This increased relatively slowly to 24.4 years by 1977, nevertheless reversing a decades long trend to earlier childbearing. It has continued to increase and stood at 27.1 years in 2000 (Smallwood 2002).

The ages at which women and men become parents has important repercussions for estimates of fertility, since a trend to earlier ages at parenthood will inflate the current fertility rate, whilst a pattern of deferral will deflate the current rate. Coleman suggests that it was earlier childbearing by women born in the 1940s which was responsible for a significant part of the baby boom of the 1960s and trends to later ages at parenthood caused the subsequent decline in annual births and period fertility rates (Coleman 1996).[5] Change in family size is an important component of fertility trends, along with changes in the incidence of childlessness.

For some writers childlessness appears to be the ultimate statement about a novel set of social relations in which individual autonomy becomes paramount. Amongst women aged 40 in 2002, 19 per cent were childless (Berrington 2004). This contrasts with a low of 10 per cent amongst women aged 40 in 1985 (ONS 1997a). This evidence is popularly cited as revealing malaise or individualism so it should be noted that the latter cohort manifests a particularly low rate of childlessness against which to judge the present. Of the cohort born in 1930 13 per cent remained childless and amongst those born in 1950, 14 per cent remained childless. Also we should recall that 21 per cent of all women born in 1920 remained childless (ONS 1997a). It is clearly premature to suggest, as some do, that significant proportions of people are 'abandoning parenthood', or becoming egocentric in an historically novel way.

Many demographers point to key factors seen to influence fertility decline. Most prominent amongst these factors are patterns of increased female participation in education and paid employment, effectiveness of contraception, particularly since the advent of the Pill, and changing ideas and values which free up people (particularly women) from traditional expectations (e.g. Bernhardt 1993; Cliquet 1991; Murphy 1993; Armitage and Babb 1996; Hobcraft 1996; Coleman 1998; Pearce *et al.* 1999). It is, notably, explanatory difficulties which remain a key theme and concern of general commentaries in the area (e.g. Bernhardt 1993; Oppenheimer 1994; Coleman 1998).

Gender issues are central to most contemporary accounts of changing fertility patterns. Changes in gendered relations are usually interpreted as an incorporation of women into the capitalist wage labour market, either in terms of a 'rationalisation' in which gender equality is increasingly realised (MacInnes 1998), or in terms of a 'catching up' where, for example, women acquire the same educational and employment opportunities which became available to men at the beginning of the twentieth century (Cliquet 1993). However, change in the relative social positions of women and men are not equivalent to equalisation. Greater female autonomy and independence and a closing of various 'inequality gaps' is a partial aspect of change but not a general one. Some theoretical positions would lead us to believe that there is a fairly direct causal relationship between improvements in women's employment and earnings position and a reduced attractiveness of procreation and childcare responsibilities (e.g. Becker 1991 and new home economics, see Irwin 1995 for critical appraisal), yet the historical mutuality of productive and reproductive processes means that it is inappropriate to search for a direct current causal relationship from one to the other (Oppenheimer 1993). Historical changes in women's relations to childbearing and rearing are important to understanding changing gendered claims to employment. Reproductive processes are reflected in the historical development of employment, such as in the massive growth of part-time employment in Britain in the second half of the twentieth century, so to construe a current direct causal relationship, from employment to reproduction, is to bracket off a key component of understanding.

The alternative perspective developed here is that we are witnessing changes in gendered positions in the reproduction of social life. Demographic changes need to be theorised in this context. The specific focus of the following is on the timing of family formation and on patterns of childlessness. The account developed is not intended as a definitive explanation of changing fertility patterns but rather reflects the more modest ambition of demonstrating the value of locating related changes as tied to a reconfiguring of gender (and to some degree generational) relations. In this way we can explore change in the social positioning of women and men and linked changes in identities as an important component of change in fertility-related behaviour.

The last quarter of the twentieth century manifested a significant shift in the ages at which women and men become parents. From the 1970s there was a reversal of a long-run trend to younger ages at family formation. Evidence on the timing of first births shows that women born from the mid 1950s onwards delayed the timing of their first birth, at ages over 20, relative to previous cohorts (Thompson 1980). Recent fertility decline is largely due to an increase in childlessness (Berrington 2004). In conceptualising deferral in the timing of parenthood and changing fertility rates we can see both new forms of constraint but also change in the contours of choice, specifically change in the current context in which people elect to have children. It was new patterns of choosing *to not have* (many) children which characterised the first fertility decline discussed in Chapter 3. Recent developments, including effective contraception, mean that typically people must make a conscious decision *to have* children and act outside the contraceptive norm. In the current context such decisions are very commonly delayed by people until they are in their late twenties and their thirties, if they are made at all. The factors shaping current change in fertility are complex (van de Kaa 1996; van Krieken 1997; Coleman 1998; Oppenheimer 1994). The focus here is on a particular component of the altered context: specifically the social positioning of women and men. I first focus on issues relating to deferral in ages at parenthood and subsequently consider the growing incidence of childlessness.

Patterns of deferral in family formation relative to prior generations are associated with change in the relative social positioning of women and men, and of different generations, by virtue of their independent access to resources (through employment, principally). Young women have significantly altered their position in respect of education and employment (e.g. Egerton and Savage 2000; Walby 1997). Expanded aspirations for autonomy and independence amongst young women are not consistent with early childbearing. Developments here are bound up with a repositioning of young women and men relative to one another, and the erosion of breadwinner divisions of labour in the last quarter of the twentieth century. From the mid 1970s the position of young men as independent earners has weakened whilst that of young women has improved, relative to young men, and to the preceding generation of women entering employment (Irwin 1995; Egerton and Savage 2000). The growing discrepancy between young men's earnings and middle-aged male adult earnings from the mid 1970s onwards, and improvements in young women's relative earnings, are linked to patterns of deferral in family formation, relative to previous cohorts. Young adults have manifested a delay in the life course timing of establishing couple households and having children. The earnings of both partners are increasingly necessary to resource new households and families at desired living standards. This appears to be the case at different ends of the earnings spectrum, so the motivations for deferral are shaped in very different contexts. Amongst the more advantaged education and employment hold a more central place within the identities of young women. Their expectations about autonomy and self-efficacy square with a desire to secure an income commensurate with contemporary lifestyle aspirations and with ideas about adequate material circumstances in which to raise children. Amongst disadvantaged, couple-headed, households women's earnings are increasingly necessary to keeping families out of poverty (Machin and Waldfogel 1994). At least in contexts where it is perceived as meaningful to plan for the future, it appears that many seek to square family formation with adequacy and linked autonomy in their material circumstances and housing arrangements (Irwin 1995). This is not all necessarily planned out in a deliberative fashion. Altered female and male dispositions towards parenthood are bound up with an altered social location in which it is economically logical and culturally normative to not have children at young ages. Thus the pattern of later ages at family formation is not experienced or considered as 'deferral'. Rather the point is to explore the articulation of perceptions and preferences as embedded in a specific context. We can develop an analysis, then, of motivations and behaviours which are not 'loosened from context' but an integral part of it. Through a reshaping of gendered and generational positions and interdependencies, the context has changed.

Another component of fertility change, the recently increased rate of childlessness, has been construed as an indicator of broad social trends towards individualism. Here it seems a commonplace, at least in popular discussions, that childlessness is an upshot of 'runaway' choices and a linked unwillingness to commit to permanent bonds of care for others (an echo interestingly of concerns about population decline in the 1930s and 1940s (Thane 1999)). Trends in childlessness have in fact been subject to relatively little research. Some have pointed to the significance of caring responsibilities and roles in kinship networks in challenging notions of increased individualism (McAllister and Clarke 1998). McAllister and Clarke place in question the supposition that voluntary childlessness is increasing since, they argue, available research indicates a constant proportion of women (around 90 per cent) born in the 1940s and up to the end of the 1960s either had, or expected to have, children (ibid.). This appears to confound the argument that we are witnessing a recent rise in deliberate intentions to avoid having children, and implies that increased childlessness is more an indirect consequence, for many, of their circumstances and experiences.

There is little research which addresses the question of why childlessness has increased. Available research offers insights based on qualitative interpretations of women's accounts of their experiences in cultures dominated by ideologies of motherhood (Campbell 1999; Gillespie 1999; Morell 1994). Where authors offer an account of reasons as to why more women are remaining childless they refer to the wider choices and opportunities available to women (Gillespie 1999) and to expanded opportunities to consider whether or not to ever have a child (Campbell 1999). The research is suggestive of the ways in which choice and constraint take on meaning within a changed cultural context. It is not simply that women are more autonomous or more free to choose than in the past. This may be the case for some groups of women but choice is a problematic concept for understanding childlessness (Morell 1994; Campbell 1999). The diversity of routes to permanent childlessness are instructive here. Campbell distinguishes two groups of women without children: those who have always known they do not want children, a factor crucial in planning their lives, and those who remain childless as a consequence of their lifestyles (Campbell 1999). This latter pattern is echoed by the women interviewed by Morell, for whom remaining childless was perceived not as a choice but as an outcome of a variety of circumstances (Morell 1994). Morell argues that experiences of childlessness reveal a society wide norm of motherhood for women (ibid.) yet in some quarters it is childlessness which is increasingly the norm.

In explanatory terms, patterns of deferral in the timing of parenthood and the increasing incidence of childlessness appear to be closely related. This is not to 'judge' childlessness against a norm of (postponed) parenting but rather to seek to locate an understanding of childlessness in the context of late twentieth-century developments. Many people had (and continue to have) children later in life than their predecessors in the post-war decades without explicitly choosing to have children 'late'. The pattern is an outcome of complex sets of processes which include change in the social location of women and men, and of different generations. Thus increased educational opportunities and expectations, and an expansion of employment opportunities and aspirations amongst women in particular, along with the increased difficulties of resourcing a new family at a preferred standard of living for many younger adults, have all contributed to deferral of parenthood. Childlessness may follow on the back of patterns of deferral in the timing of parenthood. For various individuals and couples childlessness is not explicitly chosen, but is an outcome of precisely the kinds of processes that lead to 'deferral'. Women may pass their fertile years and become permanently childless as an outcome of the same circumstances in which they did not elect to bear children. Given a constancy in the proportion of women having a single child only over the last 40 years (Pearce *et al.* 1999) it appears that those who want children and who are in a position to parent plan around the norm of two children (Smallwood and Jefferies 2003). However, there is some evidence that, because of the pattern of postponement, parenting single children may become slightly more commmon (Berrington 2004). For other individuals and couples childlessness is explicitly chosen from early on, and sought as a permanent status. It is not clear whether or not this preference has increased over recent decades. In both cases however, of being clear from an early age that one does not want children, and of remaining childless as a consequence of influences in later years, it appears that altered opportunities and bases of identity for women in particular are key to theorising the changing incidence of childlessness. Berrington suggests that through 'perpetual postponement' there is now a blurring between voluntary and involuntary childlessness (ibid.). This is to recognise that the general contours of choice and decision-making are changing. Childlessness is more common not simply as an outcome of individualistic choices but rather is bound up with new contexts of action and inaction.

The above discussion has touched only briefly on changing material aspirations, and related living costs and change in the reliability of contraception. Such changes, along with the expansion of post-16 education, are all consistent with the changing relationships discussed. Fertility declines reflect continuity of interdependence of women and men but also a reconfiguring of their relative positioning: an altered set of relations between women and men and altered gendered relations to household and family resourcing. Women particularly have significantly altered their claims to education, employment and independence since the early post-war decades. These claims are integral to changes in women's social location, and subjective position, relative to men, themes to be elaborated in section 4.3. Change in social relational ties generate altered bases for identity formation and maintenance, and altered patterns of social recognition accorded to such identity. I have argued that an important component in understanding the fertility changes discussed is the social repositioning of women and men. These shifts are less dramatic than those which characterised the first fertility decline, but are nevertheless significant.

In short, we are witnessing a change in the structuring of social reproduction, a change in the configuring of social ties. It is as an integral part of such changes that developments in patterns of fertility and family form are best analysed. This reconfiguring has opened up various spaces for independence and autonomy but it is not a process of individualisation driving fertility change. Rather we are witnessing a reshaping of gendered patterns of difference and interdependence, an altered context which has changed the grounds of 'rational' behaviours. For example, the changes in the position of adults in their twenties and thirties, most marked amongst women, are centrally important to changing fertility behaviours. Expanded aspirations for independence amongst young women are not compatible with early childbearing in the current context. *We do not see a 'falling away' of cultural contexts and rise in individualised action. To point to interdependencies and relationality is not simply to say that people 'connect' with others, but that they do so in structured, historically situated ways. It is through interrogating the reshaping of context that we can both discern the social bases of altered fertility motivations and behaviours, and develop sharper tools for analysing change.*

4.3 Gender and social reproduction

4.3.1 Diversity in women's relations to employment: the changing context

Here I move away from the focus on demographic change but continue the theme of gendered relations to employment and the family. I will focus on change in gendered employment patterns, on the erosion of the family wage claim, and on labour market restructuring and explore the reconfiguring of gendered differences and interdependencies in this context. Gender is widely seen as the key relationship, central to understanding contemporary shifts in family, work and care dynamics. First it will be useful to review some of the key developments in gendered patterns of employment over recent decades. In the following discussion and analyses I will focus primarily on women, particularly in respect of changing employment patterns and opportunities. In aggregate, women have manifested more significant changes in their employment participation than have men. However, there is a great deal of diversity and a differential rate of change across the population. Developments here have led some to suggest that it is becoming less valid to use 'woman' as a labour force category, as women's circumstances become increasingly differentiated (Humphries and Rubery 1992; Bruegel 1999). In this chapter I explore the reshaping of social reproduction and linked developments in class-related inequalities. In the next chapter I examine the articulation of values and dispositions at a micro level and general-level social changes.

If the inter-war period saw a strengthening of the family wage 'ideal', the post-war era set the scene for its partial unravelling. In the immediate post-war decades there was an assumption about the propriety – the normality – of married women's primary commitment to childrearing, and of their economic dependence upon their husbands' earnings (e.g. Roberts 1995). Ten per cent of married women were officially recorded as working in the inter-war period, and this stood at 26 per cent in 1951, at 35 per cent by 1961, at 49 per cent in 1971 (Roberts 1995) and at 71 per cent by 1991 (Walby 1997). Post-war economic growth and labour shortages encouraged employers to seek new labour sources. In the 1950s there was a large-scale recruitment from Commonwealth countries, but with restrictions on immigrant labour in the 1960s, married women were increasingly encouraged into employment (Dale and Holdsworth 1998).

Roberts describes the period 1940 to 1970 as a period of transition (Roberts 1995). In contrast to the entrenchment of women's roles in the domestic sphere in the inter-war period there was, in the context of labour shortage and broader cultural shifts, an increased expectation that married women should work (ibid.). Roberts argues that work was coming to be seen as a duty for married women, although clearly it was to be part time and organised around a primary commitment to childcare and domestic duties. Women typically worked in part-time and casual jobs, supplementing partners' earnings with a secondary income. Roberts stresses too a shift in the motivations for working amongst women. Her female interviewees had been of working age in the 1960s and 1970s. Although many stressed financial motivations to work, it was within a significantly altered context to that of their parents (ibid.). In the inter-war period unskilled households still faced severe deprivations, and in the post-war decades people enjoyed a relative affluence with general rises in living standards, full employment and increases in real wages for men. In this context, Roberts argues, the economic contributions of women were constructed as marginal. Women, then, expanded their labour force participation rate but their earnings were seen as pin money, valuable but not essential. Indeed Roberts argues that since women were acknowledged as the lynchpin of domestic survival in the early twentieth century, their loss of domestic power in the post-(second world) war context diminished the perceived value of their economic role (ibid.).

Thus, whilst the inter-war period manifested a general pattern of exclusion of women from formal paid employment, the post-war decades saw women's increased entry to employment, but structured primarily on lines that confirmed, rather than undermined, gendered difference. A question to be explored in this chapter is the extent to which gendered difference has been reshaped in recent decades. The number of women in employment rose from approximately 7 million in 1951 to 11 million in 1991. The number of men in employment stood at approximately 15 million in 1951 and 14 million in 1991. The percentage of women workers who were part time stood at 11 per cent in 1951, at 25 per cent in 1961, and 38 per cent in 1971. It remained fairly constant through the 1970s and rose somewhat thereafter to a level of around 43 per cent, where it stands today (Twomey 2002). Part-time work was considered a solution to labour shortages in post-war Britain, in a context where women's principal responsibility was deemed to lie in meeting a more or less full-time commitment to childcare and domestic responsibilities. Part-time jobs were designed in a context of givens about gendered divisions of labour: jobs for women returning to work after childbearing were designed around women's primary role as mother and homemaker. The second rise in the 'M' shaped profile of women's lifetime involvement in work reflected returns to work after childbearing which were routinely into part time jobs. Many jobs in the service sector have been constructed as part-time jobs, based on a model of women's work time as part time, secondary to childcare and domestic duties, and rooted in the historical construction of women's time as different to men's time (Creighton 1999; Beechey and Perkins 1987; Fagan and O'Reilly 1998a). Other countries which faced labour shortages effected different solutions, such as in France where women's employment was supported through the provision of day care and flexible work time arrangements (Dale and Holdsworth 1998). This 'solution' was consistent with the long-running French policy of women's integration into employment (Pedersen 1993).

In Britain employers followed gendered strategies in enhancing flexibility in their use of labour, with part-time work widely adopted as a solution to flexibility requirements in female-dominated areas, whilst shift working and overtime were adopted in male dominated areas (Smith *et al.* 1998; see also Beechey and Perkins 1987). Most part-time jobs are concentrated at lower occupational levels, and carry low pay, for example, in retailing, catering, cleaning and personal services. As well as an expansion of part-time work sectors within the economy, there has been an expansion in the use of part-time work across sectors and occupations (Smith *et al.* 1998). The British part-time solution did not square with the employment expectations of many immigrant women, especially those recruited from the Caribbean in the 1950s. The aggregate pattern of employment, and balance amongst women between full-time and part-time work, clearly reflects a white ethnic majority pattern. Holdsworth and Dale note that the growth of part-time work was based on a white model of 'proper' gender roles (Holdsworth and Dale 1997). Currently the likelihood of working part time amongst minority ethnic women is about half that of white ethnic majority women. Where women have dependent children, minority ethnic women who are working are more likely than white women to work full time, even in occupations where part-time work predominates (Dale and Holdsworth 1998).

One of the most marked, and most remarked upon, alterations in women's employment profiles over recent decades is the increase in participation amongst (married or cohabiting) mothers of pre-school children. This development has occurred from the 1980s onwards. Amongst women with children aged 0 to 4, in the years 1949, 1959 and 1969 overall employment participation rates stood at 14 per cent, 15 per cent and 22 per cent respectively (HMSO 1968, cited in Roberts 1995). The full-time employment participation rate for this group over the same years was constant at around 8 per cent (ibid.). In the years 1981, 1991 and 2001 the overall employment participation rate of women with children aged 0 to 4 rose from 24 per cent to 42 per cent to 54 per cent. The full-time employment rates across these years rose from 6 per cent to 13 per cent to 18 per cent (OPCS figures, cited in Walby 1997; and ONS 2002a).

As Humphries and Rubery noted in the early 1990s, the presence of pre-school children has become less of a constraint on mothers' employment participation (Humphries and Rubery 1992). There is a changed context of reproduction, and integral to this is a shift in norms and expectations. For example, the notion of responsible motherhood appears to be undergoing change. What has been notable over the final decades of the twentieth century is the spread of contexts in which it is the norm for mothers of young children to work in paid employment. In these contexts women's obligations to their children become less of an obstacle to paid employment, indeed for many their childrearing obligations appear to demand participation in paid work, particularly as this is linked to aspirations to furnish desired living standards. To some degree this is a continuation of the pattern identified by

Roberts (1995), but it is more extensive and applies to a larger section of the population of mothers of young and very young (pre-school) children. Notably, the trend has occurred despite limited expansion of institutional support for childcare, with most engaging in private and often informal arrangements for childcare (e.g. McKie *et al.* 2001). Work thus becomes a more continuous aspect of women's lives, more central to many women's identities (as discussed in Chapter 5), and women's earnings more significant to family resourcing (a point taken up below).

Women have increased their employment participation rates over the post-war decades, most notably around the family-building period. Their employment participation pattern has altered its shape so that a profile by age group reveals a plateau or inverted 'U' shape rather than the M-shaped profile which characterised previously higher rates of departure from employment in the family-building period and subsequent returns as children grew up. Women are more likely to work full time also, and to return to work more quickly after childbearing (Warren 2001; Dex and Joshi 1999). Women's participation rates are still below those of men but the gap has narrowed from a 19 per cent discrepancy in 1984, when women's and men's employment rates stood at 58 per cent and 77 per cent respectively, to a 9 per cent discrepancy in 2003, when women's and men's employment rates stood at 70 per cent and 79 per cent (Hibbett and Meager 2003). Where women work full time they have improved their earnings position relative to men, as revealed at both an aggregate level and at the level of household earnings (Irwin 1999a). Employment, earnings opportunities and upward mobility chances have significantly expanded for many young women in the last quarter of the twentieth century (Walby 1997; Egerton and Savage 2000). As we will see these general shifts are uneven and there is a substantial inequality.

There is a strong association between people's qualifications and their economic activity rates, a pattern which is more marked for women than for men, although it is still highly significant as a division amongst men. In 1998 86 per cent of highly qualified women ('A' level and higher) were economically active compared to 50 per cent without qualifications. Amongst men the comparable figure was 92 per cent and 66 per cent (Thair and Risdon 1999). Women with pre-school children manifested an economic activity rate of 27 per cent where they had no qualifications (of which 22 per cent were employed), and in contrast if they were highly qualified comparable women had an economic activity rate of 76 per cent (of which 74 per cent were employed).

In broad terms the post-war decades saw a clear trend to women's increased participation but this was framed largely by part-time work. This entailed limited integration given the marginal position of women within employment. However, the last quarter of the twentieth century saw some important new developments including a growth of full-time employment participation rates, and increasing employment rates amongst (partnered) mothers of young children. In the next section I consider how these changes have been conceptualised.

4.3.2 *Conceptualising continuities and changes in women's relations to employment*

In this section I will review evolving arguments regarding gender relations to work and family over recent decades. Initially developments were construed in terms of continuities in inequalities but this has given way to a recent concern with complexity and diversity, and writers have sought to better understand how change in gendered employment patterns connect to change in social organisation more widely.

Empirical research has been valuable in describing developments in female employment patterns and in illuminating some of the consequences of these developments. Changes in labour demand include commodification, and the search by capital for cheaper and more flexible sources of labour. Additionally the growth of the service sector is seen to have facilitated this shift. In respect of change in labour supply a number of key features may be cited. These include change in the availability of women as a source of labour, in turn facilitated by change in the duration of childbearing and rearing commitments over a woman's life, change in norms regarding the employment of women (especially mothers of young children), the increased take-up of educational opportunities by young women in particular, their enhanced educational success and their increasing perceived value to employers, women's own aspirations for independence and autonomy, decline in the relative level and adequacy of single wages for family resourcing with a comcomitant growth in the importance of female earnings for household income maintenance, and women's claims to greater autonomy and social participation being reflected in the labour market and the family (e.g. Humphries and Rubery 1992; Machin and Waldfogel 1994; Harrop and Moss 1995; Scott *et al.* 1996; Walby 1997; Rubery *et al.* 1999).

Has increased participation by women contributed to their integration into paid employment, or has it confirmed their marginalisation (cf. Humphries and Rubery 1992)? Many have argued that continuity of inequalities is key to understanding women's experiences. Part-time work is typically largely segregated from full-time work, carries low pay and limited prospects and employment rights, and fits the secondary earnings position and circumscribed commitment to work of the majority of women (Hakim 1996; Walby 1997). The growth of part-time employment has been argued by many to confirm women's marginal position within employment, rather than to enhance it. For example, the general message for Hakim was one of significant continuities in the extent to which women are integrated into the labour market. In 1996 she emphasised the limited extent of long-term change in women's full-time employment rates, and the very limited prospects for gender equality on the back of women's increased participation, arguing that rising part-time employment rates do not fundamentally alter women's social location (Hakim 1996).

Continuity of women's relative disadvantage has been a watchword of much research particularly through the 1980s and 1990s, along with a growing emphasis on complexity and diversity, and some recognition that the tendency to frame questions in terms of 'more' or 'less' equality may allow only a partial answer to questions about the nature of change (e.g. Baudelot 2000; Bottero 2000; Walby 1997). Research in the area of gender inequalities in employment has been very valuable in challenging notions of gender equalisation. A wealth of detailed empirical research clearly demonstrates that major continuities of inequality still confront women in the labour market. They remain significantly lower paid than men (e.g. Arber and Ginn 1995; Hakim 1996; Fagan and O'Reilly 1998; Rubery *et al.* 1999). What some have stressed in particular is a new pattern of polarisation in which a minority of highly qualified women are well positioned, effectively escaping the disadvantages and vulnerabilities confronted still by the majority of women.

Through the 1980s and early 1990s much research in the area was framed by the question of continuity in aspects of gender inequalities. The research was principally concerned with the articulation of family and employment in the context of change, especially in female patterns of employment participation, and emergent patterns of gender-related social inequality. The general picture which arose from research was one of significant change in rates of employment amongst women but, for the majority, continuity of their disadvantaged position within the labour market (e.g. Humphries and Rubery 1992; Joshi and Hinde 1993; Harrop and Moss 1995; Arber and Ginn 1995; Glover and Arber 1995; Hakim 1996; Ginn *et al.* 1996). However, the agenda of issues surrounding trends in gender in/equality, whilst immensely important, did not fully capture the nature of changes in gender relations over recent decades. A broader approach in which we can explore change in the organisation of gendered positions and the shaping of hierarchy better allows us to address the question of 'more' or 'less' equality. Recent research reveals a shift of emphasis towards the new articulation of family and employment, and a stress on new forms of diversity as well as issues relating to gender inequality (e.g. Walby 1997; Crompton 1999; Duncan and Edwards 1999; cf. Bottero 2000). The research seeks to take on board issues of diversity, complexity and contextual specificities in the (re)shaping of gender relations, and interrogates broader patterns of gender inequality and processes shaping women's vulnerability and relative disadvantage. For example, Baudelot argues:

> Rather than remain locked into the metaphor of the glass that is half full or half empty, and attempting at all costs to determine where the trends are leading, and with what intensity, it is best to look at the two contradictory components of the situation. It is helpful to view this

contradiction as the inseparably complex truth of the present time, unstable but also dynamic.

(Baudelot 2000: 319)

Others would perhaps question the appropriateness of terming more and less equality contradictory, rather it is indicative of the lack of a singular trend, and the emergence of new forms of diversity in women's (and men's) employment and life chances. In arguing that there has been a shift over the twentieth century in the system of gender relations, Walby suggests that '(t)he patterns of inequality between women and men have changed as a result, but in complex ways, not simply for better or worse' (Walby 1997: 1). How, then, can we best conceptualise change in gendered relations to employment and their consequences, and go beyond simply repeating our acknowledgement of complexity and diversity (Bottero 2000)? For many writers the answer lies in exploring the reshaping of gendered relations and treating patterns of employment as themselves linked to broader changes in the social position of women and men and change in norms about women's, and men's, roles.

4.3.3 Change in women's and men's relative social position and new inequalities

How can we best understand contemporary gender transformations? There are rather different perspectives brought to bear here. Theorists of individualisation (notably Beck 1992; Beck and Beck-Gernsheim 2002) have argued that women's employment is increasingly commodified, and that older patterns of constraint and interdependence, rooted in gender asymmetries in the family, have given way to market relations. Women, as men before, are individualised: a radical change, seemingly, in women's levels of autonomy. However, feminist theorists of gender and employment do not much engage with such arguments, emphasising rather continuities of gender inequality, but also a restructuring of context. This restructuring is not defined by a process of individualisation but rather by ongoing interconnections: a repositioning of women and men. Change in the shape of gender difference, particularly in the partial shift from a breadwinner pattern to a dual earner pattern, has been addressed as researchers seek to better delineate social change and its consequences.

Walby has replaced the terminology of patriarchy with that of gender regimes in response to criticisms of the monolithic and static nature of patriarchy as a conceptual framework (Walby 1997). She proposes that the twentieth century was characterised by a shift from private, domestically based, gender regimes, to a public gender regime. The winning of political citizenship by women in the early part of the century, and the growing demand for female labour through the post-war decades altered women's social location and public 'presence'. In the last third of the twentieth century these developments were accelerated by a series of changes. Walby highlights the significance of equality legislation and the development of equal opportunities policies and commitments at the level of state, trades unions and employers, the expansion of education and employment opportunities for young women in particular, and the lessening constraints of domestic and childcare commitments on women's employment participation. These developments have transformed gender relations, Walby argues, particularly for younger women. The gender gap in access to work and in rewards has closed for more advantaged groups but the intersection of gender with age, class and ethnicity generates very diverse and uneven consequences, constraints and opportunities, with new forms of polarisation and disadvantage emerging (ibid.). In so far as there has been an historical shift to a public gender regime, Walby highlights the salience of a generational divide. Older generations of women who grew up in the predominantly private gender regime hold very different values, and have available to them different resources and opportunities, to their current detriment. It is younger cohorts of women who are at the cutting edge of change (ibid.).

Walby also emphasises the way in which a newly extensive public presence of women has contributed to a cultural shift in perceptions and expectations regarding women's roles in society (ibid.). Women's public presence was essential to understanding the strength of the feminist movement in the 1960s, which itself contributed to a radical reshaping of gender, in part through challenging taken for granted assumptions about the natural ordering of gender (ibid.). This cultural shift in understandings of difference, the claims it engendered, and the forcing of significant policy changes fed into an altered political discourse, at a public level and at the level of individual subjectivities. As educational participation and employment opportunities have become more extensive amongst young women there is some evidence of linked shifts in their social identities, expectations and aspirations as women (Arnot *et al.* 1999; Arnot 2002; Dale *et al.* 2002).

Another influential set of ideas which has informed much recent comparative work on gender transformations is that of gender contracts (e.g. Duncan 1994; Pfau-Effinger 1994, 1998). Drawing on, yet critical of, Esping-Andersen's work on welfare regimes (1990), these writers focus on changes in the organisation of social reproduction. They draw on the notion of a 'gender contract' (after Hirdmann), suggesting that this offers a better framework for reflecting women's agency than does the more abstract concept of patriarchy. Culture is important for theorising gender relations and is part of their critique of the perceived primacy of institutional structures in shaping employment (Pfau-Effinger 1994, 1998). For Pfau-Effinger:

> [T]he orientations and actions of women and men in a social system or subsystem are founded on a gender contract; that is, a sociocultural consensus about the respective organisation of interaction between the sexes.
>
> (Pfau-Effinger 1994: 1359)

More recently, Pfau-Effinger has moved away from this model of consensus to greater recognition of conflict, struggle and negotiation (1998). She utilises the model in her comparison of contrasting German, Dutch and Finnish arrangements, with their modified breadwinner and dual earner patterns of family resourcing and employment participation, cultural patterns shaped through different processes of industrialisation in the nineteenth and twentieth centuries. Pfau-Effinger (ibid.) traces out different modernisation paths across nations as these underpin contemporary gender arrangements, and demonstrates the core importance of cultural constructions in shaping institutional arrangements. Across her comparison countries of Germany, The Netherlands and Finland she notes the increased importance of 'the employed mother' as a cultural construction (Pfau-Effinger 1994). In Britain this construction is becoming more important also, and several commentators have described an erosion of the family wage pattern of social reproduction (e.g. Fagan 2001; Warren 2001; Lewis 2002; Crompton 1999; Irwin 1995; Duncan 1994). Women clearly are far from parity with men yet their positioning in respect of employment has changed. Continuity of secondary earnings status does not mean an absence of change in women's economic position. The notion of a weakening of the breadwinner system helps locate change in women's employment patterns as linked to developments in the reshaping of social reproduction.

Developments in both full-time and part-time employment participation rates reveal important changes in the position of women relative to men. Recent changes are shown in data on household composition, employment patterns and the relative earnings of partners in couple households (Irwin 1999a). Evidence reveals change in the relative financial contributions of women and men in the resourcing of households, with an increase in the necessity of women's earnings. There have been significant changes in the relative earnings position of women and men where women are working full time (ibid.). Data reveals improvements in the occupational and earnings position of women full-time employees, relative to men, at an aggregate labour market level (Egerton and Savage 2000) and improvements in women's relative position at the household level of couple earnings (Irwin 1999a). Women remain extensively employed in part-time work, and commentators have described such jobs, and women's economic status therefore, as often marginal (e.g. Hakim 1996), yet evidence indicates an increased relative importance of women's earnings in household reproduction even where these are drawn from part-time work (Ward *et al.* 1996; Machin and Waldfogel 1994; Webb 1993). Part-time earnings of women additionally have become more important in keeping low-income households out of poverty (Machin and Waldfogel 1994) Amongst low-income households male earnings have declined relative to average earnings, and – where such men are working – their partners have increased their employment rates. As a share of household income, female earnings increased at all points across the male earnings distribution (ibid.). These authors also note increases in the participation rates as well as relative earnings of women with low-earning husbands. Evidence suggests that changing relations to household resourcing are being experienced and authored by a population more general than the privileged group to whom they are often attributed.

Various writers argue that there is a growing contradiction between reproduction and production through the latter half of the twentieth century (e.g. Siim 2000; Drew *et al.* 1998; O'Reilly and Spee 1998; Beck 1992). O'Reilly and Spee suggest we have seen a growing 'contradiction of equality' in which women seek to participate in employment and the public sphere on the same terms as men, yet are held back by their historically and culturally designated role in social reproduction (O'Reilly and Spee 1998). Bernhardt suggests that work and parenting are incompatible since they evolved as complements to each other, each role presupposes the other, at least in contexts where providing care is treated as a private affair (Bernhardt 1993). The work-life balance debate and the academic interventions there could be seen as a response to the dilemmas thrown up by this problem of fit between the demands and commitments of work and of family, a problem of fit experienced most acutely by women.

Overall the evidence indicates some significant shifts in the relative positioning of women and men. These are highly variable across the population, and not consistent with any singular trend in respect of gender inequalities. Some women are advantaged by recent developments, and in general hold an improved economic position relative to men compared to their parents' and grandparents' generations (e.g. Egerton and Savage 2000; Walby 1997; Irwin 1995). Other women have improved their standing relative to men in the same social class position. However, this is due in part to a deterioration in the position of men in low-skilled work, a position which has lost ground to rising average living standards. This class variability of change in women's and men's relative economic standing is a relatively neglected area, but an extremely important one (Warren 2000; Bruegel 1999). One of the reasons it is difficult to provide a general overview of change in women's position relative to men is because of the highly varied landscape of general social advantage and disadvantage in which women and men move.

Evidence reveals a complex picture of change. Whilst women's position has improved relative to men's, to a degree, this has both varied causes and consequences over the class structure. It is important to also highlight here that gender, as a dimension of difference and as a principle of change has varying salience. Changing relations to employment have in part been shaped by new assumptions, expectations and claims regarding women's economic potential and rights to independence. However, although women's claims have fed into change they are not a guiding principle. For many commentators the final two or three decades of the twentieth century saw a partial unravelling of prior gender arrangements, undone by economic restructuring and the market ideology of the New Right as much as by the success of women's claims for autonomy and equality. The New Right were committed, as Hobsbawm puts it, to an extreme form of business egoism, and an ideology of reduced government involvement, at least in the domain of economic management (Hobsbawm 1994). The reconfiguring of gender in late twentieth-century society cannot be separated from the marked increases in socio-economic inequality. Whilst women's altered social location, identities and claims are central to a change in the cultural terrain on which expectations are built, the shift in the political mindset and the implementation of neo-liberal economic policies from the 1970s and especially through the 1980s, clearly significantly altered both conditions of employment and people's relations to work, welfare and the social wage. 'Marketisation' is not a purely economic process and it might be deemed to reflect the ascendance of a certain set of claims, claims which helped naturalise the consequences of neo-liberal political agendas. The particular context and shaping of economic change, through deindustrialisation and employment restructuring, has had important gendered consequences.

Creighton (1999) discusses how the male-breadwinner family had mixed consequences for women and men, and so too does its erosion. Its embedding helped secure raised living standards and reconcile family and work, albeit with particular gendered consequences (and diverse ones in so far as many women may have welcomed the move away from paid labour as others regretted and resisted it, e.g. Braybon and Summerfield 1987). Yet negatively the system placed women in a situation of economic dependence and vulnerability, stigmatised those who did not fit the norm, and failed to adequately underwrite various circumstances (Creighton 1999). For Creighton, the undermining of the family wage system has had complex and diverse consequences. Its undoing has provided more space for women's autonomy, yet it has intensified the dilemma of combining family and work commitments in the absence of replacement supports outside the private domain, and it has been accompanied by an extension of poverty. Recession, economic restructuring and cutbacks in public expenditure have prevented women from achieving the gains they might have otherwise achieved with the decline of the breadwinner system. Rather:

> The potential gains of the decline of the male breadwinner family have been captured more fully by capital than by working people themselves.
>
> (Creighton 1999: 526)

Bruegel too stresses the undoing of the family wage system yet the absence of any corresponding liberation of women (Bruegel 2000). She notes the still limited employment opportunities for women at the lower end of the employment hierarchy. It was at the top end of the earnings hierachy that women's earnings improved relative to median male earnings. At the lower end the narrowing gender pay gap is largely a consequence of the worsening position of low-paid men (Bruegel and Perrons 1998). There are two distinct types of departure from a family wage system, for households at different ends of income spectrum. Economic restructuring appears to have undermined the family wage:

> [A] very uneven process and in many ways [one that] has been the antithesis of an emancipatory redistribution of income between men and women.
>
> (Bruegel 2000: 226)

In the last part of the twentieth century improvements in the position of women relative to men were parallelled by growing inequalities between households, probably exacerbating rather than easing the difficulties faced by women living with low-waged men. A partial closing of the gender gap is no simple result of the women's claims to greater autonomy and independence from men. Rubery, too, argues that the breadwinner system has been undermined through economic restructuring, and that in consequence there has been a breaking down of the link between wage claims and social reproduction costs. Change entails a disaggregation of the family wage, but this does not mean that income is linked to social reproduction costs in a more 'rational' way, as might be supposed in models of labour marketisation. Rather, through the period of neo-liberal responses and policies in the context of global economic restructuring through the 1980s in particular, the link between rewards to labour and social reproduction costs became more anarchic (Rubery 1997).

Evidence suggests that there has been a trend to increased pay differentials within apparently homogeneous groups (ibid.). Rubery argues there is no simple pattern of polarisation between the better paid at the top of the distribution and the worst paid at the bottom. Rather there is a widening of earnings inequalities spread throughout the economic system, with a trend to widening differentials within industries, within occupations and within groups of people with the same qualifications (ibid.). Rubery points to the breaking down of the link between socially embedded norms and claims on the part of labour, and patterns of remuneration. The balance of power has been tilted further in favour of employers, and a differing set of rationales has been introduced in conceptions of fairness. Rubery links this to deregulation and decentralisation in pay bargaining. There has been a move away from job-based pay to more individualised pay, with increased differentiation through performance-related pay (Rubery 1997). The Conservative administrations of the 1980s substantially reduced national wage determination in favour of organisational wage-setting. With decentralised negotiations management held (and holds) greater discretion over pay determination. Rubery highlights how changing definitions of fairness have been enshrined in new kinds of payment strategies with an undermining of traditional claims to a fair wage by labour (Rubery 1997).

In the political domain, the notion of a market 'logic' has to do with freeing up the operation of the market by removing constraints upon it: refusing to shore up social bases of cooperation where these are seen as constraints on the operation of market forces. However, in practice of course it is an ideology of market economics which guides policies and which may just as easily be seen as the ascendance of a particular set of claims. As Rubery puts it:

> Some will seek to rationalize these changes as a response to market forces, but a more relevant approach is to ask how the market for labour in the UK has been reconstituted in ways that provide the more advantaged with scope to extract ever higher shares of the available resources.
>
> (Rubery 1997: 363)

What have been the earnings-related consequences of these kinds of developments and how do they relate to the erosion of the family wage? The recomposing of gender relations and the radical restructuring of employment opportunities have been intertwined. The deterioration of many men's relative income position might be construed as simply the mirror to relative improvements in the occupational and earnings prospects of (more advantaged) women. However, it partly reflects a 'real' deterioration in the position of less advantaged men. A number of writers have commented upon how the position of low-earning men worsened in the latter decades of the twentieth century (e.g. Bruegel 2000; Bruegel and Perrons 1998; Rubery 1997; Siltanen 1994). Through analysis of earnings, based on an assessment of the social adequacy of these men in resourcing themselves and any dependents, Siltanen (1994) and Rubery (1997) show that there was a decline in the worth of male manual wages, and some improvements in the worth of female full-time wages leading to greater overlap in the earnings capacities of women and men at an aggregate level. Creighton also talks of how the costs of reproduction are now more widely spread over two wage earners as it becomes harder to support a family on a single wage, especially for less skilled men (Creighton 1999).

We can then point to both a continued salience of gender as a dimension of inequality, but also identify contexts where gender has less, or a different kind of, salience. For example, in some contexts women's economic position has become closer to that of men as a consequence of a decline in men's position. The erosion of the breadwinner model has meant a rise in a dual earner pattern in which the earnings of both adults, in couple households, are essential to resourcing households at desired living standards. Norms and values are important to the restructuring of gender, although such norms are not necessarily about gender. For example, changing norms about women's work are important and integral to the developments discussed, but so too are claims about the market and employment deregulation which have had important gendered and class-related consequences.

The latter part of the twentieth century saw a weakening of the breadwinner pattern of social reproduction. Change in the relative economic position of women and men is bound up with national and global economic restructuring which has undermined the position of those in manufacturing in Britain, and of semi-skilled and unskilled workers, as it has enhanced the position of those at the top end of the earnings spectrum. The redifferentiation of gender has occurred in this context and has been a strongly classed process. It is not simply the case that women have improved their position at the top end of the earnings spectrum whilst working-class women's position is unchanged. The position of working-class women has changed, although as Bruegel points out (1999) this is due as much to a levelling down of men's position, as a levelling up of women's position.

4.4 Conclusion

I have explored two linked domains of family and employment and argued that changes across both are bound up with a social repositioning of women and men. Theorists of individualisation have posited that expanding choices and spaces of autonomy underpin recent changes in fertility and family form, and have shaped the second demographic transition of the late twentieth century. There is an implicit if not overt argument of a loosening of agency from structure. In contrast, some theorists of the first fertility decline, discussed in Chapter 3, located radically new kinds of choices as inseparable from change in the shape of social ties and interdependencies. In doing this they develop an analysis which reveals the mutuality of agency and structure even whilst the latter is changing in unprecedented ways. Changing contexts altered the grounds for choices and decisions, and altered motivations and behaviours. So too in the late twentieth century change in the relative positioning of women and men, and of generations, has become part of an altered context of choice, action and inaction. Change in generational relations, to a degree, and in gendered differences and interdependencies have been crucial to understanding altered contexts and motivations engendering changes in family forms and patterns of living. The argument was developed through a consideration of trends to later ages at parenthood and the increased incidence of childlessness. Late twentieth-century changes revealed not individualisation, but reconfiguring: a shift in the social positioning of gender groups, and particularly in the positioning of women. New motivations, choices and behaviours link strongly to these changes.

In the domain of gender and employment, extensive research has generated rich empirical data and linked insights into gender inequalities and gender restructuring. Through the 1980s and early 1990s many researchers focused on the question of whether or not women had closed the equality gap with men. This concern has continued but it came to be framed within broader questions about the shape of new forms of complexity and diversity. In this way theorists have sought to locate changes in gendered patterns of employment as an aspect of wider economic and social restructuring. Key issues here have been the erosion of the family wage pattern of social reproduction, the rise in women's employment participation and increased earnings contributions to household resourcing, and the link to changing class-related inequalities. Women's position has changed relative to men's in quite marked ways since the 1970s. This is linked to a changing pattern of interdependence in the reproduction of social life, and changing norms and expectations regarding gender difference.

How are recent patterns of continuity and change in the gender order experienced and authored at the level of individual perceptions and actions? How does the current configuration of social positions and diversity relate to individuals' values and dispositions? A particularly interesting and important question at the current time is what people see as the right thing to do in respect of organising work and care in the family-building period. This is a key site for research since it is a point of very significant changes in women's employment participation over recent decades. In Chapter 5 I include a micro-level perspective and develop analyses of social position and linked dispositions. In the reshaping of attitudes and social identities we can see the meshing of social norms and changes in the social order and not their chronic disjuncture.

5 Disposition and position

Norms, attitudes and commitments to children, work and self

5.1 Introduction

Values and beliefs seem to be more important in society now than they were in the past. Reflection, choice and decision-making are all foregrounded as central to human social life and seen by some to be more important now as severe economic hardship has receded and allowed more space for choice, and as cultural mores have tumbled leaving people less deferential and more free to 'be themselves'. However, it is misleading to separate out values and social structural processes in this way: the latter are about more than constraint. They are not best construed as a framework which boxes people in with more or less room for manoeuvre. Rather social structural processes are as much about the shaping of choices and the contours of what is deemed choosable, and possible.

In this chapter I explore how perceptions, attitudes and values at the level of the individual link to diverse contexts. The analysis is of the dispositions and identities of women with young children, a group which has manifested some important changes in their relations to work, care and family. There has been a significant expansion of work amongst mothers of pre-school children. There is, of course, a good deal of diversity and recently some writers have suggested a growing disalignment between values and preferences, and the contexts in which people find themselves. I will argue that claims of a disalignment do not stand up. There is general coherence between subjective assessments on the one hand and circumstances and experience on the other. Indeed taking the notion of discrepancy as a puzzle to be resolved, rather than as a sufficient description of social arrangements, can enhance our understanding of social structural complexity. An understanding of contextual diversity in attitudes and values, and change in such diversity, is itself a contribution to gaining a more nuanced understanding of structure, and people's position within it.

In Chapter 4 I explored the repositioning of gender. Here I take as a focus links between the diverse social positions of women and men, and their dispositions: how they perceive and evaluate the right thing to do in respect of work and care commitments. I focus on the commitments and perceptions of parents of young (pre-school and primary school-aged) children. Empirical data is drawn from the British Social Attitudes survey and from quantitative and qualitative data generated through recent research by the ESRC Research Group for the Study of Care, Values and the Future of Welfare ('CAVA') (Williams 2001). The evidence cuts against the notion that contemporary social change entails an historically new kind of separation of the subjective and objective, and it is argued that such a conceptual separation is untenable. The analysis reveals some of the ways in which work has become more central as a part of the lifetime identities of women, that is throughout the period of family-building and parenting young children. This is not general but it is more common, and helps to reveal the mutuality of norms and subjectivities and extant social relations, in the midst of change, indeed as an integral component of change.

In the first part of this chapter I explore general evidence collected in national level attitudinal surveys, as reported in the literature and through analysis of recent British Social Attitudes Survey data. This will be followed by analysis of new empirical data generated as part of the CAVA research project. The analysis shows the value of researching the patterning of attitudes and beliefs and that we can use subjective data in helping further our understanding of social structural diversity. Qualitative evidence provides insight into individual level experience and enhances understanding of social identities and commitments and how these are manifesting change, part of the broader repositioning of gender and the increased importance of a work identity amongst women with children. These different levels of analysis all offer a lens on the meshing of social structural relations and norms in the current context of change.

5.2 Attitudes, values and social structure

Recent research in the areas of parenting, employment and childcare has stressed the importance of norms in people's decisions and actions in these domains. There is a general perception that normative issues have been under-acknowledged and insufficiently researched, and there is a growing literature on diverse subjectivities and their link to new forms of diversity in family life, in childrearing and in gendered roles (e.g. Hakim 1996, 2000; Duncan *et al.* 2003; McRae 2003; Williams 2001; Himmelweit 2002; Marks and Houston 2002; Hattery 2001; Thomson 1995).

Hakim advocates preference theory, a model which holds parallels with individualisation theory, and for which she has been widely critiqued. Hakim stresses the social significance of historical change in economic prosperity, with an ending of absolute economic want as a life and death issue as it was, for many, in the past. She also stresses the importance, especially for women, of sophisticated means of birth control. Her argument is that such developments have made people more free of structural constraint, and in a position to choose and determine their own fates in a way which was not conceivable in the past (Hakim 1996, 2000). However, what is particularly problematic in arguments of a shift to a new kind of reflexivity, a new salience of choice and value, is the presumption that the current significance of values entails their 'loosening' from structural processes. This separation has clear expression in preference theory:

> Our thesis is that lifestyle preferences and values are becoming more important determinants of behaviour, relative to economic necessity and social structural factors.
>
> (Hakim 2000: 80–1)

Rather than rethink our understanding of structural processes we are enjoined to see them as less relevant. This is arguably a feature of the sociological turn to agency more generally. People may be 'free' of past constraints, but in respect of how they live their lives they remain embedded within contemporary structural processes, as did their forebears. Structure is not just about frameworks of opportunity and constraint, it is also about the shaping of contexts of social action and volition, about when and why choices are meaningful.

For her critics Hakim presents an over-individualised and inappropriately voluntaristic theory of human behaviour (e.g. Duncan *et al.* 2003; Blackburn *et al.* 2002; Tomlinson 2003; Bruegel 1996; Ginn *et al.* 1996). Hakim foregrounds the sociological significance of choices but social diversity means that the very contours of choice and constraint vary (e.g. Duncan and Edwards 1999; Glucksmann 2000). Without analysis of experience and context, choice holds limited explanatory purchase.

Part of the impetus behind recent, principally qualitative, research in the areas of family, kin and commitment has been the concern that we need to more precisely contextualise individuals' values and the ways in which moral choices and negotiations are made in care decisions and employment decisions (e.g. Duncan *et al.* 2003; Williams 2001; Mason 2000; Silva and Smart 1999; Duncan and Edwards 1999). The emphasis within research by the ESRC Research Group for the study of Care, Values and the Future of Welfare (CAVA) has been on the context and texture of social interaction and on understanding the links between moral judgements and social practices.[6] The research helps to reveal the ways in which people are moral beings, embedded in webs of relationships and, when confronted with moral ambiguities in their conduct and relationships, seek to do 'the right thing'. The research then challenges models of uniform rationalities and usefully positions 'values' not as something simply held, possession-like, by individuals, but as something often in process, evolved in concrete circumstances and contexts (Williams 2001; Mason 2000).

There remains a gap in our understanding of the general social landscape of diverse contexts. There is of course a wealth of quantitative attitudinal research on issues relating to family, work and welfare (e.g. Scott *et al.* 1998;

Jarvis *et al.* 2000; Bonoli *et al.* 2000). Such research offers important insights into diversity, and continuity and change in attitudes, yet these studies offer a very broad-brush description of social diversity.

In some respects the current emphasis on norms and values within the literature on care and work is part of an ongoing critique of structuralist perspectives in which social location, allegedly, was seen to determine interests and values. However, as we have seen there is broad concern that we have inadequate tools for conceptualising and analysing structural processes (e.g. Bradley 1996). The new interest in norms and values has been productive and has offered a range of insights but the emphasis on contexts has not been matched by research on their links with the broader social structure. Recently commentators have stressed the need to improve theories of how norms and the social order mesh together (Duncan *et al.* 2003; Crompton 2002; Himmelweit 2002). *The empirical data analyses developed in this chapter show an important strand in the mutuality of norms and the social order, specifically the coherence of position and disposition at the level of individual social actors.*

To clarify the analytical perspective some definitions are helpful. The empirical analysis of much of this chapter focuses on attitudes and dispositions. Attitudes are more specific than values, and in many respects may be considered as 'generated data', offered in response to direct questions about how things are or should be. Responses to attitudinal statements, perceptions of how things are, respondents' priorities and so on, tap into dispositions, that is, into orientations that may be more mutable than are values. However, responses are not mere 'artefacts' of imposed meaning, and reveal a clear pattern of co-variation with material and situational factors, a co-variation which requires us to reinterrogate recent arguments of disjuncture between subjective and structural processes.

Norms provide a framing set of assumptions on which people draw, usually implicitly, in their choices or judgements about forms of moral conduct and in their perceptions about appropriate behaviours, and rights and responsibilities. The contemporary reworking of gendered norms forms part of the context of this chapter, and will be addressed directly later on. This reworking is manifest in particular in the repositioning of women and men in household resourcing and the more routine expectation, across an expanding section of the population, that women with young children will engage in paid employment. The evidence shows us that changing norms can be usefully understood as integral to recent changes in women's and men's positioning in society and relative to each other.

The chapter develops some general arguments regarding the articulation of attitudes, values and the social order. In contrast to some recent arguments of their disjuncture, it will be argued that diverse dispositions, and attitudes regarding 'the right thing to do' are closely linked to social location. The analysis feeds into a more general argument: that recent treatments of normative processes as autonomous from structural relations are misplaced.

Subjectivities are not more autonomous of the social interaction order than in the past, but remain an integral part of that order, even in a time of rapid change. *We should not 'conceptualise away structure', but construe and analyse it as a dynamic process in which the subjective and normative dimensions of social life are meshed with extant material social relations.*

5.3 Attitudinal change

5.3.1 A comment on attitudinal data

The discussion in this section is not intended to provide a comprehensive overview of attitudes to work, care and home life over recent decades, an area which has seen extensive commentary and analysis (e.g. Crompton *et al.* 2003; Scott *et al.* 1998; Scott *et al.* 1996; Hakim 1996; Dex 1988; Martin and Roberts 1984). Rather it is intended to give some sense of continuities and changes in general attitudes, and provide context for the subsequent discussion of diversity, and the link between attitudes and behaviours. Before embarking on the presentation of attitudinal data it is useful to offer some prefatory comments about the nature of such data, and on the way in which it provides a very particular lens, as do other kinds of data, on the processes in which we are interested (cf. Mason 2002).

Attitudinal data is sometimes treated (in journalism especially, but not uniquely) like a thermometer, an instrument to measure the collective temperature, a kind of average of 'our' outlook on crucial issues. There is a tradition of critiquing notional publics (e.g. Wright Mills 1959). There are plenty of critics of attitudinal surveys, in particular many find fault with the superficial nature of attitudinal statements. This is a fair criticism. Attitudinal questions do not necessarily tap into deeply held values. However, the patterned nature of such preferences reveals real insights into dispositions and social diversity.[7] Analysis of patterns of attitudinal data can help challenge, rather than simply reproduce, prior analytic categories and assumptions where these in fact hide more than they reveal.

There is, in the uses of attitudinal data, a less reflected upon tendency to 'average out', across quite broad populations of respondents. We are often presented with a fairly aggregated picture of attitudes, sometimes disaggregated by sex, and age group and other standard social indices. It is important to be wary of the homogenising tendency which often accompanies generalised descriptions of attitudinal data. To get the most out of such data it will be especially useful to focus on those groups for whom the questions and issues have the most direct salience, and to explore patterns of variation in some depth.

5.3.2 *Changing attitudes to gender roles*

In her review and careful assessment of women's attitudes towards work and home life from the 1940s to the 1980s, Dex (1988) warns against the risks of oversimplification. She draws on different sources of survey data and emphasises the significance of population diversity in the former as well as the latter period. What changed over time was not the range of views but the frequency of their occurrence. In 1940 one could find as diverse a set of attitudes towards work and care responsibilities as one might find 40 years later, but Dex provides evidence which shows quite clearly a change in the relative frequency of different attitudes with a general shift towards a more liberal or positive attitude towards women working.

In respect of the question of breadwinning and linked gender roles, the 1943 Government Wartime Social Survey conducted interviews of working women, the majority of whom thought that women should cease working upon marriage (ibid.). In data from the government Social Survey of Women's Employment in 1965, Hunt revealed strong opposition to mothers working, with 78 per cent of women stating that a mother of pre-school children should stay at home (Hunt 1968, cited in Dex 1988). Taking up the story of attitudes to breadwinner patterns from 1980 onwards it is clear that in general there has been a significant shift away from accepting a breadwinner imperative.

Dex compares data from the 1980 Women and Employment Survey (Martin and Roberts 1984) with parallel data produced through the 1984 British Social Attitudes Survey (BSAS). The following 'breadwinner statement': 'A husband's job is to earn the money; a wife's job is to look after the home and family' had a ratio of agree to disagree responses of 46:33 in 1980 compared to 32:51 just four years later. Dex notes the samples are not fully comparable and errs on the side of caution, concluding alongside other evidence simply that there was a move by women to more liberal attitudes over the period. However we can see a marked continuation of the trend to disapproval of the male breadwinning statement through later BSAS data. The same breadwinner statement (slightly rephrased: 'a man's job is to earn money; a woman's job is to look after the home and family') was asked within a battery of questions on gender roles within the BSAS.[8] The percentages of women agreeing with this statement stood in 1989 at 26 per cent, in 1994 at 21 per cent and in 2002 at 15 per cent (Crompton *et al.* 2003). The equivalent figures for male respondents across the three points in time stood at 32 per cent, 26 per cent and 20 per cent – a more or less parallel decline from a slightly higher base (ibid.). The steady decline over recent decades here would seem indicative of a stable shift away from sanctioning the male breadwinner 'requirement'. It is also notable how many respondents '*strongly* disagree' with the statement (20 per cent in 2002), given that BSAS attitudinal statements generally draw milder 'disagree' (or 'agree') responses.[9]

Another statement, the 'income contribution' statement: 'both the husband and wife should contribute to the household income' reveals a constant pattern of responses over recent years. In the 1989 BSAS 57 per cent of female respondents agreed, a similar proportion responding the same way to a slightly reworded question (from husband/wife to man/woman) in 1994 when 59 per cent of female respondents agreed (Scott *et al.* 1996). In 2002, 58 per cent of female respondents agreed. Only 14 per cent disagree and a sizeable 26 per cent neither agree nor disagree. The latter is a useful reminder of people's reluctance to 'commit', as implied by the word 'should' within the statement, and the likely preference of some respondents for a solution which is dependent on people's circumstances (which obviously are not given in the attitude questions). Notably 60 per cent of men think women should contribute to household income – a rare example of men being just as 'liberal' as women when it comes to attitudes to gender roles. At first glance it might seem that both the breadwinner statement and the income contribution statement are tapping into the same issues. However, responses to the former reveal a shift in attitudes whilst responses to the latter reveal a constancy of attitudes. I would suggest that the contrast reveals an ongoing liberalism (at least in the last quarter of the twentieth century) about both partners contributing to household income, but a growing rejection of any presumed breadwinner 'requirement', that is a rejection of the asymmetry presented in the breadwinner question.

Crompton and her colleagues offer an analysis of difference across age cohorts and explore the significance of cohort replacement as a driver of general attitudinal change. In 2002 over 80 per cent of young women (aged under 30) disagreed with the breadwinner attitude statement, in contrast to 32 per cent of women in later life (aged 70 and over) (Crompton *et al.* 2003). The authors argue a process of attitudinal change is driven principally by cohort replacement. This is as we would expect. If younger women in particular are manifesting new patterns of behaviour we might reasonably predict that they too will most clearly manifest new attitudes.

In recent decades women have changed their social position more strikingly than have men (Egerton and Savage 2000; Walby 1997; Irwin 1995). The attitude statements more typically invite judgements about women's proper roles than about men's, since men hold a more stable and constantly typical pattern of commitment to employment around the family-building period than do women. Women have increased their labour force participation rates around the family-building period with a marked increase amongst mothers of young children (as reviewed in Chapter 4). General attitudes towards women's roles and towards appropriate patterns of behaviour amongst parents run broadly in parallel with these changes (e.g. Dex 1988; Crompton *et al.* 2003). So, for example, when asked whether a married woman with children under school age ought to work or stay at home, in 1965 78 per cent of female survey respondents thought she should stay at home, and in 1980 60 per cent of respondents thought she should do so[10] (Hunt 1968; Martin and Roberts 1984, cited in Dex 1988). In the 2002 BSA survey, 46 per cent of female respondents thought that women with a pre-school child should stay at home.[11] Notably the earlier and more recent figures compare closely with actual participation rates.

When asked whether a married woman with children of school age ought to work or stay at home, in 1965, 20 per cent of female respondents thought she should stay at home, in 1980, 11 per cent thought she should stay at home. In the 2002 BSAS question, only 4 per cent of female respondents thought such a woman should stay at home. Over two-thirds thought she should work part time. The notion that a mother of school age children *should* stay at home has more or less evaporated.

In general men reveal less 'liberal' attitudes towards gender roles (e.g. Crompton *et al.* 2003; Scott *et al.* 1996). In respect of the questions about mothers' appropriate 'place' described above, however, the differences between women and men are fairly slight. In the 2002 BSAS survey 51 per cent of men thought a mother of pre-school should stay at home, and 7 per cent thought a mother of school age children should stay at home.

The above data refers to aggregated responses across the population of women and of men. If we focus just on the experience of women and men for whom these issues are of much more immediate concern, that is parents of young children, we might find a rather different distribution of attitudes. BSAS (2002) data reveals that amongst female respondents who themselves have a child under school age, 35 per cent think women in such a position should stay at home, that is 11 per cent less than across the female population as a whole. Amongst male respondents with a child under school age, 44 per cent think mothers with pre-school children should stay at home, being more conservative than the women, but somewhat less than the rest of the male population. Having young children of one's own serves as a proxy for being a member of a relatively recent cohort of new parents. It is clearly evident that such respondents will favour mothers being in work compared to older respondents. Additionally, the fact of having one's own young children, and of being a member of a relatively recent cohort of new parents, sets women apart from the population of women as a whole more than it does men. It is women who have changed their social position, and linked identifications, more than have men. Additionally the differences across the population remind us of the variable salience of the issues across the population. We should note that people will likely be more influenced by proximate circumstances and experiences than by the attitudes of distant others. Attitude questions which tap experience fairly directly are more useful, analytically, than those which do not. Generalised attitudes may be of some interest in taking the national pulse but hold more limited use in understanding the actions of different parts of the social body.

The above discussion of change is indicative rather than comprehensive but gives a sense of a shift to more 'liberal' attitudes across the population; specifically people are less likely to disapprove of mothers' employment. This shift in attitudes may make for a more generally tolerant environment, relevant to women's decision-making and actions. However it is not a direct cause of increased participation. Indeed attitudinal change may be largely a consequence rather than a cause of changed patterns of behaviour. It is time to move on now from examining population-wide attitudes, whose salience may be quite limited and very diffuse. It is pertinent to consider in more depth the variable patterning of attitudes amongst those for whom the issues have the most direct salience.

Again here we can observe a good deal of consistency between attitudes and experience. It is notable that some recent writers who share this focus have taken up an argument that beliefs have become more freed from context and structural constraint and are consequently more important for understanding behaviour than they were in the past. I will be arguing that it is more helpful to see attitudes as a lens on social structural diversity and complexity rather than as more autonomous from social structure. There is notable continuity between disposition and position, but the relationship is most clear when we have a sufficient conceptualisation of people's social position. Indeed analysis of attitudes and dispositions can contribute to an improved theory of social structural diversity.

5.4 Attitudes and diversity

There is extensive evidence on patterns of co-variation between people's attitudes and their behaviours in respect of gender and parenting roles, work and care (Alwin *et al.* 1992; Thompson 1995; Marks and Houston 2002; Hattery 2001; McRae 2003; Crompton *et al.* 2003). Alwin and colleagues were agnostic regarding the the nature of causality here although many writers have placed an emphasis on beliefs (attitudes or preferences) as having a significant role in shaping behaviours (e.g. Marks and Houston 2002; Hattery 2001; Hakim 2000). They are all aware that stated attitudes may be a rationalisation of behaviour, or possibly created through experience. However, they all offer evidence that attitudes, or in Hakim's argument preferences, play a significant role in shaping people's work and care decisions. In such accounts attitudes and preference are seen to have an important independent role in shaping behaviours, specifically in the childcare and employment participation decisions amongst mothers. Thompson concludes that whilst social and economic factors differentiate mothers who work and mothers who do not, and availability of childcare is very important:

> [W]hat most distinguishes working from non-working mothers is their attitude towards women and work.
>
> (Thomson 1995: 83)

This echoes Hakim's argument that women have choices in a way they did not in the past (Hakim 2000). However, analysis of causal direction, from beliefs to behaviours, is not definitive within the literature but somewhat speculative. For example, Thomson identifies diversity of belief within three groups of full-time workers, part-time workers and homemakers, and an association between within-group variation and women's stated preparedness to return to work if they had access to ideal childcare. This patterning suggests to Thomson that attitudes are not merely a reflection of own labour market position, and she argues that women's beliefs condition, and partly determine, their behaviours. This is a plausible enough statement, but it does not follow the empirical evidence she presents, in which various factors remain uncontrolled. It may be that there is a coincidence of attitude and experience that can be explained only with reference to prior variables. Indeed it is likely that the notion of a general causal model is inappropriate: causality may be context-specific. For the moment I will explore co-variation between stated attitudes and respondents' experiences, a pattern of association which parallels that revealed in other studies and data sets. This coherence can help us to shed light on the shape of social diversity.

To preface the empirical analysis, first the evidence reveals a clear association between respondents' attitudes to mothers' responsibilities and their own circumstances and experiences. Additionally, those with a consistently pro maternal care ('homemaker') attitude are in similar social positions.[12] Furthermore, evidence on seemingly homogeneous evaluations across subsamples of middle- and working-class women shows, on closer inspection, a pattern of diversity in line with differential opportunities. There is no evidence here of attitudes being divorced from social location.

The first analyses below show evidence of a strong association, as we would expect, between attitudes and experience, and circumstances. The two attitudinal questions referred to here were part of a battery of questions drawn from the International Social Survey Programme component of the British Social Attitudes Survey (included in 1989, 1994 and 2002). In all the tables presented below the terms 'agree' and 'disagree' are aggregates for responses to both 'agree' and 'strongly agree', and 'disagree' and 'strongly disagree' respectively.

Women who are themselves currently mothers of young children are less likely to consider that a child will suffer as a consequence of his/her mother working, than are the population as a whole (Table 5.1). Focusing just on those who are currently mothers of pre-school children, we can see a strong association between respondents' attitudes towards the likelihood of a child suffering if their mother works and their own pattern of working. Of those in work 16 per cent state a child with a working mother is likely to suffer, whilst 75 per cent disagree. Relatively few women in this group give the neutral response. In contrast responses are much more evenly spread over the three categories amongst women who are currently looking after the home full time. Here, in stark contrast to the working mothers, 37 per cent disagree that a child of a working mother is likely to suffer. We can see also from the table that level of qualification is associated with the pattern of responses, clearly more highly qualified women are less likely to agree with the statement (at 12 per cent) than women with lower-level or no qualifications (at 28 per cent).

Table 5.1 Distribution of responses to BSAS attitude statement shown by all, and by female, respondents' own status and qualification level (BSAS 2002; author's analysis)

A pre-school child is likely to suffer if his or her mother works

	Agree	*Neutral*	*Disagree*	*N*
All respondents	36%	20%	43%	1984
Mothers of pre-school children	20%	18%	61%	146
Mothers of pre-school children				
in work	16%	10%	75%	83
looking after home	28%	35%	37%	43
Mothers of pre-school children				
A level and higher qualifications	12%	16%	72%	76
GCSE and lower/no qualifications	29%	21%	50%	70

Note: Not all the percentage figures sum to 100 since 'not answered' is recorded for up to 4% of respondents on the questions shown.

We can look also at the distribution of responses to the question about whether or not women should work or not at different stages in the family life course. Table 5.2 shows the aggregate pattern of responses.

There is general consensus about the appropriateness of working when children are not present, or older, and a strong favouring of part-time work when women have school aged children. Responses are most evenly differentiated by the question of women's appropriate work/care behaviour when there is a child under school age. Focusing then just on the question regarding the behaviours of mothers of pre-school children, Table 5.3 shows the responses of mothers of pre-school children within the sample, disaggregated by their current labour force status and qualification level.

Table 5.3 reveals the clear, although not general, association between respondents' attitudes and their own circumstances and behaviour when they themselves had pre-school children. Working mothers favour work (clearly part-time work even where they worked full time) and homemaker mothers favour homemaking. Sixteen per cent of homemaker mothers of pre-school children felt that a woman in the same situation should work, and 64 per cent felt that she should stay at home. In contrast amongst working mothers shown here 66 per cent felt such a woman should work whilst 16 per cent felt she should stay at home (a ratio of 4:1 homemaker women favour staying at home, a ratio of more than 4:1 working women favour working). Clearly there is little evidence here of a dissonance between experience and attitudes, rather a noteworthy consistency. There is also evident in the table an association between level of qualification and stated attitude although this is more muted compared to the association between work experience and attitude.

In furthering the analysis of the links between experience and attitudes I now turn to the Life as a Parent data set, generated by the author. The Life

Table 5.2 Distribution of responses to BSAS attitude statement shown by all respondents (BSAS 2002; Park *et al.* 2003)

Do you think women should work outside the home full time, part time or not at all under these circumstances?

	Work full time	*Work part time*	*Stay at home*	*Can't choose*
After marrying and before there are children	78%	8%	1%	11%
When there is a child under school age	3%	34%	48%	12%
After the youngest child starts school	15%	66%	5%	12%
After the children leave home	62%	19%	1%	15%

Note: N = 1984.

Table 5.3 Distribution of responses to BSAS attitude statement shown by female respondents' own status and qualification level (BSAS 2002; author's analysis)

Do you think women should work outside the home full time, part time or not at all under these circumstances? – when there is a child under school age

	Work full time	*Work part time*	*Stay at home*	*Can't choose*	N
Mothers of pre-school children	5%	43%	35%	15%	146
Mothers of pre-school children					
In work	8%	58%	14%	16%	84
Looking after home	0%	16%	64%	18%	44
Mothers of pre-school children					
A level and higher qualifications	9%	42%	26%	17%	77
GCSE and lower/no qualifications	1%	42%	44%	11%	70

as a Parent research into attitudes, care and commitments took as a focus the experiences, perceptions and behaviours of parents of young school children aged 4 to 7 years, and was conducted through the ESRC Research Group for the Study if Care, Values and the Future of Welfare (CAVA). The Life as a Parent sample locales were chosen with reference to specific dimensions of social diversity, profiling Leeds city wards with reference to socio-economic indicators and taking the 'catchment' neighbourhoods of targeted schools as locales for the study.[13]

Parallelling the BSAS data, the Life as a Parent data also shows significant continuities between attitudes and social position. For example, in respect of the question about whether a mother of a pre-school child should work or stay at home, of those who had themselves stayed at home over half felt such a woman should stay at home, whereas amongst those who had themselves worked when they had pre-school children, fewer than one-fifth felt a woman in this position should stay at home (see Irwin 2004 for details). We can use the new survey data to examine some issues relating to the care of school aged children, and do so through a different kind of question, specifically here from a vignette question, of interest for the present discussion.

As we saw in Table 5.2 most people in the BSA survey state that in general women should work *when their youngest child is school age*, the vast majority suggesting that (in response to an abstract and generalising question) such women should work part time. Whilst an abstract statement about what 'women in general' should do suggests a 15 per cent 'approval rating' for full-time employment amongst this group in the 2002 BSAS data, in practice nationally 26 per cent of women with children aged 5–10 work full time (or did so in 2001, reported by ONS 2002a). This may reflect a greater liberalism than the compulsion implied by the attitude statement. Often people may wish they could answer such generalising questions with an 'it depends . . .' response. Vignettes offer a more detailed scenario to respondents and arguably give us a slightly more subtle insight into respondents' opinions.

One of the vignettes used within the Life as a Parent survey sought to elucidate what people judge to be the best way for a mother of a school-aged child to balance employment and childcare commitments when they are given more detail and contextual information about options, desires and constraints.

The vignette was as follows:

> I will now read out another dilemma.
>
> Sue and David have one child and they do not plan to have any more. The child is about to start reception year at primary school. David works full time and Sue works part time. An opportunity to apply for a new job has come up and Sue would very much like this job, but it is only available on a full-time basis. However, their child minder could take the child to school and pick her up and look after her until 6 o'clock each day. Sue is trying to decide whether or not to apply for the job. What should she do? Should she:
>
> A. Apply for the job?
>
> B. Stay in her part time job so she can drop off and collect her daughter and be with her after school?
>
> Do something else?
>
> *If answer is – do something else*: what would that be? (open ended)

Of the 96 female respondents, 87 gave as their answer A or B, and of these a two-thirds to one-third majority answered B (a ratio of 58 to 29). Women who are currently working full time, and the most highly qualified women, are marginally more likely than not to favour the full-time option for the vignette character, in contrast to the part-timer and homemaker respondents who clearly favour the part-time option. Table 5.4 shows this distribution.

Table 5.4 Women's responses to vignette, by labour force status and by qualification level (Life as a Parent Survey)

	Own current labour force/carer status				
	Work full time	*Work part time*	*Full time looks after home*	*Other (unemployed/ sick/disabled)*	*Total*
Sue should:					
Apply for f.t. job	9 (47%)	13 (31%)	4 (14%)	3 (43%)	29 (30%)
Stay in p.t. job	7 (37%)	24 (57%)	23 (82%)	4 (57%)	58 (60%)
Do something else	3 (16%)	5 (12%)	1 (4%)		9 (9%)
Total	19	42	28	7	96
	Level of qualification achieved				
	Degree/ higher degree	*A level*	*Lower/ vocational*	*None*	*Total*
Sue should:					
Apply for f.t. job	9 (47%)	5 (26%)	11 (28%)	4 (22%)	29 (30%)
Stay in p.t. job	7 (37%)	10 (53%)	27 (68%)	14 (78%)	58 (60%)
Do something else	3 (16%)	4 (21%)	2 (5%)	0 (0%)	9 (9%)
Total	19	19	40	18	96

Note: The column percentages aid comparison but are bracketed since the absolute numbers are small.

So far the evidence suggests a broad correspondence between circumstances and attitudes, which is as we might expect. However, some writers as we have seen argue a growing importance of choices and preferences in shaping behaviour and actions. Where this has been subject to empirical research it has been argued that it is where attitudes and preferences are most strongly and consistently held that they will have the greatest causal impact (e.g. Hattery 2001; Hakim 2000). There is a risk though that such attitudes and preferences are treated asociologically: we cannot locate them or analyse their provenance. For example, Hakim identifies a homemaker group, that is women who have a primary, and orienting preference for homemaking over work. Such women, she argues, exist across the social spectrum. This she takes as evidence of the relative fixity, and historical continuity, of such a preference, and as suggestive that such a preference is primary (Hakim 1996, 2000). It is certainly plausible that some women will indeed seek only a full-time homemaker role, seemingly against the odds (at least of current sociological predictive capacities). However, what should we read into this? We cannot always 'locate' values but this stems from their complexity rather than their randomness, and further analysis often uncovers close connections between social location and perceptions. As with Hakim's evidence, the data here reveals homemakers to be spread across a diverse social spectrum. As discussed next, however, the Life as a Parent sample shows those with the most consistent homemaker attitudes were all in very similar social circumstances.

To identify respondents who were consistently 'pro maternal care' (or 'homemaker') in their attitudes I take responses to the three survey questions discussed already within this section. The three questions were the child-suffer statement as described in Table 5.1, the woman's place statement as described in Table 5.3, and the vignette question. Female respondents (who formed the majority of survey respondents) were classified as 'pro maternal care' if they identified the 'homemaker' solution to the two attitude statements and if they also identified as best the part-time work option within the vignette. Out of the Life as a Parent sample of 96 mothers, 14 fell into the category of pro maternal care. We might see these women as being the most committed homemakers, at least in their general attitudes (preferences were not directly addressed in the questionnaire). For commentators such as Hakim (2000) and Hattery (2001) it is women with consistent homemaker commitments we might see as most likely to realise their preferences. It is there in particular where Hakim (2000) and Hattery (2001) see values as having a primary influence in shaping behaviours.

In the Life as a Parent data members of the 'pro maternal care' subsample were all concentrated in relatively constrained circumstances. None held qualifications above O level or GCSE level. In contrast, amongst the remainder of the sample, 38/82 did so. Taking qualification level as an indicator of social position we can presume that, in general, employment opportunities will be relatively limited for this group, a likely constraint then on their actions. An analysis across the school catchments shows that 10/14 pro maternal care respondents were concentrated in white working-class neighbourhoods. The average age of these women when they had their first child was 22, in marked constrast to the average age of 26 at first birth for the rest of the sample. Again this is consistent with a pattern of relatively limited opportunities within employment. Such women have typically worked at some point at least and social class membership (based on current, or last held job) shows these women to be concentrated in RG social class III non-manual, or lower. Only 1/14 belongs to class I or II, compared to 28/82 of the rest of the sample. These women then appear to be relatively constrained in respect of their employment opportunities, but they are not necessarily amongst the most disadvantaged. They typically live with a spouse or partner, and the latter are typically working. These women with 'pro maternal care' attitudes are less likely than average to be working and where they do work, it is part time. In only one case out of fourteen is it described as being 'for essentials', in contrast to over half of the rest of the sample of working women.

In general then we can say that those who are consistently 'pro maternal care' in their attitudes are positioned very similarly to one another. They are white, working class, typically with a partner who is working. Their social circumstances limited their choices with respect to employment opportunities but also to some extent facilitated consistent pro maternal care attitudes. It is of interest to note within the 2002 BSAS data that it is within the lower half of household income groups, *but not amongst the lowest*, where mothers are most likely to express the most 'pro maternal care' attitudes (as measured by the same two BSAS attitude statements discussed here). Again this is consistent with seeing such attitudes as associated not simply with 'constraint', but with a combination of constraint and a perceived relative adequacy of household resources.

The argument of Hakim is that because ostensibly similar preferences cross the social spectrum, so circumstances clearly do not determine choices. She argues that choices now are more primary in shaping outcomes in mothers' work and care decisions (Hakim 2000). However, we cannot adequately understand social diversity if we disconnect choices, and perceptions, from circumstances. Continuities between attitudes and social location are in clear evidence within the data sets examined, as elsewhere. Diverse vantage points and dispositions are congruent with varied social locations. The evidence should reorient us to reflect further on the coherence of subjective evaluations and how people are positioned in social space. Can we then use evidence on perceptions to help us improve the ways in which we can analyse social diversity? The next section explores this question with a focus on aspects of socio-economic advantage and disadvantage, with reference to perceptions of appropriate care for children as it varies by their age.

5.5 Attitudes and inequalities

Duncan and his colleagues (2003) maintain that understandings of good mothering transcend class and income differences. So whilst these authors come from a very different theoretical angle to that of Hakim, a parallel dilemma of explanation emerges, in the seeming dissociation of value and circumstance. Is it simply that a uniform value has been found, or would a more differentiated understanding hold greater analytic purchase? To address this question I will consider further the responses to the vignette as described above, and a follow-up question. I have described the tendency for respondents with degree level qualifications to favour the full-time option more than the other groups. Still, though, nearly half the graduates favour the part-time option. This pattern echoes the argument of Duncan and his colleagues – that a group of highly qualified middle-class women are seemingly not distinguishable from working-class women in their homemaker orientation (ibid.). It also seemingly echoes Hakim's argument that the same preferences can cross the social spectrum. Does the data imply that we have uncovered a uniform construction of maternal responsibilities that cuts across class-based social inequalities? The analysis below shows that the construction is not uniform, but hides a diversity within. Uncovering this diversity reveals that attitudes correspond closely with different social locations. The diversity reflects differing perceptions of how care commitments (practical and moral) should vary over a child's early years.

After providing an answer to the vignette described earlier, respondents were asked: 'Why do you think this is the better solution'?[14] Those who had said that 'Sue should stay in her part-time job so she can drop off and collect her daugher and be with her after school' were then asked:

> 'Would it have made any difference to your answer if rather than *starting* at primary school the child had been at school a few years?', and then: 'Why do you think that?'

For these respondents the distribution of responses disaggregated by qualification level is shown in Table 5.5.

Table 5.5 Responses to vignette follow-up question, 'Would it have made any difference to your answer if rather than starting at primary school the child had been at school for a few years?', by respondents' qualifications level (Life as a Parent Survey)

	Yes	*No*
Degree	6	1
A level	5	5
Lower	11	16
None	5	9
N	27	31

Amongst those who favour the part-time option we can see again a clear qualification level gradation on notions of what might be appropriate behaviour when the child is older (but still at primary school). It is notable that those with degree level qualifications stand apart in almost uniformly altering their recommendation as the child grows older. We can explore some of the substance of this pattern through considering the responses to the subsequent open-ended question.

All the following quotes are taken from respondents who say that the character in the vignette should stay in her part-time post. The first set of responses is from respondents qualified to degree level. Six out of seven of these lived in predominantly white middle-class neighbourhoods.

Having stated they preferred the part-time 'solution' to the vignette dilemma they were asked why:

> Q: Why do you think this is the better solution?
> A: To get a bit of the best of both worlds. I think kids like being taken to school and parents also like doing it. You can become very disconnected if you never pick up the kids.
>
> (White, married, degree, 3 children aged 6 and under, homemaker/student, Registrar General Social Class, RGSC III NM)

> Q: Why do you think this is the better solution?
> A: Because she can go for the full time job later when her child is settled and more confident. Reception year is very important and can set a precedent for the rest of the years at school. By 6pm both you and the child would be too tired and have no real time for each other.
>
> (White, married, degree, 2 children, works 16–20 hours, RGSC II)

> Q: Why do you think this is the better solution?
> A: To be involved in the school. To know the child's friends, and to know she is settled. It's very tiring to carry on until 6.
>
> (White, married, degree, 3 children, works 16–20 hours, RGSC II)

Of these and the other high-qualified respondents opting for the part-time solution, 6/7 say that their part-time recommendation would change if the child had been at school for a few years. The following responses were made when they were asked why:

> 'Children become more independent as they become older.'
>
> (White, married, degree, 3 children aged 6 and under, homemaker/student, RGSC III NM)

> 'The children's lives become much more independent. They get themselves to school and back independently.'
>
> (White, married, degree, 3 children, works part time 26–30 hours, RGSC II)

> 'It might make a difference if the child is settled and has after school facilities.'
>
> (White, married, degree, 2 children, works 16–20 hours, RGSC II)

> '[The] child would already be settled at school, and secure. The child would be older physically and emotionally to cope with the long day.'
>
> (White, married, 3 children, degree, works 16–20 hours, RGSC II)

This kind of response is not completely 'contained' within the high-qualification category, although as we have seen it relates strongly to it. The following quote shows a similar attitude held by a woman who had no qualifications. Interestingly her child is at the same school as children of mothers cited above. This respondent's part-time recommendation would change to the full-time one if the child had been at school for a few years:

> 'Because when they are little they like the security more. When the are older they are more confident and know (their) mum's coming back at a certain time. The younger they are the more they want their mum there.'
>
> (Married, 4 children (one pre-school, one primary school, and two young adult), no qualifications, full-time homemaker, RGSC III NM)

The following quotes are from mothers with children at schools in neighbourhoods which were almost uniformly white, and working class. Respondents here generally held few qualifications, and as we saw earlier people here tend to be more 'pro maternal care' in their attitudes and relatively constrained in their employment opportunities. Like the respondents cited above, these women also recommend the vignette character should give priority to time with her child, but in contrast they see this as the right thing to do, it seems, *throughout* the child's primary school years. Their recommendation would not change if the child had been at school for a few years. For example:

> '[She] needs to spend time with her children [it] doesn't matter what age they are.'
>
> (White, married, 5 children aged 10 and under, no qualifications, homemaker, last job: RGSC III M)

> '[You] don't have kids to give to somebody else. It's a long time for a child to be with a childminder.'
>
> (Cohabiting, 2 children (1 pre-school and one school age), works part time (11–15 hours), has NVQ level qualifications, RGSC III NM)

> 'You still need to spend time with your children whatever age they are.'
>
> (Cohabiting, 3 children (7 years and older), homemaker, no qualifications, last job RGSC IV).

> 'Because kids need their mum at home whatever age they are. They need them to cook their tea and stuff.'
>
> (Lone parent, 2 children, white, no qualifications, never worked, age 23)

> 'Your child has to come first. I have been offered full time work from September when my son starts but while he is (at) primary I will not do this.'
>
> (Cohabiting, 4 children, unspecified vocational/professional qualification, works 25–32 hours on shifts, RGSC III NM)

These women appear to believe that mothers' exclusive care and commitment, at least in the circumstance described, should extend right across a child's primary school years. This contrasts with responses by the highly qualified, more advantaged women described above. It seems very likely that the highly qualified women possess opportunities for strategic employment decisions, and hold aspirations for themselves as workers, and careerists, independent of their commitments to their children. In contrast a more limited scope for strategic employment decisions is consistent with holding moral commitments which lie for much longer with the exclusive care of children. Thus perceptions which at first appear uniform, and independent of social difference, turn out to have a significant link to social location, with commitments seen through a temporal, life course lens, their patterning consistent with very different class-related positions and likely trajectories.

Duncan argues that in respect of research into mothering identities and moralities there has been limited engagement with issues of class, and he seeks to understand the articulation of mothering identities, and decisions around work and care, with class diversity. Through his analysis of the CAVA Mother, Care and Employment project data Duncan argues that class matters, but finds a complex situation in which mothering ideologies and work and care preferences do not directly cleave around social class distinctions nor availability of human capital (Duncan 2005). For example he identifies two middle-class groups distinguishable by their contrasting attitudes to the appropriateness of working or being a full-time carer when children are young, arguing that 'aspirations and identity are in this way autonomous from access to the labour market' (Duncan 2005: 68). A similar split is in evidence amongst working-class respondents.

The fact that patterns of behaviour and values do not straightforwardly map directly onto class divisions again initially begs the question of discrepancy between social position and belief. Duncan (2005) properly treats this as a puzzle, and seeks to resolve the contradiction by foregrounding cultural and relational factors, and seeing class as embedded within. Class differences in mothers' actions, he argues, refer not simply to structural divisions but to more nuanced social identities, referring in particular to the perceived importance of career, biographical experience, relations with partners, and norms as these are developed within social networks (Duncan ibid.). The very diverse cultural and historical contexts of coalmining and textiles areas in which interviews were conducted mean that there is no necessary linking of class with any particular outcome in respect of mothers' employment patterns (ibid.). As we saw in Chapter 3, these different working-class occupations were historically associated with very different divisions of labour and associated assumptions and expectations surrounding women's employment participation.

It is clearly problematic to try and capture identity and aspiration in economic class groupings. However, if generalised measures of class have so little purchase on identities, aspirations and values one could ask whether or not it is time to drop such a limiting categorisation. Generalised class categories are simply too crude to capture the complexities of experience across diverse local labour markets (Szreter 1996; Bottero 2004). In Szreter's historical analysis subjectivities and labour market processes are not autonomous. The different organisation of production, and of local labour markets means that historically a very different division of labour in working-class households obtained in coalmining districts and in textiles districts, linked to very different perspectives on appropriate gendered and generational roles, and different patterns of reproductive behaviour and so on (Szreter 1996). As Duncan himself notes, cultural expectations that are integral to local labour markets and divisions of labour are centrally important parts of the social fabric. The gap between aspirations and identities on the one hand and class divisions on the other appears to say more about the flaws in the class schema than it does about a discrepancy between cultural and material processes (cf. Bottero 2004).

What I have sought to show throughout the chapter so far is that the strong links between subjective views and experience reveal a great deal of coherence between them. *The argument that values have somehow become a new kind of motor of social change leaving behind the structural does not stand up.* Analysis of diverse dispositions and identifications reveals not a disalignment or discrepancy with social structure. However, what it does is highlight the need for a sufficiently differentiated conception of structure. So far I have sought to explore links between dispositions and extant material social relationships and diversity. We have seen an alignment between the two. Importantly this is in evidence in a period of some significant social changes in gendered, and especially women's, relations to work and care. In the final section of this chapter I reflect further on change in gendered positions and women's identifications around work and care, with reference to qualitative data. I present the evidence as part of an argument of continued changes in 'the normal thing to do'.

5.6 Gendered positions and identities in a context of change

Looking at the continued extent of women's participation in low-paying and part-time jobs it has been concluded by some that women's circumstances are characterised by continuity more than by change (Hakim 2000; Arber and Ginn 1995). It is true that overall women's position has changed in a relatively muted way if one just looks at this position through the lens of employment participation rates. However, this would be to understate the changes in women's (and to a lesser extent, men's) social position, a development discussed in Chapter 4. A primary focus on employment rates risks missing analysis of the altered position of women in society and the altered meanings of work as a component of women's identities. Greater 'acceptance' of women's employment revealed in attitudinal data reflects not simply liberal tolerance (although it does in part), but it is also linked more closely to a shifting configuration of need, aspiration and gendered commitments.

In Chapter 4 I discussed change in gendered economic and social positions. It is not simply a case of women being 'drawn in' to employment as their male partners' bring home a poorer wage, or less security. Rather the change in women's position relative to men should be construed also in terms of changing identities, and change in the placing of work in the lives of women. It would be easy to overstate the suddenness of this change. After all, Roberts (1995) identifies a similar pattern in her review of experiences between the 1940s and 1970s. However, an important development in the last decades of the twentieth century was the normalisation, and routinisation, of work amongst mothers of young children across a growing proportion of the population.

In the rest of this section I explore perceptions of the appropriate commitments of mothers, with reference to qualitative data available through other recently generated primary data. The Mothers, Care and Employment (MCE) project (led by Professor Simon Duncan) was a qualitative study conducted as part of the research by the ESRC Research Group for the Study of Care, Values and the Future of Welfare (CAVA). It was conducted across different locales in Yorkshire and Lancashire. Parents (mostly mothers) of children aged 14 and under were interviewed, with a particular focus on issues of value and people's sense of 'doing the right thing', in respect of caring for their children (Duncan and Saugeres 2000; Duncan *et al.* 2003). Thanks to Lise Saugeres for conducting the semi-structured interviews and to Simon Duncan for making available to me the qualitative data.

Analysis of data from the Mothers, Care and Employment Study allows us to further reflect on general developments in the relative position of women and men, and the recomposing of interdependence, and income earning roles at the level of household reproduction. This is reflected in a pattern of dispositions in which work is a central component of the women's identities, and not 'set aside' in the family-building period. It seems likely that the salience of work as a crucial component of women's identities has a greater spread across the population, and that it is growing amongst groups for whom it has traditionally been a less definitive experience or expectation.

Change in the relative positioning of women and men entails change in women's identities in particular. Work is very significant in women's identities; partly as two incomes are increasingly required for household resourcing, but also as women increasingly lay claim to autonomy. The CAVA Mothers, Care and Employment interviews reveal a significant work ethic amongst women who are mothers of young children. This is a feature of middle-class respondents, many of whom see work as a core part of their identity. But it is also a theme for many working-class respondents with more circumscribed opportunities and perhaps more circumscribed motivations for work. Women hold work as more central to their identities, and more mothers, including working-class mothers, have a work-related identity as well as a mother identity. The MCE evidence reveals the very routine nature of work amongst women, and suggests that it would disrupt their sense of themselves if they were to stop work fully through the family-building period.

Even amongst the relatively few women defined by Duncan and his colleagues as 'primarily mother' (Duncan *et al.* 2003) who express clearly their full commitment to full-time parental care for their children, there is a clear sense of paid work as a core part of their identities. For example, Theresa (Burnley, GCSE level qualifications) encapsulates what Duncan terms a 'primarily mother' orientation:

> 'I believe if you have children you should fetch 'em up yourself rather than like you get your career mums who can go out to work and somebody else has fetched your child up and I don't believe in that really.'

Nevertheless this woman returned to work as a health care assistant when her child was 10 months old. She has a job share arrangement with her husband, both doing 25 hours as a care assistant. She was asked:

> Q: And you say that that is because you found it difficult to be just at home?
>
> A: Yeah. Yeah I found it hard work, I needed to see other people and do other things as well as be at home. I needed to be myself as well as being a mum.

That is, whilst her commitment to care may be paramount, she still sees work and its sociability as core aspects of her identity.

Others expressed further dimensions of why work is so important to them. For example, Jessica said:

> 'I work so that I can give my son everything that I've never had and so that I can provide for him and if he wants anything he can have it, not to spoil him but to make sure that . . . we can provide a decent standard of living.'

In discussing her return to work when son was young she said:

> 'I wanted to go back to work. I don't know why, but I did. I think it were, it were important for me to get back to being that person, not just being me little boy's mum.'

Another respondent who encapsulates the 'primarily mother' orientation was Christine, who said:

> 'I couldn't see t'point of having a child and leaving him with somebody else.'

Christine was from Barnsley (a traditional coal mining town, and therefore a cultural context in which we might expect the 'primarily mother' orientation to be common). She has five children aged from 4 to their late teens, and has worked fairly extensively in unskilled (factory and cleaning) jobs through family-building. Her desire for work is financial. It is of course though not possible to separate out notions of need from cultural expectations of adequacy, in turn linked to both partners' contributions. It is also not possible to separate out her seemingly pecuniary motives for working from other aspects of her identity, reflecting it seems an important place of work within her identity. Initially she expresses the financial value of work, but it becomes clear that this is not purely utilitarian, but links to her desire for a significant degree of economic autonomy from her husband:

> Q: So . . . the fact that you went back full time when you had the three children, . . . was it mostly financial or was it because you actually wanted . . .
> A: No, financial, financial, it were financial, yeah, yeah.
> Q: Any other reasons for you to be working?
> A: Just financial, it's just scary . . . how much things cost and like I wanted a bigger family and me husband wanted a bigger family but to be able to support a big family I felt like we had to keep, I had to keep working ye know.

And clearly she works very hard, not just for supporting others but for her own independence (this was a common theme of female interviewees). When she is asked questions about her husband getting involved with childcare she says:

> '[H]e is away through week, but he does help Saturdays and Sundays but – my husband always, always wanted me to stop working yeah. Ye know, this were always a bit of friction between me and A. 'cos he'd always say we'll cope and we'll manage ye know but I were always, I've always had money so I were always scared of just relying on his wage and then I'd say yeah, but what happens when I want summat and what happens if I want to do summat or I want to buy a new coat . . . do I ask you for money, I says: "I don't think it'll work out like that" and he says "yeah yeah of course you ask me" but ye know, it's not, I can't. I've always had a job, from 19 I've always worked and I've always had me own money.'

As well as her earnings being important for meeting expectations regarding living standards, to work seems an important part of her identity, and the kind of role model she wants to be for her children:

> 'I want my children to work, I want 'em to work, I want 'em to do good at school, as good as they can ye know, and try and, try and get on.'

So even amongst those who have few qualifications and express Duncan's 'primarily mother' orientation it is notable that very strongly expressed care commitments are consistent with holding a very significant work ethic. A sense of paid work appears to be a core component of the identity of a wide spectrum of women who have young children. It is common for this ethic to be bound up with women's desire for independence and autonomy.

As well as the importance of work to these women's sense of themselves and their self-esteem, it is notable that their views were not necessarily mirrored by their husbands who, like Christine's, tended to 'fall in' with their wives' plans following a position of doubt. The expressions here seem illustrative of the differential rate of change in women's and men's social positions, discussed in Chapter 4. One example of a husband 'falling in' with his wife's desires is evident in the responses of Lisa, mother of five children aged from 4 years old to 'college' age. She works from 4.30 to 9.30 p.m. through weekdays, and did so since her youngest was a year old, primarily for financial reasons but she also enjoys the sociability. She is a machine operator at a bakery, and plans to go to college when her youngest child starts school.

When asked if her husband was supportive when she started work she said:

> '. . . when I first started for t'first few weeks he didn't like it – and we did have a few arguments and I says "look, we either argue over t'fact that we don't see each other and you're tired and you're coming home and seeing to t'kids or we argue over money". I says "it's like Hobson's Choice, which would you prefer?" And he says "I know you're right," he says "carry on, we'll give it a bit longer" and he's fine now, got used to it, the routine and there's no problem at all, he's quite alright with it.'

Another respondent, Hannah, revealed a fairly extreme version of a very marked discrepancy in both opinions and power of husband and wife, and the importance of economic position within that balance:

> 'I was under his power when he got the job and moved in and he was the bill payer, it's like – he took control and undermined me and you feel worthless when they do that . . . being kept like that is terrible on your own self esteem. So I'd gone back to work and I started to lose weight, get more confidence about meself 'cos I'd got me baby weight still on

> me, and then money were coming in and it were like he'd say "oh no, I don't want that, I don't like this" and I'd say "well get stuffed" and he's like – the power changed because – I was then his equal and he couldn't belittle me and he behaved, the behaviour of a man when you can equal 'em is a lot better, if they get you under their power they will abuse it, without a doubt and – we'd been, I wouldn't give t' job up then, no matter, if he could support and I thought – I've done it when the child, when I didn't want to work, I've gone through the pain barrier, I'm now gonna stick with it.'

The interview data here is illustrative of individual level experiences in a way that quantitative data cannot be, but is also indicative of general themes which are revealed through the general level numerical data. From the 1970s there has been a marked rise in the employment rates of partnered mothers of young children. Work has become a more routinised experience around the family-building period. The evidence indicates that it is a larger section of the population for whom this is so. Work is a more core component of women's identities across the life course, and this includes a significant section of working-class women, who may be relatively disadvantaged in their employment prospects. *The qualitative evidence shown here squares with evidence on gendered differences revealed in aggregate level trends: that women are more at the forefront of change than are men: pushing it through desires for work-based independence and the ability to shape family living standards as much as reacting to changed exigencies of economic need.*

I have argued that there is a coherence between subjectivities and contexts, and that social change is about the reshaping of these contexts. Women are not newly individualised. The normative and material are intertwined. We have seen how norms, dispositions and aspects of identity link to an altered configuration of gendered relations to work and family. It is important to stress though that 'coherence' between attitudes and circumstances does not mean that experiences are without difficulty. The content of contemporary work life negotiation engenders high levels of stress for particular groups (Crompton *et al.* 2003). Jessica, an interviewee in the MCE project, gives voice to the dual faceted disposition of women who are seeking to manage their commitments in this context. She is reflecting on the upcoming birth of second child:

> 'Half of me's gonna be wanting to be at home and half of me's wanting to be at work and I don't know whether I can handle that, I don't know whether I can cope being at home all t'time but then I don't know whether I can cope being back at work and leaving two [children].'

Additionally there is a clear sense of compromise: that with so many demands and commitments it is difficult to ever feel that one is excelling in any one of them.

> Hannah: I do love me job, I couldn't do full time because – personally don't feel I do anything well because – I'm a mother, and I'm a wife, I'm a housekeeper so I don't feel that I can give, I'm good at me job, I know I am but I know I could be a lot better, but I struggle between all three, it's like a balancing act . . . I do.

The best one can do is the best in the circumstances. This may be an existential problem to some degree but the demands on those with full-time jobs and extensive childcare commitments also throws into focus a systemic problem – that in the context of changing gendered relations to work and care social institutions frequently still hinder rather than facilitate people's commitments and endeavours.

5.7 Conclusion

We have seen a growth of research into values, and into why people choose whether or not to work when they have young children. We need to better understand the changing contexts in which people's choices and decisions are shaped. Through the latter part of the twentieth century we have witnessed not only a change in the structure of opportunity and constraint for women, and men, but a shift in their social identities and location. This means that employment has become, in many contexts, a more routinised aspect of women's experience across the life course (of family building and childcare), deemed more 'necessary' as part of maintaining household resourcing against desired living standards, and deemed more 'natural', more a part of women's identities. The position of both women and men has changed, and they have new relations to employment and to household resourcing and, to a degree, to each other. Women are positioned, and have positioned themselves, at the forefront of change, in part through forging claims to greater autonomy.

In the chapter I have explored empirical data on gender roles, and parenting, in the post-war period and analysed data from the 2002 British Social Attitudes Survey, and from other survey and qualitative research. I argued that diverse attitudes are strongly associated with social circumstances. Seeming discrepancies between the two identified by other writers appear limited in light of the analysis of social diversity. The data presented here shows a clear alignment between attitudes towards work and care and social location. Additionally consideration of values articulated through qualitative data reveals cohesion between disposition and position. That this pattern of mutuality is evident in a period of significant changes in women's employment patterns is sociologically very important. General level data reveals the growing numerical importance of employment amongst mothers of young children, and the general evidence suggests the increased importance of employment in women's identities. The qualitative data explored here accords with this expectation and gives insights into the experiences of women whose social similars, a generation ago, would probably have seen work as a less significant aspect of their identity. We can see a reconfiguring of gendered social positions and their link to changes in social identifications, aspirations and norms.

Over this and the last two chapters I have explored issues in the analysis of social change. The particular focus has been on gendered relations to work, care and family, We have seen how explanations of change have faced difficulties due to a separation of norms and material social relations. Recently theorists have emphasised a weakening of structural forces, or made little headway into conceptualising the links between the social and the normative. I have developed analyses across historical and contemporary contexts which reveal a meshing of social relations and norms and values. The normative realm is an integral part of social structural pattern and process. I turn now to some other domains of social life. We find there similar problems of explanation, notably a presumed gap between subjective experience and perceptions of that experience, and 'objective' social structures. Again we need to better conceptualise the social contexts through which individual level subjectivities and macro level structural processes mesh. And again, this is not simply a case of analysing a 'missing' middle layer, but a broader, and more interesting, conceptual issue.

6 Life course transitions and the changing landscape of opportunity and constraint

6.1 Life course and social change

6.1.1 Introduction

Recent decades have seen very significant changes in the shape of the life course and, in particular, in the experience of people in different life course stages. Later life has been dramatically extended as a period of post-retirement for many, with increased longevity and lowered ages of exit from the labour force. Youth as a period of partial dependence has also been significantly extended as young people manifest a delay relative to their predecessors in the attainment of material independence. How can we best understand these developments and analyse them with reference to the societal context of which they are a part? Many writers, whilst providing insights into aspects of experience of youth and of later life, work with a model in which subjective experiences and objective structures do not 'fit'. So, for example, a lack of awareness of structural oppressions reveals the effectiveness of ideologies of individualised responsibility. As we will see such a model projects onto people its own failure of explanation. A way forward is needed. We urgently need a better theorisation of the contexts of subjective experience and how they mesh within a broader structure.

Sociological research into later life has been shaped by a concern with the disadvantaging and poverty of older people. In conjunction, much research has sought to conceptualise the social location of later life: how this life course stage is constructed as a life course stage apart, and older people treated as 'other'. I explore constructions of the position of later life, and research on aspects of older people's identity, and argue that by virtue of the analytic categories being used, later life is inappropriately positioned 'at the edges' of society. Categories which enshrine a concept of difference reinforce, rather than locate, the difference, and similarities, of later life. Recent arguments of an undermining of difference as an outcome of fragmentation and individualisation posit an identity crisis for older people. However, there is limited empirical evidence in support of such a position. A more adequate account of older people's social experiences must focus on the specific milieux in which people's sense of self and identity is formed. In such an account older people would not appear as a class apart, or at the edges of the social order.

The chapter then moves to a consideration of continuity and change in the social positioning and experience of youth. Perhaps since youth researchers have long been exercised by the question of class reproduction, there is a strong sense in the literature of diversity and inequality. I describe changes in the relative positioning in youth and the processes and social relations underpinning this change. I explore recent arguments of a dissonance between young adults' perceptions and sense of being responsible for their fates on the one hand, and their highly structured and class-related social trajectories on the other. Any 'dissonance' between the particular and the general stems from seeking to make too direct a connection between the two, and insufficiently acknowledges people's diverse social locations and linked subjectivities. Restructuring of youth reveals consistency between subjectivities and social location, even though the contours of youth have changed.

Analysis of life course processes is crucial to developing a dynamic account of individual experience and to theorising social change. Hardy and Waite comment that life course research has a tangential relation to analyses of social change (Hardy and Waite 1997). This limited connectedness is unfortunate. It may not be wholly surprising given the diverse research agendas of people engaging in life course research, but it is an important problem in need of redress. The issues hold relevance beyond the domain of 'life course studies', which often have a rather particular take on life course issues. In fact life course processes are implicit across a wide arena of social research. There is growing recognition of life course processes in, for example, recent analyses of poverty and inequality (Falkingham and Hills 1995; Ellwood 1998; Leisering and Walker 1998). To adequately conceptualise change in the shape of life course trajectories requires analysis of processes underpinning life course differentiation and patterns of interdependence between those in different life course stages. This would allow exploration of restructuring as an integral part of social change (Irwin 1995). Over recent decades life course restructuring has combined with a general reshaping of inequality, and their articulation should be more fully analysed.

6.1.2 Theorising life course transitions: contours of debate

It is difficult to point to any coherent body of literature of 'life course studies', in sociology or elsewhere, yet life course-related issues are increasingly recognised as crucial to understanding people's experiences at a micro level and to understanding general, macro level, patterns and processes. This is true within sociology and in the realm of social policy. The idea of the life course draws attention to the limited value of chronological age, *per se*, as a sociological variable, and offers a framework for interrogating the historically specific nature of different life course stages, and the kinds of social processes and assumptions which shape the experience of people in these life course stages. Researchers have explored the social and historical shaping of biographies, or lifetime trajectories, and the processes involved in shaping the experience of particular life course stages and in shaping transitions through significant life course events and turning points (Kohli 1986; Anderson 1985). In recent decades there has been particular concern with transitions between youth and adult status. Research there has focused on the restructuring of youth transitions, and some writers stress a prolonging of the partial dependence of youth as young people's claims are increasingly met through parental resources and less through access to independent income (Jones 2002; Bynner *et al.* 2002; Furlong and Cartmel 1997; Irwin 1995; Roberts 1994; Jones and Wallace 1992). Other research has focused on the recent very significant changes in patterns of exit from the labour force and the experience of retirement, and change in the nature of intergenerational relations (Riley *et al.* 1994a; Kohli *et al.* 1991; Arber and Ginn 1991). A good deal of social policy research lately has explored trajectories into, and out of, lone parenthood, locating change in the prevalence of this family form as integral to the changing norms and material bases of demographic behaviour (e.g. Leisering and Walker 1998). Although it is not usually explicitly designated life course research, we can also note the significant growth of research in the area of childhood and later life. Some of the work in these areas has explored historical developments and changes in the contours, and experience, of these life course stages (e.g. Hendrick 1997; Thane 2002).

It is valuable to think of the relevance of life course issues in different ways, depending on the problem at hand. Many advocates of a life course perspective are interested in a temporal analysis whose focus is with individual trajectories, traversing historical time and articulating with social structure (e.g. Riley *et al.* 1994b; Elder 1974). We can also construe the life course as a lens on the social ordering of age-related difference, in very rough terms a tripartite structure differentiating childhood and education | adult work life and childrearing | later life and retirement (e.g. Kohli 1986; Anderson 1985). Here we can see the life course as a structure of difference and of related ties of interdependence and assumptions about the nature of a proper social order. The twentieth century saw a normalisation of a tripartite life course progression through education, work and retirement (Kohli 1986; Anderson 1985). Kohli describes this pattern in terms of moral economy to indicate its social and historical making and the importance of assumptions about proper divisions of labour and allocation of tasks and rewards in modern society (Kohli 1986). Some writers have argued that the latter decades of the twentieth century manifested an entrenchment of age-based difference and linked inequalities. Others argue that the period manifested an erosion of the tripartite structure of the life course and linked social arrangements, with a pattern of diversification and individualisation of life course trajectories, and a blurring, even collapse, of life course divisions (Bauman 1995;

Castells 1996; Phillipson 1998). It is to these contrasting interpretations that I now turn.

For a number of writers the tripartite structure of education, work and retirement both reflects and reinforces an age-related structure of social inclusion and marginalisation. Sometimes the life course is described as, roughly, a structure of inequality, which reveals differential access to citizenship rights and to meaningful social participation (Kohli 1986; Hockey and James 1993; Priestley 2000). This view has informed much of the new sociology of childhood (e.g. James and Prout 1990), debates about the transition from youth to adulthood, and discussions regarding the marginalisation of those in later life (Turner 1989; Featherstone and Wernick 1995). Childhood and later life are positioned, in cultural representations and in social and institutional constructions, as dependent statuses and as social locations that deny children and those in later life full social participation or a proper measure of dignity. In contrast, independent adulthood is positively valued, carrying social status and prestige (Turner 1989; Hockey and James 1993). There is a clear parallel, in these constructions, with the positioning of disabled experiences in modern society. The latter is seen by some to designate a broadly parallel location of social marginalisation (Priestley 2000).

Hockey and James (1993) argue that participation in paid employment is fundamental to social identity and prestige, and that those not so engaged are marginalised in a variety of ways. They maintain that a growing ideology of individualism increasingly marginalises those around the perimeters of the productive sphere and stigmatises 'welfare' groups. Independence is highly valued, dependence increasingly problematic. 'Vertical' lines of cleavage, which separate life course stages (and structure access to paid employment), become the markers of social differentiation and inequality. Their argument is that in a work society, where paid employment remains key to social inclusion, children, (unemployed) youth, the elderly and disabled people are marginalised in various ways. Hockey and James see exclusion from independent (working) adulthood as a social location that is popularly perceived as entailing dependence, and consequently a form of disadvantage. Similarly, Turner maintains that the low status of the young and the old is a function of age varying reciprocity and social exchange over the life course (Turner 1989). The picture parallels that of Hockey and James, with social status and prestige located in people's (popularly perceived) position with regard to reciprocity.

The model of life course-based stratification focuses our attention on how social citizenship rights are biased in respect of age and life course stage. Citizenship claims clearly have an important, and under-theorised, life course dimension. However, life course divisions, as markers of inequality, offer a partial take on social arrangements. A dynamic account of the processes shaping inequalities requires a broader treatment of life course processes, and analysis of how these mesh with classed and gendered processes as these operate throughout the life course and shape very different, and unequal, lifetime trajectories (Irwin 1999b). In contrast to arguments of age stratification a number of writers have argued that divisions between 'youth' and 'independent adulthood', or between the latter and 'old age' have become increasingly blurred in recent years. Some writers here posit a pattern of individualisation and fragmentation in which life course structures are much less fixed than through the first three quarters of the twentieth century, and people are more authors of their own biographies, making diverse decisions regarding education, personal commitments, employment routes, retirement and pension options and so on (e.g. Furlong and Cartmel 1997; Phillipson 1998).

We are witnessing a growing diversity in later life course transitions. However, arguments of individualisation and fragmentation which have been advanced to describe both youth to adult, and later life transitions, refer not only to new patterns of diversity but also usually to a new dissonance between subjectivities and identities on the one hand, and social structural processes on the other. In contrast I will argue again that we can delineate the mutuality of subjective and objective. We can do so by understanding 'objective' extant social relations as composed of diverse (subject) positions, rather than as an overarching description of social reality. The mutuality of subjective and objective is an important part of an account of social change.

Later life and youth are brought together in the chapter to aid exploration of life course differentiation. Not only do they share a linking life course theme but also there are parallels across the specialist literatures, not least in the difficulties faced by analysts in locating these life course stages as integral to wider social relations. In both areas we need acknowledge life course differences as outcomes of social processes and as subject to change. In both we can enhance our understanding of the links between subjective experiences and perceptions and extant social conditions, and use this to help in mapping the nature of social diversity and linked inequalities.

I now examine later life as a life course stage and explore its conceptualisation. Much of the literature here has focused on the social positioning of later life and the shaping of attendant disadvantage and inequality. Problems have arisen through the use of metaphors of social diversity which are overreliant on notions of life course difference. Consequently difference becomes a starting point of analyses and is not adequately located, as discussed in Chapter 2. Difference is a partial account only of the processes shaping later life and its experiences and inequalities.

6.2 Later life

6.2.1 Locating later life

A general feature of much literature on later life is the importance of better 'locating' later life, with a view to improving understanding of ageing and ageism and their intersection. In Chapter 2 I argued that social differences are sometimes assumed: taken as a starting point of analysis rather than an outcome of underpinning processes. Although the differences of later life are mostly conceptualised as outcomes of social processes, particularly of economic, social and cultural constructions of difference, diverse analytic frameworks have entailed metaphors which tend to overstate difference. This is discernible in the theories of age stratification discussed above (Hockey and James 1993; Turner 1989), in arguments that cultural attributions of difference underpin the *othering* of later life (Elias 1985; Featherstone and Wernick 1995), and in theories of a generational culture gap (Dowd 1986). It is also discernible in theories of intergenerational conflict (reviewed in Phillipson 1998; Irwin 1996; Arber and Ginn 1991; Ginn *et al.* 2001). In addition recent discussions of identity contain elements of 'othering' which inappropriately characterise 'the elderly' as a group apart. Theories here are not without value, far from it. They highlight important processes, not least of all the deeply significant and deleterious ageist assumptions and stereotypes extant within society, its institutions and in people's outlooks. However, in seeking to better understand processes of othering, many theories overstate the explanatory virtue of categories of life course *difference*. We need to more fundamentally challenge the scope of the category of old age or later life as an analytic tool, and locate it as one which can give only partial insights into identity, social experience and structures of inequality.

It is useful to indicate some contours of change in later life over recent decades. Across many Western societies the latter decades of the twentieth century manifested a growing concentration of paid employment amongst those aged 20–55, with a prolonging of periods of non-employment which characterise early adulthood and later mid-life. Evandrou and Falkingham (2000) document the patterns of labour force entry and exit for successive cohorts of men, who enter the labour force later and leave earlier, and have lower participation rates across the working life course (Evandrou and Falkingham 2000). The period from the 1970s to the mid 1990s saw striking declines in employment participation rates amongst men in their late fifties and sixties. In the UK, amongst men aged 60–64 in 1975, 1985 and 1995 respectively, economic participation rates declined from 84 per cent to 53 per cent to 50 per cent. Men aged 50–59 in 1975, 1985 and 1995 respectively, manifested a decline in their economic participation rates from 94 per cent to 82 per cent to 73 per cent (ONS 1997b). The trend amongst women is less clear. Through the same period there was a decrease in economic participation rates amongst non-married women aged 55 to 59, whilst amongst married women in this age group there was a fluctuating pattern, with rates at around 53 per cent (ibid.). Trends to declining ages at exit from the labour force in this period were Europe-wide. Economic recession and the management of unemployment and reduced demand for labour by governments and industry lie at the heart of explanations of the trend to early exit in the latter quarter of the twentieth century (e.g. Phillipson 1997; Kohli and

Rein 1991). There are signs that this trend may be reversed as consequence of a relatively buoyant labour market and growing concerns about future pension arrangements. The period from the mid 1990s to 2003 has seen an increase in employment rates amongst men and women aged between 50 and state pension age (ONS 2004).

General conceptual arguments about life course difference take insufficient account of continuities over the life course, and of evidence of a closing gap between pensioners and workers (Dilnot *et al.* 1994). Both suggest the model of life course stratification, documented near the outset of this chapter, is unhelpful. In respect of the first, class-related continuities in income over people's lifetimes are widely documented (e.g. Ellison 2003; Bardasi and Jenkins 2002; Midwinter 1997; Arber and Ginn 1991). As well as class-related continuites, continuities in gendered inequalities are evident, as asymmetries in work and care have translated into very differing entitlements in retirement and high levels of female poverty (Arber and Ginn 1991; Ginn *et al.* 2001). These lifetime continuities must be central to an adequate conceptualisation of the 'location' of later life, since it is no less diverse than, say, mid-life and just as circumscribed in its analytic purchase on highly varied social experiences. Yet also, arguments of growing inequality within cohorts are important if we are to adequately theorise later life (Goodman *et al.* 1997). The 1980s and 1990s saw a widening gap in the incomes of rich and poor pensioners (Ellison 2003). Evandrou and Falkingham (2000) point to a growing polarisation amongst the retired population of the future, as a consequence of a number of factors. This includes the growing emphasis on private pensions, and the diverse patterning of employment amongst the current working age population, with a significant proportion having experienced extensive unemployment notably those made redundant or those entering the job market in the 1980s. Developments in the housing market too have underlain extremely mixed financial fortunes which will translate into retirement inequalities (Evandrou and Falkingham 2000). The increased risk involved in private pensions, tied to the fortunes of financial markets, increases insecurities across the board (Zaidi *et al.* 2001).

Although the discussion here is no more than indicative, the general point is that continuities over the life course are very important to conceptualising later life, and its inequalities. Recent transformations in the experience of later life can be fully understood only with reference to these class- and gender-related aspects of diversity. Older people may be positioned beyond the labour market and may be 'othered' and subject to demeaning stereotypes, or simply to indifference. However the relative fortunes and experience of older people are not separable from the historical contexts in which people age, the employment, pension and general policy contexts which shape retirement, and their positioning within specific milieux: social networks, family, diverse social and economic activities, and so on. These factors are bound up with significant inequalities across the population and through which the experience of later life is mediated. Barnes *et al.* (2002)

highlight the association between material resources and levels of social participation and sense of personal fulfilment (ibid.). Specific issues confront those in later life, and the categorisation of later life captures important facets of shared experience. However, as the evidence cited above shows, seeking to locate later life as a distinctive position or identification is full of difficulties. Writers often work with particular metaphors of the social structure seeing older people 'at the margins'. We need a more sufficient understanding of how older people are just as integral to society as anyone else. This will come from a move away from classifying older people as a group, since this has little more purchase than classifing the working age population as a group. It also requires that we understand the limitations and misleading nature of a metaphor of older people looking back on a society they are leaving behind.

6.2.2 Ageism, life course differentiation and identities: the categorial othering of older people

Writers from a range of perspectives have elaborated processes seen to position older people at the margins of society, subject to modes of social and cultural exclusion. The thread has run through disengagement theory, political economy accounts, and structured dependency theory, and more recent accounts of age stratification (see e.g. Vincent 1995 and Phillipson 1998 for reviews). As in other sociological domains there has recently been a growing stress on agency, on culture, and on the diversification of prior age-based norms and trajectories through retirement and later life.

Many theorists of later life have explored various processes seen to shape the marginalisation and relative disadvantage of older people in contemporary society. Their approaches emphasise life course and generation based divisions, particularly with reference to economic (work|retirement) divisions as well as linked cultural expectations. The arguments here are very valuable yet I would suggest that they overstate life course difference and understate the importance of life course processes in shaping inequalities.

I have already indicated at the outset of this chapter that models of life course stratification usefully focus attention on the life course variability of social citizenship rights yet perspectives that treat life course divisions as markers of inequality offer a partial take on social arrangements. There is a tendency to both see cultural presumptions about dependence and independence as mapping onto distinct life course stages, and to see ageist assumptions as underpinning diversity and inequality over the life course. I have argued elsewhere that the model of life course-based inclusion and marginalisation has tended to under-theorise the coherence of work and welfare processes and the mutuality of different life course stages (Irwin 1996, 1998; see also Turner 1998). The model of age stratification understates the importance of continuities across the life course and of great diversity in later life. Clearly, as age stratificationists argue, ageist assumptions are built into institutions and cultural attributions of difference to the detriment of older people as to society more generally. However, we need a more differentiated understanding of the shaping of life course processes and the disadvantaging of many older people.

Theories with a cultural emphasis have also identified the difference and relative disadvantage of later life and sought to explain it with reference to cultural processes of othering. A number of writers argue that, in the cultural imagination, and in social and economic institutions, there is an association between the presumed 'effects of ageing' and the nature of older people (e.g. Featherstone and Wernick 1995; Biggs 1993; Elias 1985). Just as theories of disability identify cultural fears of distance from the able-bodied ideal, so perceptions of distance of 'the elderly' from this ideal generate cultural ambivalence, if not hostility from other age groups. Relatively trivial physical manifestations of difference turn into markers of otherness. Through the post-war decades in particular retirement provided a ready cultural marker of 'old age'. Institutionalised patterns of differentiation across the life course (e.g. work | retirement) reveal an age-segregated society and reinforce, as well as draw on, ideas about differential competencies (e.g. Hockey and James 1993; Riley *et al.* 1994). Additionally, some argue that existential anxieties surrounding death mean that there is a further embedding of the idea of older people as 'other'. For Elias, social distancing and ageist sentiments are rooted in forms of psychological repression and death denial (Elias 1985) whilst for Marshall there is a society-wide devaluation of those seen to be temporally proximate to death (Marshall 1986). Others stress a cultural 'denial' or avoidance of reminders of ageing, deterioration and death and a linked cult of youth and youthfulness in contemporary society (Mellor and Shilling 1993; Willmott 2000)

The cultural valuing of youth is not only a reaction, allegedly, to fear of ageing, but is also seen to shape people's experience of growing older. Self-identities which are presumed to be bound up with youthfulness diverge from bodily appearance and capacities as people age. Such a tendency has been described in terms of a mask of ageing, the mask being the ageing body or 'exterior' which hides the true, young, spirit 'within' (Featherstone and Hepworth 1991; Turner 1995). However, youthfulness is a narrow metaphor for describing continuities in a person's identity: perhaps a plausible metaphor for physical and physiological vitality and vigour, this is only one aspect of subjective self-identity. For Biggs, if there is a contradiction in the experience of old age it lies less in the gap between an individual's self-identity and body and more in the gap between personal wants and an increasingly restrictive social environment (Biggs 1997). It may be inappropriate to simply dismiss the idea that older people still feel young inside or feel betrayed by their bodies. However, alternative metaphors could equally well be used to signify continuities of identity over a person's life course. There is an absence of empirical and analytic support for the argument that youthfulness captures people's sense of self. In consequence the idea of a mask of ageing, where the old are 'not as they seem', itself inappropriately positions the elderly as different.

In summary, various theories of how later life is to be located overstate the value of later life as a category and position older people 'at the margins' by virtue of the analytic categories being used. There is a parallel tendency in some discussions of later life and subjective identifications, discussed below.

There has recently been a growing interest in research exploring directly the aspects of identity and the experiences and perceptions of older people (e.g. Minichiello *et al.* 2000; Wray 2003; Kaufman and Elder 2002; Hurd 1999). This research provides some rich empirical evidence. However it is interesting to note that here there is again evidence of researchers using categories which seem to position older people as different in an *a priori* way. We can see that respondents and interviewees seem to often disavow the categories into which analysts seek to place them. Some writers describe this 'non-compliance' as a form of resistance or as a contradiction. Many people's dismissal of being described as 'old' may indeed reveal resistance to societal designations and assumptions of what it means to be old. However, it may also tell us, importantly, that the category does not adequately capture the experience or identity of older people. Rather than suppose they are overtly resisting classification as 'old people', it may be that in many contexts this is not experienced as a defining identity. People's perceptions then, do not necessarily denote resistance to being positioned on the margins. More straightforwardly, they are very often a description of routine actions. Because older people's location in a broader structure is misconstrued as being 'at the edges', older people's non-compliance with designations as old, or being 'old-like' is read as resistance. The alternative interpretation is to see their perceptions and self-identification as entirely consistent with a social positioning no less within the social structure as anybody else's. Ageism, and resistance to it, or disavowal of it, are important processes, but by no means sufficient as a general account of the positioning and experience of those in later life. Some examples illustrate the problem.

The meaning of old age is socially and culturally saturated with negative metaphor and meaning so it should come as little surprise that people do not typically embrace it as an identity. Rather they appear to accept it as an adequate description of their experience when they acquire the characteristics associated with old age, particularly illness (Kaufman and Elder 2002). Kaufman and Elder argue that older people say they do not feel old, and that people adjust upwards their life expectancy as they get older. A 60-year-old, they say, may not even hope to be alive at 80 yet 'as she approaches 80, she is likely to reevaluate her desired longevity' (p. 175). This, they say, 'may be a strategy for resisting old age, and approaching death' (p. 175). However, what is not explicit in the analysis is that people will not typically orient themselves to non-proximate or non-imminent events. It may be more valid simply to see them as not embracing the categories researchers see as relevant, rather than as resisting these categories. If what is meant as 'old' is not felt as relevant in an immediate sense by people in their day-to-day lives we need not see them as 'resistant'. The fact that identities often do not tally with the category of old reveals not a dissonance between perceptions and social location but rather a gap between perceptions and the prior categories of the analyst. Rather than 'force' a fit between perceptions and social location by presuming people are resisting their position, a more economical explanation is that their actions fit their social position. We need a better understanding, then, of their social positioning.

Another example of 'non-compliance' with the category old is identified by Hurd (1999). In her study of older people involved in a seniors' centre in Canada, she describes how older people presented 'keeping active' as an important part of their 'not-old identities' (Hurd 1999). She argues that older people resist ageist stereotypes and

> the solidarity of the group and the shared belief in the importance of remaining vigorous serves to encourage and buttress the 'not old' in their quest for vitality even as they confront their own mortality on a daily basis.
>
> (Hurd 1999: 428)

There is a risk that some behaviours that would be treated as normal and unremarkable amongst other life stages take on a different quality where people are older. However, for many older people 'keeping active' might be deemed no more remarkable than for other life course groups. Whilst 'keeping active' is a situation with which many older people identify this might be better construed as reflecting the lack of a clearly defined social role for older people, rather than necessarily as an aspect of resisting 'being old'. It is apt to remain sceptical that this marks out older people as 'resisting the ageing process'. Hurd also notes that some of her respondents were not wholly open to their peers about deteriorating health, and speculates that this too can be read as resisting a designation as 'old'. However there could well be other reasons for non-disclosure of illness. In Hurd's analysis, motives and behaviours are deduced on the basis of presumed social positioning and its salience for actors (being near the end of life). But older people may simply not routinely orient themselves in this way. A more convincing metaphor, and model, would not position older people 'at the edges' of society.

In contrast, in her study of the experiences of women from different ethnic groups, Wray describes older female respondents in terms one might use to describe women in any life course stage. For example, she considers those with health problems and who also exercise control and agency and notes that 'this ability to *get on with life* is not simply a feature of growing older, rather it is present throughout the life course' (Wray 2003: 518). In this kind of analysis we are not required to see age as a defining, nor even necessarily relevant, dimension of people's identities, experiences, motivations and behaviours. Its importance will be variable, and partly itself shaped by the nature of the experience and interactional context in which people find themselves. Wray critiques Western conceptualisations of 'successful ageing' in terms of maintaining independence and autonomy, and emphasises, first in relation to minority ethnic women and then in respect of white majority women, autonomy is linked not with independence, but with interdependence, connection with others and social participation (ibid.; see also Barnes *et al.* 2002). In short we should not presume later life as singular, or singularly problematic, social location.

The argument so far is that the 'difference' of later life is often overstated, and associated with a metaphorical positioning of older people on the edges of society, 'looking back' or resisting their designation. Arguments of difference are overstated in general descriptions of life course patterns, whether age stratification, or cultural bases of difference, and in some accounts of older people's identities. I have criticised the notion that older people's identities and perspectives are somehow out of line with their social location. Rather we need to incorporate their perceptions and experience as part of a more adequate conceptualisation of their social location. This sits in contrast to an argument that there is a new kind of disarray evident in later life as older institutional securities of retirement are seen to fall apart and give rise to a crisis of identity and meaning in later life (Phillipson 1998). Like a number of others Phillipson discerns a process of individualisation and fragmentation in the move away from collective arrangements. This is reasonable as a description of policy, of the diminishing value of state provision and of trends towards customised pensions and more individualised arrangements (also Ellison 2003). However, individualisation is also used by Phillipson to describe subjective change and a growing existential gap confronted by older people. Phillipson argues that the twentieth-century life course pattern is now collapsing. New patterns of diversity he sees as quite chaotic. Through much of the twentieth century, Phillipson argues, later life was a relatively marginalised position, yet it provided a stable end to the life course, one which was constructed as meaningful, entailing a set of recognised claims about social rights and citizenship (Phillipson 1998). However, the latter quarter of the twentieth century manifested an unravelling of the previous arrangement (of a stable, normative, tripartite, structured life course). This occurred partly through a break up of the institution of retirement, partly through merging for many with long-term unemployment. In consequence he argues, drawing on Guillemard, 'an individual's working life now ends in confusion' (Guillemard 1989, cited in Phillipson 1998: 61).

Phillipson sees a shift from a secure identities residing in 'a retirement self' to a postmodern self that is riven by insecurity. Post-war compacts and the institutionalised 'commitment' to underwrite pensions, and a linked cultural compact of solidarity across generations have been undermined since the 1970s, but nothing meaningful has replaced them. He argues that there has been a fragmentation of routes from paid work to retirement, and much more diverse trajectories along with a less determinate framing of retirement and old age (whether economic, cultural or social). In consequence there is a much greater openness and indeterminacy, and a linked crisis of identity for ageing people, with an absence of meaning surrounding later life. This, he argues, is damaging for individuals and for society as a whole. Additionally there has been a growing cultural emphasis on 'personalised' solutions to public problems, such as private pensions. In consequence we have seen a growing individualism and privatisation, a decline in cultural solidarity or continuity across generations and over the life course, and newly emergent patterns and processes of social exclusion. For Phillipson, later life now occurs within an indeterminate space, a social and cultural vacuum. This generates a crisis of identity amongst older people and a linked crisis about the meaning of later life. He offers a moral critique arguing that later life is rendered invisible or newly problematic in current society and marginalised in new ways. To tackle this crisis we need new conceptual and policy tools, argues Phillipson, ones which can better capture the links between social structures and individual lives in a time of change.

However, in his argument of 'thinned out' identities there is no clear-cut evidence, nor guide to what such evidence would look like. He argues that:

> Older people have moved into a new zone of indeterminacy, marginal to work and welfare.
>
> (Phillipson 1998: 138)

and

> in the case of older people the conditions for securing identity have been drastically changed over the past 20 years. Achieving a secure sense of self has become one of the biggest challenges in later life: the postmodern self is one riven by insecurity and this is especially the case in the period defined as older age. The central argument of this study is that . . . we seem to have undercut a language and moral space which can resonate with the rights and needs of older people as a group.
>
> (Phillipson 1998: 51)

Phillipson's argument of a lack of moral and social vision is well made. We have seen a growth in inequalities amongst older people, and the continuance of significant material insecurities for many. However, it is far from clear that those in later life are the vanguard of postmodern insecure selves. Phillipson's notion of an emergent crisis of identity amongst older people seems to require an analytic correspondence between individual's identifications and experiences, and macro level institutional arrangements and societal discourse. Yet identity is an aspect of people's selves made through intimate relations, networks, significant others and broader social relations and positioning. The institutions in question, such as post-war pension arrangements, and cultural ideas about a generational contract, form only a subset of the latter. Phillipson overstates the case in deducing that the erosion of macro institutions also undermines the bases of identity. Diversity and identity will be best understood not in terms of 'fragmentation' and relative confusion but by incorporating within analysis the levels at which people construct meaning. Meaning construction is shaped by life course differentiation, but this does not overwrite other dimensions of social experience, particularly the immediate milieux in which, and relationships through which, people (young and old) live their lives.

In the above discussion I have argued that we can observe a gap, within analyses, between subjective experiences and social structures. This gap follows in part from modes of analysis which overstate later life difference, and this hinders explanation of social experience and diversity. I turn next to the transition from youth to adult status. Again, here, there is a gap in some analyses between subjective experiences and social structures. This is exemplified in arguments of individualisation which are used by some theorists of youth. To fully understand the social position and experience of youth we must locate it as integral to broader social arrangements. Only in so doing can we properly identify and analyse processes reshaping this life course period.

6.3 Restructuring the transition from youth to adult status

6.3.1 On the allegedly expanding gap between subjective and objective

A critical engagement with theses of individualisation has been a characteristic feature of the literature on youth, and on the transition from youth to adult status over recent years. Many writers maintain that there has been a marked increase in social diversity, and a marked growth in the perceived scope and significance of choice. However, characteristically writers also emphasise the continuity of older processes shaping inequality and its social reproduction. I review some of these arguments below. The arguments are important and hold value in shedding light on the persistence of structured inequalities and on the processes shaping their reproduction. They highlight how in contemporary times young adults appear to confront a much more open set of choices and possibilities. I discuss a problem in how we are to best conceptualise change. This problem is sometimes acknowledged within the literature but I give it a quite extended treatment, since its redress helps enhance our understanding of the reshaping of transitions from youth to adult status. The problem stems from a broader problematic within the literature – how to conceptualise the structure – agency link. Some writers posit a tension, if not a contradiction, between new kinds of openness, and individualised 'options' on the one hand, and structure and constraint on the other. This contradiction is seemingly squared through an argument of a gap between objective structures and subjective understandings. The gap is filled conceptually by deducing an individualised outlook or ideology. If people believe they are agents of their destinies they will not see the structures which oppress them and restrict their opportunities. The alleged dissonance between objective and subjective can endure because a pattern and ideology of individualisation persuades people of their own responsibility and efficacy despite clear 'objective' evidence of constraint. For Furlong and Cartmel individualisation is the ideological glue which sticks together agents and structure, as the former misconstrue the nature of the latter and hold themselves responsible for their social fortunes or misfortunes (Furlong and Cartmel 1997; also Arnot 2002, Rose 1999). Such arguments rely on an untheorised connection between individual perspectives and subjectivities and objective indicators of diversity and inequality, with insufficient specification of the contexts in which individuals 'move' and act, and experience themselves as actors.

A discrepancy between objective structures and subjective perceptions of structure is not necessarily contradictory. We could rather construe a differentiated structure in which people necessarily hold diverse viewpoints about a wide variety of things, including their own experience and efficacy. It need not be at all contradictory that we see agentic identities (where people see themselves as authors of their own lives and biographies) combined with quite narrow structurally shaped limitations. A central argument of this chapter is that we need to analyse the partiality and specificity of individual viewpoints not in a *distinct* cultural/ideological realm but rather seek to understand how they are continuous with, and link with, diverse social locations. I argue that the changing experience of youth and early adulthood reveals no new dissonance between subjective and objective, and that we can clearly delineate continuities between them, where the objective is construed in a disaggregated way, in terms of diverse social positions.

The alleged gap between subjective and objective appears greatest at times of social change. Its diagnosis stems from a tendency to jump levels of analysis, and not locate the embedded and specific nature of human experience and perception across diverse milieux and contexts. Before examining aspects of perception and subjectivity amongst contemporary young adults I will briefly delineate some of the more significant contours of change in the positioning of youth as a life course period.

6.3.2 *Restructuring youth transitions*

Youth as a life course period has manifested considerable change across the last 40 years or so. These are well documented and here I draw out some key processes shaping change in the experience and social location of youth, and some issues regarding how this change in life course structure links to a reshaping of social inequalities. There has been a prolonging of youth as a period of partial dependence, and a pattern of deferral in the attainment of 'adult' independence by cohorts leaving school through the last quarter of the twentieth century. Change in the experience of youth and early adulthood is in part about a repositioning – a shift in the location of youth relative to other life course stages, and altered assumptions about appropriate roles, responsibilities and divisions of labour (Irwin 1995). These changes link to developments across various domains, including those of family, of employment and career, and education and the relative importance of qualifications. I explore these areas very briefly below to indicate some of the main contours of change in the experience and social position of youth and early adulthood in the space of a generation. Even through this brief review we can see how a reshaping of the life course contributes to changing patterns of class-related inequality.

The prolonging of the partial dependence of youth, and patterns of deferral in family formation, reflect a change in the relative positioning of young adulthood as a social location, and an undermining of claims to independence at a young age. The pattern of deferral in the age at departure from the parental home, in the age at establishing an independent household with a cohabiting or marital partner, and in the age at becoming a parent is well established. These changes in the organisation of transitions from 'partial dependence' to independence are bound up with shifts in the social position of young women and men, including changes in their ability to independently access resources. Patterns of deferral in the attainment of material independence and in the acquisition of family obligations through family formation has been both forced and facilitated by change in the relative positioning of different generations, and shifts in gendered differences, identities and expectations (Irwin 1995). The change in relations between generations is not simply an affair internal to the family. Rather household divisions of labour, and related (gender and life course varying) claims and obligations, are embedded in the organisation of access to, and rewards from, employment. The example of change in transitions from youth to adult status reflects an altered positioning of life course groups in the reproduction of social life.

The very major increases in house prices over recent decades have meant that the resources for securing independent lifestyles at young ages have become harder to access. Thus the ability of young adults to procure resources for household and family formation has changed. The reduction in young men's earnings and relative improvements in young women's has been part of the more general trend away from breadwinner/secondary earner patterns of household resourcing towards dual earner patterns, discussed in Chapters 4 and 5. The increased import of young women's wages to household formation is also in line with shifts in the identities and expectations of young women regarding the relative importance of career and family in their young adult lives (Irwin 1995; Walby 1997; Brannen and Nilsen 2002). In addition the pattern of deferral reflects long-run changes in family structure, in which the prolonged partial dependence of youth can be 'afforded' by parents in a way it was not historically.

Young men have become more disadvantaged relative to men in mid life, whilst young women have improved their position relative to young men (Irwin 1995; Egerton and Savage 2000). The overall position of young workers has improved in absolute terms in the latter decades of the twentieth century, whilst it has declined relative to that of older workers (Irwin 1995; Bynner *et al.* 2002). There has been a significant decline in the availability of skilled craft apprenticeships and jobs from the 1970s onwards. Previously this formed a significant employment route for young working-class men (Roberts *et al.* 1994). Amongst young women aged 18 to 24 there has been a shift away from administrative and clerical jobs towards typically lower-paying sales and personal service jobs (Bynner 2002). As Bynner and many others have argued the vocational route in the labour market has diminished significantly. Emergent age-related patterns of employment point to a significant shrinking of employment opportunities for post-school-age teenagers. Unsurprisingly, perhaps, such demand as there is exists even more exclusively than hitherto for unskilled labour (Elias and Pierre 2002).

Another key component of the changing experience of youth, and change in the social posititi‌on of youth and young adults is the extension of education across a significantly increased proportion of the population. Current political understanding and discourse encourages a belief that education is the key to a competitive, inclusive and liberal society, and not least important that it is crucial for individual citizenship and social mobility. Some have asked whether it is inequalities in educational outcomes which are entrenching employment inequalities. However, whilst qualification level remains an important indicator of relative success in the labour market, we should not treat qualifications as a simple index of human capital with the associated notions that individuals carry attributes which are valued by a neutral labour market. As Elias and Pierre (2002) suggest there has been a change in how the labour market 'values' certain factors that contribute to earnings levels. Bynner offers evidence that qualification levels strongly differentiate employment outcomes, and do so in a more marked way amongst cohorts born in 1970 than they did for cohorts born in 1958. Young people without qualifications now are more likely to be locked into a disadvantaged position within the labour market, from which it is difficult to escape especially given the decline in work-based career routes (Bynner *et al.* 2002; Roberts 1994).

Some writers stress how decisions at age 16, and linked educational outcomes, are critical to early life course trajectories, and young people's position into their early twenties, and probably have a lasting influence (Jones 2002; Hobcraft 2003). Hobcraft uses data from the British National Child Development Study (a cohort survey of a sample of children born in 1958) to document the ways in which experiences between 16 and 23 are strongly associated with adult disadvantage. Not only are childhood disadvantages 'transmitted' into adulthood, but experiences in late adolescence and early adulthood (including notably educational attainments) have an additional and lasting effect (Hobcraft 2003). The evidence indicates a widening inequality, and the entrenchment of the long-term difficulties and marginalisation of those who leave school with few qualifications.

In sum, there has been a repositioning of youth as a life course period through the latter part of the twentieth century, and a pattern of deferral in the attainment of material independence. In conjunction there have been important changes in the employment opportunity structure. The developments amount not to straightforward diversification, nor individualisation and increasing choice but to new forms of inequality and, importantly, a narrowing of opportunities at the minimum school-leaving age. Perhaps the most deleterious consequence is that for those who do not follow the standard educational route (at least to 17+ qualifications) there are fewer resources typically available to them and a greater risk of being disadvantaged and of remaining so. The broad picture of economic changes described above points to changing contours of opportunity and constraint. Young people are positioned differently to how they were a generation ago. The options available to them are different, how they can best proceed is different and if they do not have qualifications, a passport which allows at least some movement or mobility, then they are likely to remain more disadvantaged, and in the depressions of an increasingly variegated social landscape.

6.3.3 *Youth and the mutuality of social position and disposition*

Beck's thesis of individualisation (1992), and his argument of an elective biography, in which people make choices and decisions at many more junctures in their lives, has been influential amongst contemporary theorists of youth. Furlong and Cartmel engage extensively with Beck's work and are strongly influenced by the individualisation thesis but they insist that class remains as strong as ever as a predictor of life chances. For them the crucial development in late modernity is a shift in subjective orientations:

> [W]hile structures of inequality remain deeply entrenched, in our view one of the most significant features of late modernity is the epistemological fallacy: the growing disjuncture between objective and subjective dimensions of life.
>
> (Furlong and Cartmel 1997: 4)

They argue that there has been a breaking up of collective transitions, and with growing diversity in people's life experience their perceptions of social bonds are weakened. Diversity and a new range of opportunities available for people serves to render opaque social cleavages and, therefore, the reproduction of inequalities (Furlong and Cartmel 1997). The authors provide a metaphor through which to contemplate alteration in the articulation of social structure and perceptions of that structure. In the post-war decades, they suggest, we might see young people's trajectories as if they were making train journeys bound for different destinations, where their journeys were dependent on class, on gender, and on educational attainment. In the current era we might better imagine young people as car drivers, constantly faced with decisions about which routes to follow, and seemingly in charge of their journey, yet in fact bound for largely pre-determined destinations despite change in the metaphorical mode of travel. That is, inequalities prevail but are increasingly opaque as a consequence of new forms of diversity and a new cultural context through which social awareness of structural inequalities is undermined. This leaves individuals more likely to see their fate as an outcome of personal responsibility (ibid.). For Furlong and Cartmel, 'whereas subjective understandings of the social world were once shaped by class, gender and neighbourhood relations today everything is presented as a possibility' (ibid.: 7).

As with Furlong and Cartmel, so Arnot (2002) presents individualisation as a good account of the rise of the individual as the perceived locus of social affairs. Again the change in subjectivities identified by Arnot is accompanied, in her argument, by a continuation of class, 'race' and gender as determinants or shapers of social inequalities. Arnot stresses too the divisive effect of the ideology of individualisation, with its pernicious effect upon the disadvantaged who are blamed, and increasingly blame themselves, for their situation (also cf. Ball *et al.* 2000 and Rose 1999). This pattern of responsibilisation means that the working classes 'are no longer entitled to a 'sense of unfairness' since everything is the responsibility of individuals' (Arnot 2002: 218).

Disadvantaged groups are seen to internalise structural oppression. The process of individualisation is seen to normalise choice and individual responsibility and in so doing it legitimates, and thus helps secure, class reproduction. This stress on objective continuities and subjective changes raises a number of questions. Furlong and Cartmel, and Arnot, are right to stress that 'objective' *general* structures and individual apprehension of such structures do not map directly onto each other, yet is is not clear that a closer fit was ever general as a basis for collective action (Cannadine 2000; Savage 2000). It is far from clear that late twentieth-century patterns of diversity have newly undermined 'awareness' of structural inequalities. As I have argued earlier, an enduring feature of the nature (and culture) of hierarchy is that it teaches people to 'know their place' and to routinely not orient themselves towards, nor be reflexive about, general structural inequalities. It is far from clear that in modern societies there has ever been an isomorphic relationship between structural inequalities and perceptions of such inequalities. As indicated, historical interpretations of political action, and its absence, throw doubt on the novelty of this apolitical understanding. It is also salutary to remind ourselves of the long pedigree of youth research documenting much the same thing in different contexts. For example, in the 1960s and 1970s writers addressed how social processes secured the reproduction of class inequality, but then the process was discerned in socialisation and the delimitation of expectations (e.g. Roberts 1968). One difficulty here is talking of perceptions in such a generalising way. There is an analytic jump between structural level processes, and their (mis)apprehension at the level of the individual. I argue that we need to reflect further on how to locate diverse subjectivities and perceptions. Then we can move to a level of analysis in which we can understand the complex connections between diverse social positions and an overall structure. Some writers on youth in transition have indicated the value of such an analysis.

Roberts and his colleagues wrote an influential article in 1994 in which they described contemporary processes in terms of 'structured individualisation' (Roberts *et al.* 1994). They describe a pattern of diversification, noting the very varied careers through education, training and employment amongst young people. Like the writers described above they discern a dual process of structured inequality and its reproduction on the one hand and perceptions of choice and individual efficacy on the other hand. However, we need not see a gap, or inconsistency between these 'levels' of the social. Rather, they are different aspects of the same state of affairs. Extant constraints coexist with perceptions of opportunity:

> The young people's own experiences did not normally make them feel there were rigid boundaries to their opportunities.
>
> (Roberts *et al.* 1994: 51)

In other words we can understand that people may believe themselves to be authors of their biographies to a large degree, yet the spaces within which they are 'authors', and exercisers of choice, are fairly closely circumscribed.

We can see how young people's perceptions are linked to the contexts in which they have grown and in which they now find themselves, and from which they orient to the world. Ball and his colleagues (2000) seek to explore the specifics of individuals' experiences and their place in a general and diverse social landscape. They offer rich accounts of young people's life stories, within a longitudinal qualitative analysis. The following quotes from two girls interviewed for the study illustrate continuities between social position and disposition. They are indicative of a diverse social space in which different positions are linked to different social dispositions, including people's sense of personal efficacy, and of their capacities to be effective agents.

Debra was a working class respondent, raised by her sometimes abusive lone mother. She was long-term unemployed and lived in small council flat. She describes her experience in fatalistic terms:

> 'I take it day by day. I don't make plans because they are always messed up anyway. I am not the kind of person to make plans because when I

make plans they never work and then I get upset, so its not worth making plans see' (Debra at age 15, Ball *et al.* 2000: 48).

'I live life everyday. I've always said that you know. You never know what's round the corner, so don't make no plans because they will come falling down round your head. Take it a day at a time, I do' (Debra at age 19, Ball *et al.* 2000: 48)

In contrast Rachel, a middle-class respondent, with professional parents, describes her experience of sixth form college and how it helped her achieve a place at the University of Cambridge:

'I've seen it at Riverway . . . people . . . have that extra bit of confidence and they can speak as if they really know what they are talking about, even when they don't. And when I first went to Riverway I found it off-putting . . . , but then I just listened and learned how to be like that too and it's a bit of an act really. I know that you need to be like that at Cambridge, its how it works, you have to be able to like, fight with words and that is what I learned at Riverway. You have to come back at people with words, and show how you won't be beaten and that and that is what I did and I got offered a place' (Rachel, Ball *et al.* 2000: 84).

For the relatively disadvantaged young woman cited above choice is clearly not routinely a meaningful dimension of her experience. For the advantaged young woman cited above assumptions, resources and expectations seem to guide her choices in such a way that, again, we might say choice is closely circumscribed. She is more 'free' to make choices given the resources available to her yet there are strong pressures, both internal and external, to stop her making the wrong kinds of choices – the 'right' choices (ones which will maintain her middle-class trajectory) are second nature stemming, for example, from familial and school level assumptions and expectations (cf. Reay 1998a; Bourdieu and Wacquant 1992). In addition the quotes from these young women in very different circumstances help reveal how very different kinds of disposition, here in terms of personal efficacy, link to diverse class-related positions.

Others are also critical of the notion of an individualised elective biography and seek to better understand the provenance of individual choices and decisions. Nilsen and Brannen directly address the structure–agency problematic and argue that people will necessarily stress choice and agency in the stories they tell about themselves. People are not routinely oriented to, nor typically particularly aware of the external and structured forces that shape their lives:

When structural forces and personal resources . . . support one another there is a tendency for the structural resources to take on an 'invisible' quality.

(Nilsen and Brannen 2002: 42)

The ensuing lack of an orientation to the social forces shaping one's life stems from such 'invisibility', embedded in normal social processes and not in novel patterns of responsibilisation.

Further evidence on the links between position and perception is present in another recent research project (Gillies *et al.* 2003). Here a generational dimension is revealed as young adults and their parents describe their perceptions of the formers' transitions to independence. Gillies and her colleagues stress the 'embedded' nature of young adults' accounts, particularly the relational and interconnected nature of young people's understandings. The researchers argue that for young people describing their experiences, growing up was a process of taking control of their behaviour and accepting responsibility for their decisions. Young people saw themselves as at the centre of their transition, as agents or authors of their progression to adult status. In contrast, interestingly, their parents emphasised their children's physical changes and the continuities they saw in their children's personalities as they progressed from childhood to adulthood. Young adults highlighted the ways in which they had changed since their childhoods, whilst parents reflected on consistencies.

We can see these differences as unsurprising outcomes of the interviews but it is pertinent to remind ourselves that young people may more than any other life course group emphasise agency and 'the cult of the self' since this surely has a social apogee in this life course stage. Gillies and her colleagues stress that the individualism expressed by the youngsters 'was clearly contained within a wider social context, characterised by interdependent family relationships' (ibid.: 47). We can also usefully extend discussion of something which remains implicit within their account: young adults and their parents are positioned differently and can be seen as offering different 'vantage points' on the question of transition to independence. The young adults naturally enough experience themselves as being agents in a context where boundaries are widening and the scope for their action expands as they seize greater autonomy and responsibilities. Parents have a more 'sociological' understanding of this transition, having some social distance from it (and probably themselves engaging in a fair degree of reflexive analysis about their children's position and how, as parents, to best relate to it). The vantage points of youth and parent are very different but they are not contradictory; we can see them as consistent if we understand that the players hold different perspectives on the events under discussion. Again diverse values and perceptions can shed light on people's social positioning within a highly differentiated social space.

6.3.4 Youth, transition and altered norms and opportunities

There has been a prolonging of the partial dependence of youth, and recent evidence highlights a shrinking of opportunities for low and unqualified youth since the 1970s. It is this changing landscape of material opportunities and linked assumptions about the central role of education and academic qualifications as guarantors of economic success which mean that certain options are closed off and a new 'common sense' emerges. In this new common sense academic qualifications are increasingly seen as a good thing for all, a passport to employment success, even whilst the UK experiences a shortage of skilled manual labour.

Through the 1980s and 1990s the prolonging of the partial dependence of youth meshed with the reshaping of occupational opportunities and class-related inequalities to produce new divisions and patterns of marginalisation. The meshing of class, gender and life course processes have produced an altered landscape of opportunity at an aggregate level, and become part of a new common sense about appropriate choices and decisions for young people. This does not mean that young people are necessarily disadvantaged by these processes, the impact of which is highly varied. What we see at a general level is the reshaping of opportunity and constraint, and of the contexts in which young people make choices and decisions.

Furlong suggests that the separation of qualitative and quantitative approaches has stood in the way of an enhanced understanding of the (changing) experience of young people (Furlong 1998). Clearly it will be valuable to develop further research which works at different levels of analysis, particularly in linking insights at the micro level (of experience, perceptions and subjectivities) with analysis of changes in the social location of youth and in the linked reconfiguring of life chances for different groups of young people. We already see through available evidence the clear continuities between subjective views and the contexts in which people find themselves. This runs counter to the notion of a growing gap between 'subjective' perceptions and 'objective' conditions. The analysis of mutuality rather than disjuncture entails treating objective conditions in terms of a highly differentiated social order, and one that is subject to change. It is likely that research into identity, perceptions and value will retain its current fascination. It is important that such research orients 'out', with confidence that subjectivities offer a lens on structure. To ensure they do so requires full analysis of the contextual nature of subjectivities, and of the composition and reshaping of diverse contexts.

6.4 Conclusion

In this chapter I have looked at the social positioning and experiences of two distinct life course stages: youth and later life. Hardy and Waite have commented on the paradox that life course research has tended to hold a tangential relationship to analyses of social change. A more satisfactory analysis of life course stages treats them not only as distinct stages on institutionally organised trajectories but as an integral part of social arrangements.

Theorists have sought to shed light on the social positioning of later life. Within the literature older people have often been positioned as different or 'at the margins', disadvantaged materially and disrespected culturally. The 'difference' of later life is assumed within much research, including that which seeks to locate difference. I argued that the analytic concepts and categories tend themselves to enshrine assumptions about the social difference of later life. This is evidenced in general descriptions of aggregate arrangements and in accounts of aspects of older people's subjectivity and identifications. In the former, older people come to be positioned as different to the 'rest' (or certainly, to independent working-age adults) in part as an outcome of the analytic categories in use, such as age stratification or cultural difference metaphors, which overstate the homogeneity of life course stages, and exaggerate the significance of life course cleavages over life course processes. In some accounts of older people's identifications, presumed differences shape the analysis of data on attitudes and perceptions. In fact often people's perceptions reflect not a pattern of resistance to marginalisation, but the failure of analytic categories to encapsulate their experience and social location. We need to move away from analytic categories which inadvertently position older people at the margins of society to analyses which better locate the specificity of disadvantage, and its articulation with ageing and the life course.

In respect of youth recent decades have seen changes in the positioning of youth, a change bound up with a reconfiguring of difference and interdependence across gender and generation. Youth researchers are more exercised by intra-cohort inequalities than theorists of later life, with many emphasising continuities in structures of inequality. However, this stress sidelines the significance of class- and gender-related structural changes in the distribution of opportunity and constraint across the population of young people. Some, then, have underplayed change in the patterning of inequality, but have exaggerated change in the *nature* of social processes. In such arguments there is a new dissonance between subjectivities and extant social relations, as youngsters are 'responsibilised' and increasingly see themselves responsible for their circumstances. A gap between subjective and objective is seen to be filled by an ideology of individualised choices and personal responsibility. In contrast, I have argued that we should understand the lack of direct correspondence between 'subjective' and 'objective' as an outcome of standard social processes, and as a puzzle which is resolved by adequate analysis of diverse contexts. It is simply the case that social actors do not, in their routine actions and reflections, take a 'bird's eye' view of the general social structure and their place within it.

In this chapter I have argued that social positioning is bound up with different contexts and perspectives on society. In the next chapter I further develop this theme with reference to ethnicity and perceptions of belonging and difference. Again we see the importance of understanding how people are placed, through linked material and normative processes.

7 Ethnicity and contexts of belonging and exclusion

7.1 Introduction

In respect of 'race' and ethnicity, recent decades have seen a significantly altered landscape of difference. Although anti-racism became more firmly placed on policy agendas in the latter part of the twentieth century, to some degree it has given way to claims of cultural difference, recognition politics and a discourse of multiculturalism. Some argue that the emphasis on difference and diversity comes at the expense of effectively analysing or challenging power differentials, racism and hierarchy (Alexander 2002; Amin 2002; Hall 2000; Hesse 2000; Solomos and Back 1996). The dominant emphasis on difference has raised concerns that hierarchical and oppressive social relations are inappropriately flattened in social analyses (Alexander 2002). In conjunction, some argue that whilst there was a broad acceptance of challenges to colour racism and notions of biological hierarchy, a racist 'code' of social understanding is still extant through the racialising of cultural difference (cf. Hall 2000; Solomos and Back 1996; Modood *et al.* 1994). In this logic, a majority 'our' culture is normalised in contrast to minority 'their' cultures, or 'their' ethnicity. For some, then, there has simply been a shift in racist constructions, not a weakening of such constructions.

The renewed interest in cultural diversity and difference raises new kinds of question about the nature of ethnic identification and boundary formation, and racism. Racism and ethnicity are key issues in debates about difference and its construction. Frequently there is an emphasis on cultural process, and a relative neglect of the ways in which such process links to social relations (Solomos and Back 1996). The question arises as to how cultural and evaluative constructions link to social contexts. Additionally authors not infrequently assume the uniform salience of categories of ethnic difference and treat them, along with racist discourse at a general level, as a starting point of analysis. Evidence is then interpreted through presumptions of racialised, if not always racist, beliefs. For example, recent research into ethnicity and schooling, and cultural constructions of difference, operate with an assumption of the general salience of racialised beliefs in interpreting teachers' and pupils' expressed attitudes (see Foster *et al.* 1996 for a review).

In contrast some authors have highlighted the importance of developing theories which can help illuminate the intersection of cultural constructions of difference on the one hand and material circumstance and social position on the other (e.g. Solomos and Back 1996). How do cultural processes shaping ethnicity and racialisation intersect with social contexts? How and why does the salience of ethnicity, or the prevalence of racism, vary across contexts? These are central questions to be addressed in this chapter. In it I draw on primary data and secondary sources to explore how certain patterns of association and interaction, and the contexts in which they take place, render ethnicity and 'race' salient as dimensions of cultural difference and inequality, and elsewhere work against constructions of difference. The analysis moves us beyond generalised accounts of ethnicity and racism to a more nuanced and sociological understanding of the shaping of cultural difference and its link to social contexts.

7.2 Locating difference

In Chapter 2 I argued that difference is a useful concept – but a partial one, at least in the ways it is used. Whilst there is wide-ranging emphasis within the literature on the processes shaping difference we need a more sufficient analysis of those processes. There is a tendency for discussions to become framed within the terms of difference, and for difference to be taken as a point of departure. Where this happens there is clearly a risk of essentialising groups – that is to say that members of any particular group tend to have some specific character or nature – whether it is a biological one or a cultural one. Consequently, as various writers indicate, analysis becomes asociological (e.g. Maynard 1994; Jenkins 1997). Maynard highlights what she sees as the risks of emphasising difference over unity, and notes another problem endemic in focusing exclusively on difference, arguing that: 'There is therefore a need to shift the focus of analysis from difference alone to the social relations which convert this difference into oppression' (Maynard 1994: 20). In this Maynard echoes others who are concerned with difference, power relations and hierarchy (e.g. Brah 1992). However it is also worth noting that Maynard seeks to 'balance' the focus on difference with a focus on 'parallel' processes; whether those that convert difference into oppression, or those that generate unity as opposed to difference. Alexander makes a parallel point (Alexander 2002). She argues that the cultural and academic discourse around difference and multiculturalism underplays the importance of social structure and of racism in shaping experiences and generating inequalities. The emphasis on difference has different manifestations across analyses of African-Caribbean and Asian ethnicities in Britain (ibid.). This has entailed a focus on *political difference* in respect of African-Caribbean identities and the social positioning of African-Caribbean people, and a focus on *cultural difference* in analyses of Asian ethnicities. A new common sense has, Alexander argues, entailed a 'disavowal of structure' and a neglect of material disadvantage, racism and aspects of commonality across minority experiences:

> The too easy valorization of an increasingly inward-looking and (apparently) self-defining 'difference' has led not only to the erection of seemingly insurmountable boundaries between Britain's African, Caribbean and Asian communities, which are empirically unsustainable, but has denied its more subtle ramifications for the way in which we think about these communities. Difference may be in, it may be all there is, but it is applied differentially to communities and often obscures as much as it reveals.
>
> (Alexander 2002: 553)

Alexander is right to argue 'difference' as a concept can hide as much as it reveals. However, 'difference' is not 'all there is'. For Alexander, defining social life and division in terms of difference requires analysis of its absence as if it were an opposite:

> [D]ifference must be able to account for elements that run apparently counter to it, to be able to make space for articulations of 'sameness'.
>
> (Alexander 2002: 568)

It is important to 'make space' for the absence of difference. To do so requires that we illuminate the processes which shape difference as a salient feature of social life: when, where and why is it present or absent? *However, we should not take difference as a starting point nor allow difference to frame the terms of debate*. It is useful (to a degree) to consider difference but we need to conceptualise it as a *specific* outcome of social processes, processes which may or may not render difference a salient dimension of social life and experience.

There are parallels between my argument that we need to locate difference and focus on the processes which give rise to difference (and perceived similarities) and those of Anthias (1998, 2001). Anthias argues that a singular focus on 'difference' may encourage empiricism, in which we take assertions of difference at face value, and discern a diverse and fragmented world (Anthias 1998). Additionally, categories of difference, such as ethnicity and gender, are often treated as causal, rather than as an *outcome* of social relations. Rather, Anthias argues, we need to consider processes of differentiation and identification. For example, how is the salience of some categories established? Under what conditions do actors see themselves in these terms? How do categories emerge as hierarchical?

Some critics observe that the focus on difference may itself entail majoritarian assumptions, since it is sometimes the difference of minority groups which is problematised, with the implication that the majority or dominant position is normalised (Maynard 1994; Anthias 1998). However, if the analytic focus is on the processes shaping difference, rather than difference *per se*, this should not happen. Indeed such an analysis will help illuminate normative assumptions, and locate majoritarian perspectives as not neutral but precisely as assumptions, and claims.

Walby argues that theorists who address the issue of difference have tended to present an abstracted account which is inadequately grounded in real social relations. We need to go 'beyond the simplicities of "community"' (Walby 2001: 123), that is, beyond abstracted notions of group identity, difference and group claims to a more grounded analysis. In this chapter I seek to develop this kind of more grounded analysis.

Part of the argument then will be for an illumination of diverse contexts in which 'race' and ethnicity may or may not be marked out. I will consider evidence on patterns of association and interaction, and linked cultural ideas and assumptions. Clearly, though, differential recognition, racist practices, and marginalising sentiments do not depend solely on diverse contexts of interaction and association, and local cultural lore. It is important to conceptualise how such contexts are embedded in a wider structure which generates pressures towards hierarchical differentiation.

Studies of 'race' and ethnicity, it has been noted, tend to focus on minority ethnic experience and to identify the 'othering' of such experiences, to analyse the construction of difference as a legitimation of hierarchy and so on. However, recently there has been some growth of a literature which looks at the meaning of majority 'white' ethnicity and identity. Frankenberg observes the 'apparent emptiness of 'white' as a cultural identity' (Frankenberg 2000: 448) and argues that, nonetheless, 'racism shapes white people's lives and identities in a way that is inseparable from other facets of daily life' (ibid.: 451). For Frankenberg, whiteness is a location of structural advantage, and 'refers to a set of cultural practices that are usually unmarked and unnamed' (ibid.: 447). The implicit, embodied and taken-for-granted nature of 'whiteness' means that white experience becomes naturalised and normative. In a majority white society, white people typically associate with other white people, and normalise that experience. In parallel, Dyer (1997) argues that:

> White people have power and believe that they think, feel and act like and for all other people; white people, unable to see their particularity, cannot take account of other people's; white people create the dominant images of the world and don't quite see that they thus construct the world in their own image.
>
> (Dyer 1997: 9)

Of course we need be very cautious in talking about majority white experience, since this is no less crude than speaking of any general minority experience. However, the central point is important: that majority normalising processes push towards a marginalising of minority differences. Some argue that linked 'white' assumptions amount to racism. Indeed they often do amount to racism, but it is imperative to understand when, where and why this is the case and to appreciate where and why it is not the case. To presume the former, that in a racist society all individuals are racist, is to commit an error of categorisation, and it is to misconstrue the processes shaping very diverse experiences. Iris Young (1990) offers an interesting and valuable account of processes shaping marginalisation in the United States. She argues that racism has changed its location, but not its nature. However, there is a risk that in her analysis she reifies difference and racism, insisting that they are everywhere. Young argues that over time social 'positions' in respect of race and ethnicity have altered, whilst values pertaining to race and ethnicity are largely unchanged. (In this we have another version of the argument that conditions and consciousness are out of step.) The suggestion by Young, but echoed elsewhere, is that racist ideas have gone 'underground' as public and civic discourse has rendered unacceptable expressions of racist sentiment. Behind closed doors, in private and/or in people's minds if not their utterances, racist sentiments, and other hatreds continue, largely unchanged. As with sexism, homophobia, ageism and disablism, racism has gone underground, and exists less at the level of conscious awareness, but continues as 'unconscious aversion' (ibid.). Young argues that we need understand and address the psychological mechanisms which generate prejudice and fear of 'the other', through perceived threats to security of the psychological self. She argues that we are uncomfortable with difference, we need shore up a notion of our self as a unitary category, and difference is perceived as a threat to our (distorted) notions of 'wholeness'.

The psychological dimensions of perceived difference are clearly beyond my remit here. But we need to take seriously the argument that racism, and other modes or prejudice, have gone underground. People may not express racist sentiments for fear of social opprobrium. However, it is surely a mistake to accept this as a generalising statement. Sniderman and Carmines (1997), again in an American context, draw on empirical survey data to argue that the view that prejudice and racism continue as before but have simply 'become hidden' is too simplistic. Certainly much extant racism, prejudice and ill-will will not be picked up in, say, attitudinal surveys or in general public statements. However, Sniderman and Carmines argue, it is not appropriate to jump from accepting the veracity of the existence of hidden racism to presuming that 'nothing changes' (Sniderman and Carmines 1997).[15] The notion of hidden racism is useful, but partial and homogenising. It seems unlikely, given change in the social positioning and circumstances of ethnic minority and majority, relative to one another, that there has been no cultural shift, merely a generalised but superficial suppression of prejudice.

Racism is a core aspect of the lives and experiences of minority ethnic groupings, yet we cannot sufficiently understand marginalising experiences solely in terms of racism. It has also to do with how minority cultures, groupings and individuals are positioned within society, and such positioning is often an outcome of implicit social processes as much as overt racist practices. Additionally we should not suppose that the relevant unit of experience and analysis is always the individual. Some people will experience 'difference' in particular times and places as, for example, they move across different normative contexts. In general, however, minority groups are positioned as different, and experience difference, in a more systematic way than majority groups. It is important to analyse the 'systematising' of difference, and how this generates 'routine oppressions'. But it is also important to research non-oppressive, routine, interactions to understand that oppressions are not 'everywhere'.

In the following I argue that 'difference' emerges at particular junctures. This pattern helps reveal the coherence of social processes shaping difference. My argument is that an understanding of ethnic identification requires a theorisation of the shaping of diverse contexts. Empirical evidence reveals the significance of social interaction and social milieux in shaping people's perceptions, in the context of asymmetries marked, and partly made, by racism. Drawing on some key empirical studies I will explore links between culture, dispositions and perceptions and extant social relations. How do ethnic identifications and experiences of belonging and difference, and racism, link to the social milieux in which people conduct most of their daily lives? I explore also how perceptions of difference have variable salience across the experiences of diverse individuals and also *within* individuals' experiences, and how this relates to context. I will further consider how minority individuals' perceptions of cultural difference are often linked to expressions of marginalisation.

7.3 Practice and perception

In this section I present some empirical evidence on perceptions of identity and belonging, drawing on data from the CAVA Transnational Kinship Study (Mason 2004; Smart and Shipman 2004), and from a study of changing ethnic identities by Modood *et al.* (1994). Modood and his colleagues argue that ethnic identities should be understood in terms of distinctive cultural practices, and in terms of how minorities believe they are treated by the majority (Modood *et al.* 1994). In parallel Jenkins describes ethnicity as partly an expression of what goes on within group boundaries and the external categorising or imposition of difference (Jenkins 1997). In the analysis of data to follow I will explore expressions of identity and belonging, and where possible examine this in relation to evidence on patterns of association and interaction. I will also present evidence on how ethnic minorities' expressions of identity and belonging are often contingent, that is reflexively linked to context and sometimes made in relation to partial exclusions. I will not be looking at evidence of distinctive religious and cultural practices but more precisely at articulations of difference as they relate to patterns of association, and to the general, asymmetrical and sometimes racist context in which such patterns obtain. The qualitative evidence examined in this section is drawn from open contexts, that is there is no scope for analysing networks or patterns of association beyond that which can be surmised from individuals' accounts. In a later section I will explore research with a direct focus on contexts in considering further the articulation of cultural constructions and social relations.

The CAVA Transnational Kinship study examined family obligations and networks across kin, within and across national borders, amongst Pakistani, Indian and Irish households. For the different groupings a limited number of families were identified through a snowballing method, and interviews were carried out amongst family and kin. The sample then does not purport to be representative on any quantitative measure, but rather was designed as an in-depth study, focusing on caring networks across generations, and perceptions of the adequacy of state support, within a strategically chosen urban context. The research was not designed directly to illuminate the issues under consideration here. Consequently I will be presenting and exploring data on a particular set of issues, about belonging, which were explored with the Pakistani sample. They were all resident in Bradford when the fieldwork was conducted, in 2001.

Respondents were not asked explicitly about identification, or discrimination but they were invited to relate their feelings about living in Bradford, about Pakistan, and about belonging, or not, to a community. Reflections on belonging provided some interesting themes for exploration. Analysis of the interview data with a focus on issues of 'belonging' suggested a rough patterning to the diverse responses. Expressions of belonging lay on a spectrum. At one end were those who held strong emotional (and associational) ties to Pakistan, seeing Pakistan as home, alongside a limited sense of belonging in Britain. I describe these respondents under a heading 'Pakistani belonging'. At the other end were those who clearly identified Britain (or, at least, Bradford) as home, and Pakistan as, at most, a secondary home. I place these under a heading 'British belonging'. However, for the most part respondents lie between, and I have characterised them as having a 'dual faceted belonging'. (I use the term dual faceted belonging since the term 'dual belonging' may suggest a tension or 'in-betweenness' which would be inappropriate). These 'heuristic' analytic categories are rather blurry, and blend at the edges. Their purpose is to help organise the data and they allow us to draw out some interesting themes. Expressions of belonging relate to perceptions of belonging and of 'home', often couched in terms of kin ties, other social networks and to holding 'outsider' status. The latter 'positioning' varies for different respondents, but it is generally described in a quite circumscribed way, an aspect of quite particular experiences. In exploring ethnic minorities' perceptions of 'belonging' and identification it is pertinent to emphasise that white majority British people might not unequivocally identify with Britain, and may identify more readily with other, for example more local, geographic units.

The following data is drawn from a series of interviews conducted by Dr Yasmin Hussain, and thanks are due to her and to Dr Jennifer Mason and Professor Carol Smart for access to the qualitative data. The first respondents quoted below are grouped under the heading 'Pakistani belonging'. This was a small and quite specific grouping, and their allegiances to Pakistan far from surprising given the strength of their links there, and/or the newness or partial nature of their residence in Britain. In this, these respondents hold a quite particular position within this small sample.

Zarqa is 26 and came to Bradford from Pakistan four and a half years before the interview, and after marrying her British-born husband, through an arranged marriage. She does not work, and lives with her husband in his parents' house, along with his brothers and their wives. She speaks at length about the importance of duty to relatives, both her own and her husband's. Her mother and four siblings live in Pakistan, whilst another four siblings live in Britain. She describes the importance of family connections for her 3-year-old daughter:

> Zarqa: We took her with us to Pakistan. She saw Pakistan and was very pleased. Now she is very young. We will take her again when she is grown up.
>
> Q: Why is it important for you to take her to Pakistan?
>
> Zarqa: She should know where her parents were born and which is our real country. The country belongs to her father and grandfather. That is our real country. We are here only to earn money and work.
>
> Q: Did you come to earn?
>
> Zarqa: If my husband works it is the same thing.

Other respondents describing similar sentiments were both female, and older. One, Fatima, co-resides in Bradford with her sons and in Pakistan, with her husband. She is 62. She speaks in terms of a clearly perceived difference between 'us' (Pakistani) and 'them' (white British). Shamshaad aged 51, with four children aged 13 to 24, migrated to Britain as a young woman to join her husband, has not worked in Britain, and does not much like Britain. She observes many positive features to British life, law and society yet expresses no sense of belonging:

> Q: Do you want your children to keep their links with Pakistan the way you have?
>
> Shamshaad: We wish that. Pakistan is our country.
>
> Q: Yes.
>
> Shamshaad: As we love our country and the people of Pakistan, we want our children to have the same love. That is our country. This country belongs to the English people.

In contrast a relatively clear-cut description of British belonging, more or less unproblematically in their accounts, was given by some interviewees. Clear expressions of this were provided by two young adults, both of whom were students.

Iffat is female, 19 years old, was born in Britain, has family and relatives in Bradford and around Europe, lives with her family in a predominantly white area, and is a student at Bradford University. She was asked about her sense of home:

> Q: But what is home then?
>
> Iffat: Here.
>
> . . .
>
> Q: Where are you told is your home?
>
> Iffat: Here, Bradford, definitely Bradford. Its weird because my friends and stuff they normally say Pakistan.
>
> Q: Do they?
>
> Iffat: They'd actually say this is their home this is where they were born and raised but our parents' home is Pakistan. I think that's why they call it back home but I can't call that back home because I don't see that as home.

Similarly, another young woman, Bushra, who is 18, born in Britain, a student living with her parents expressed a similar sentiment:

> 'Home to us is this, it's what we've grown up with, that's [Pakistan is] home as well but this is what we've been living all our lives. That is just like a second home but obviously from my parents' point of view its different.'

The next respondents articulate more directly aspects of dual faceted (or multi faceted) belonging and identifications. Their perceptions help highlight a pattern in which singular categories of 'nation' do not effectively capture felt identifications.

Asia is female, 34, single and works as a development officer at an Asian disability advice centre. Her father maintains strong ties with family in Pakistan, and owns land there, and spends much of his time there. She was asked if she would consider living in Pakistan herself, and she said:

> 'I think it's more difficult to work there as well and we would just find it difficult to live there. We are Pakistani by origin but we're not Pakistani by nature any more, our upbringing is not like that and mind set is different, I think we would find it very difficult to adjust.'

Rashid is male, aged 27; born in Britain he lives with his parents and his Pakistan-born and raised wife. He reflected on the generational dimensions of belonging:

> Rashid: This is my country just as my parents' country is Pakistan.
>
> Q: Do other people tell you that Pakistan is your home?
>
> Rashid: They say that we're Pakistani, but they don't say that Pakistan is our home.
>
> Q: Do you feel that Pakistan is your home?
>
> Rashid: No.
>
> Q: But you are Pakistani?
>
> Rashid: Yes by descent; I'm also Arabic by descent but Saudi Arabia isn't my home.
>
> Q: What does your Pakistani-ness do for your identity?
>
> Rashid: It's very important, it defines who I am. I can never lose my skin colour, I can never lose my cultural ties, and I can never forget who I am. I'm not English or European; I'm Asian and Pakistani. Apart from that I live in the UK, this is where I was born, this is where I stay, work and this is where I live, and this is my country.

As with Rashid, many others expressed a dual faceted belonging, seeing Britain or England, or more definitely Bradford, as home, yet also expressing in quite strong terms the significance to them of a Pakistani identity and sense of belonging. These expressions were often intermingled with expressions of contingency of belonging in Britain, and perceptions of racism and discrimination, both actual and potential.

Nazia is female, aged 29, was born in Britain, her husband moved from Pakistan to Britain when they married, she has A levels, works as an administrator, has 3 children (aged 1 to 8), and lives in a predominantly Asian area. Nazia seems to hold an unequivocal sense of Bradford/Britain as home, and sees herself as fully integrated; yet she also describes a 'contingency of belonging', a sense of being positioned outside of white majority norms to which she is required to orient herself if only at particular junctures: specifically in her decription of how she would interact with an employer as opposed to someone 'in the community'. Nazia's account bridges my categorisation of 'British belonging' and 'dual-faceted belonging', expressing both statements about 'belonging' in Britain which are at one point seemingly unequivocal, and at another contingent on circumstance. The former relates to a line of questioning around issues of belonging, the latter to questioning about identity.

Q: Do you think you will stay here or go to Pakistan?

Nazia: Stay here.

Q: Why is that?

Nazia: Because it's my home, I wouldn't go and live in Pakistan.

Q: Why not?

Nazia: I don't have a sense of urge to go abroad, I've got in-laws there but that's about it. If there was nobody to look after them and I couldn't get them here, I would have to go and live abroad. Under any other circumstances, I wouldn't want to move from here. This is where my family is, where my friends are, my way of living is, my roots and everything. I consider this is to be my home.

Q: Are your roots not in Pakistan?

Nazia: No, my roots are here.

Q: Do you think you are integrated into this society?

Nazia: Yes.

Q: To what extent are you integrated into this society?

Nazia: Everywhere and in everyway, born, bred everything's done here. That's the way we've integrated.

Later in the interview, when asked how she defines herself, she responds:

Nazia: It depends on who I am talking to, if I went to an employer, I'd say I was British. If I am talking to somebody in the community I'd say I'm Pakistani.

Q: Why do you think it's important to define yourself as British, when you're outside the community?

Nazia: I think there is still discrimination when you go out and say you're Pakistani. I think a person automatically gets a different impression, than when you say British.

Q: Have you ever experienced that?

Nazia: Personally I haven't and I don't think I'd like to either. We're British because we've been brought up in this country and we were born in this country. At the end of the day we're still Pakistanis.

Q: What makes you Pakistani?

Nazia: Because that's our culture and that's our background. That's where our parents have come from, we're Pakistanis aren't we? We live in a British society and we abide by British rules and that's why we call ourselves British, but yet we are Pakistanis.

Q: Do you ever feel that it was a mistake for your parents to come to the UK?

Nazia: No I don't feel it's a mistake, it's not our country it's just a country that we live in. We could easily be living in any other country in the world, it could be anywhere. The thing is at the end of the day we have a good standard of living which we wouldn't have got if we were living in Pakistan.

The next three respondents also manifested a dual faceted belonging, and reveal a felt contingency of that belonging in terms of insider and outsider status. Noreen and Shameem express this in terms of a sense of, or desire for, belonging when faced with 'othering' experiences, which strengthens their Pakistani identity. Zahid expresses his outsider status in terms of his experience in Pakistan: he is 'Pakistani at heart', yet does not feel himself to particularly belong in Pakistan. The responses here are also interesting since they reveal aspects of felt belonging within and across communities, and across experiences. This orientation parallels Bradley's (1996) notion of 'active identity' in which some particular identity (or facet of identity) has salience in particular situations or interactions.

Noreen is female, 24, was born in Pakistan and moved to Britain with her family at age 3; she lived in Pakistan for a year at age 14, and lives in a predominantly Asian area of Bradford. She offers a somewhat mixed expression of belonging when asked directly. Whilst she unequivocally identifies England as 'her country' she clearly also feels a strong allegiance to Pakistan and it is expressed in terms of the felt contingency of belonging in England:

Q: Which do you feel is your country, England or Pakistan?

Noreen: England.

Q: Do your brother and sisters feel the same way?

Noreen: Yes, even more so for them than it is for me.

Q: Why?

Noreen: Because they don't really know much of Pakistan at all, I think I've got more of a feeling for Pakistan, my mum says it's because I was born there.

Q: What's that feeling you have?

Noreen: It feels like Pakistan's yours, you get told so often that England isn't your country that you start to believe it.

Q: Who do you get told by?

Noreen: By the media, the National Front.

Shameem is female, 33, was born in Britain, holds a higher degree, lives in Bradford in a predominantly Asian area, and she works in Leeds. She articulated clearly two of the issues being highlighted here. When asked whether she felt part of a community she identified a mix of communities to which she felt she belonged: relating to work, to residence and to the Muslim community. When asked whether she felt part of the Pakistani community where she lives she talked about the contingency of identification, noting that identification with a community may vary and is just one aspect of multiple and complex affiiliations:

> '[I]identity isn't hard and set, it just depends what mood you're in or what is the current situation.'

She expressed her identification with Pakistan in large part in terms of her minority status in Britain. She was asked if her religious faith strengthened her links with Pakistan and she said:

> 'I think my link with Pakistan is more to do with my self identity in terms of who I am in relation to being here in Britain being from a minority group. I sort of also have like a dual nationality that I feel because you know sometimes my sense of belonging here, I feel that okay well at least I have some sort of Pakistani heritage and therefore some links with Pakistan. It's almost in like a very idealistic perception of: well if this place is no good for me then I can go there.'

Zahid is male, 29, married to Zarqa who came to Britain from Pakistan following their arranged marriage. (Zarqa is quoted above, under the heading Pakistani belonging.) Zahid was born in Britain, has an MSc and works for the local authority. He was asked in interview if he would live in Pakistan, and he replied that if he had the money he would love to stay there, referring to the weather and the relaxed atmosphere as reasons for this. He was then asked 'Would you go anywhere else other than Pakistan to live?' and the following discussion ensued:

> Zahid: Not really, I think the attachment with Pakistan is we are Pakistanis at heart and even in England we have this constant reminder that we are Pakistani so there is that issue, but in Pakistan when you go there they don't see you as Pakistani they see you as a British Citizen.
>
> Q: Why don't they see yourself as a Pakistani?
>
> Zahid: Because your culture is different your language is different, even your behaviour is different to what you eat, your dress sense is different and you're not fitting into their norm so in that respect you are different to them, here you look at it from a race point of view that you can be British but never English in the same way – there is yes you are Pakistani because

> your parents are from there or your family is there but the way you think and the way you behave and your attitudes, values and beliefs are not necessarily the same as the people there, we used to find that even within close family.

Zahid was asked whether he considered himself to be part of a community, and on his positive response:

> Q: Which community?
>
> Zahid: Different communities really, at home just the family network, outside the family there is Muslim friends there's the local community like neighbours or people who I interact with at mosques or shops, then beyond that there's different projects that I might be involved with like voluntary work, at work you have English friends, Asian friends. I don't think, I can't pinpoint it, as this is my community I think you can fit into different networks of people.

Some interviewees, then, gave a strong expression of Pakistani identification, and of British belonging. Such 'belonging' is often couched in terms of Britain as 'home', a birthplace and birthright, yet also in terms of felt exclusions, and the marginalising effects of discrimination and racism. Another issue arising from the data relates to the significance to people of diverse communities in which they 'moved'. I will be further exploring these themes through other empirical evidence below. In the CAVA data, though not directly designed for such an analysis, there is some evidence that patterns of association and interaction, their homogeneity and density, or diversity and looseness, ground people's sense of themselves, the ways in which they identify, and their sense of belonging. For example, unsurprisingly, some of those with particularly strong connections to Pakistan, such as Zarqa, having migrated from Pakistan quite recently, or Shamshaad, who lives in Pakistan for part of the time, may identify most clearly with it and feel somewhat distanced from British contexts, despite their residence in Britain. Young students who unproblematically describe Britain as home may be immersed in networks and patterns of association which cross ethnic boundaries and render them less salient. Between these two ends of the spectrum of expressions of belonging many articulate what I call a dual faceted belonging. Here people's sense of belonging relates to the particular contexts in which they find themselves. Belonging is often expressed in very concrete terms of kinship ties, and ties into other social networks and geographical spaces. It is also often described as having a contingent component, being expressed in relation to experiences, or anticipation, of racism and discrimination.

Greater reflexivity regarding ethnic identification and one's position in society probably follows from contexts in which majoritarian normalising assumptions press against, and render contingent or problematic, minority people's sense of belonging. In this way there is a systematising of majority/minority normative asymmetry. However, through the CAVA data we have seen how, within the one minority Pakistani grouping, there are many diverse perceptions of belonging and identification, and some evidence that these link to diverse social positions, networks and patterns of association in which people are embedded.

To further address these issues I turn now to the analysis of different generational patterns of sociality and contact and their links to diverse identifications made by Modood and his colleagues (Modood *et al.* 1994). (This qualitative study, and the linked social survey were conducted for the Policy Studies Institute so I will at times refer to it as the PSI study. I will refer to evidence from the linked survey (Modood *et al.* 1997) as the PSI survey.) The PSI research is of interest because it also reveals some of the ways in which perceptions and identities relate to diverse social positions. Despite Alexander's (2002) concerns about the different representation of Asian and Caribbean minority groups it is clear that the positioning of these groups in Britain is both heterogeneous but also distinctive, across ethnicities and across generations. It is informative to compare this diversity since it, too, sheds light on the articulation of social positioning and ethnic identity.

The PSI study explored diverse Asian and African-Caribbean identities, as articulated across different generations. In the study generation was defined in relation to where people had been born and raised, to age 16, so first generation refers to those who migrated to Britain, and second generation to those who had been born in Britain (Modood *et al.* 1994). The characterisation of 'South Asians' as a single grouping is a very broad brush description, with the PSI study including interviews with Pakistani Muslims, Bangladeshi Muslims, Punjabi Sikhs and Gujurati Hindus. Caribbean identities too are diverse. However in the summary account which follows I will generally (following Modood and his colleagues) refer to Asian and Caribbean ethnicities, since the broad brushstrokes should not detract from the main arguments being developed, and hopefully do no injustice to obviously diverse religious, ethnic and country affiliations.

The 'first generation' South Asian respondents in the PSI study were typically involved in close networks and organisations centred around the temple or mosque, and they socialised quite exclusively with family and friends who were members of the same ethnic group. Modood and his colleagues describe the presence within this grouping of a 'taken for granted' point of view, which followed from sharing so many aspects of life, experience and meaningful contact. It was quite unusual for close friendships amongst first generation Asians to cross ethnic boundaries (Modood *et al.* 1994).

In contrast second generation patterns of contact across South Asian ethnic groupings were very different (ibid.). There was less meaningful contact here with extended family: commitments to family remain very high but this was more often restricted to immediate family and kin. Social contacts through work and through education are more extensive, and more important. The generation gap, more significant in times of change, is clearly marked. Nevertheless, patterns of cultural distinctiveness and the continuance of boundaries between Asian ethnicities and white British ethnicities remain important amongst second generation Asians (Modood *et al.* 1994, 1997). One might say that patterns of association and networks cross these boundaries more often for second than for first generation Asians, yet the boundary itself remains quite strongly marked. Why? Because the most meaningful social relationships which people hold typically occur on the same side of the boundary, amongst those similarly positioned.

Amongst some religions and traditions marriage is in effect a marriage of two families, not just two individuals. Traditionally Hindus and Sikhs marry within their own religion (Modood *et al.* 1994). Amongst Muslims, marrying someone who would convert to Islam is deemed acceptable. However, it is not common. In the PSI study first generation respondents emphasised the importance of maintaining family ties and obligations across generations and saw this as possible only within the context of a shared religion and culture. Such attitudes coincided also with a belief in the importance of children being happy: tradition should not necessarily prevail over such happiness (Modood *et al.* 1994). However as the authors of the study point out the latter attitudes had not really been put to the test since marriages crossing ethnic boundaries remain unusual.

Amongst second generation interviewees in the PSI study, a more individualist ethos prevailed over the ethos of family and religious ethnicity. However, in many respects the outcomes were the same. Second generation young adults saw partnership and marriage in terms of individual compatibility, yet because such compatibility is felt to be largely dependent on cultural outlooks and what people hold in common, marriage within ethnic groups remains the norm. A Gujurati interviewee in the PSI study (Modood *et al.* 1994: 74) said:

> 'What's important to me if I want to go out with anyone is that we get on, that we have strong common interests. I couldn't say that of a white or black person because I am strongly Gujurati. So if I did go out with someone, it would have to be someone I could get along with and that person could only be Gujurati.'

Whilst second generation Asians emphasise personal choice there is still a high level of conformity to Asian cultural norms and expectations. This is partly an upshot of processes in which perceptions of compatibility follow the contours of ethnicity and religion. It is partly due also to some deference to parental expectations and community norms, and the perceived value of continuing cultural ties and distinctions. Data gathered in the 1994 Fourth National Survey of Ethnic Minorities shows the extremely low level of partnerships across Pakistani or Bangladeshi and other ethnicities. Of children with both parents co-resident, only 1 per cent of children with a Pakistani or Bangladeshi parent also have a white parent (Modood *et al.* 1997). Modood and his colleages argue that 'marriage continues to be a principal means of affirming and maintaining an ethnic identity amongst the South Asian groups' (Modood *et al.* 1994: 80).

What is marked in the evidence presented is the distinctiveness between Asian and Caribbean groups. They hold a somewhat different social positioning relative to the white majority. In aggregate they manifest different patterns of association and interaction, and so too different perceptions of Britishness, belonging and exclusion. These facets of experience are interlinked in important ways and to some extent they are mutually made, indeed diverse facets of the same social processes. Amongst Caribbean interviewees in the PSI study, and in constrast to Asian people, marrying across ethnic boundaries was quite widely taken for granted as a possibility. This reflects the common occurrence of mixed partnerships: the PSI National Survey revealed that 39 per cent of children with a parent of Caribbean ethnicity also had a white parent. In the PSI Survey people were asked whether members of their ethnic group would mind a relative marrying a white person, and whether they themselves would mind. Amongst Caribbean respondents, 12 per cent respondents said they would mind (5 per cent minding a little, and 7 per cent very much) in contrast to 51 per cent of Pakistani respondents (11 per cent minding a little, and 40 per cent minding very much). Twenty-four per cent of white people said they would mind if a close relative married a person of ethnic minority origin (10 per cent minding a little and 14 per cent minding very much) (Modood *et al.* 1997).

Amongst Caribbean interviewees, partnerships and marriages across ethnic 'borders' were seen in terms of compatibilty and attraction, and ethnicity and cultural difference was much less of an issue than for Asian people (Modood *et al.* 1994). The principal reservations and concerns for African-Caribbean interviewees were to do with perceptions of intolerance and racism directed at couples in 'mixed marriages'. First generation interviewees felt that individuals might face racist attitudes not just generally but amongst family and friends, and even from the white partner in the last analysis. Second generation interviewees were more positive, although still expressed some concerns about racist attitudes. Amongst Caribbean interviewees, then, inter-ethnic marriages were mostly seen positively and concerns were expressed in terms of perceived racism. In contrast, amongst Asian interviewees the primary concern expressed was about maintaining cultural continuities (ibid.). Choice of partners, the authors argue, is declining as a boundary marker between Caribbeans and white Britons.

Friendship patterns also revealed differences across South Asian and Caribbean ethnicities which broadly parallel those identified above. As noted, first generation Asians did not typically have non-Asian friends. Most second generation Asians had non-Asian friends, and their lives typically involved more diffuse patterns of contact than amongst first generation, especially through work and education (ibid.). There was a much greater commonality of interests crossing ethnic boundaries. Nevertheless close friends tended to be also Asian. In part this had to do with commonalities of background, and shared concerns, and in part it had to do with racism and experiences of exclusion, pressing towards formation of closer friendships within ethnic groupings. In contrast Caribbean respondents held stronger patterns of friendship across ethnic boundaries. A clear majority of Caribbean respondents, both first and second generation, had friends from different ethnic groups. Such friendships were deemed close for half of the first generation and two-thirds of second generation Caribbean respondents (ibid.).

These diverse patterns, of family relations, and patterns of inter-ethnic marriage and friendship relate to expressions of belonging. Constructions of compatibility reflect notions of 'we-ness': who 'we' refers to, and what 'we' share. In the PSI qualitative study, Asian expressions of 'we-ness' and identifications are made in terms of culturally grounded patterns of ethnic and religious distinction, and Caribbean expressions of we-ness are made in terms of reactions to racism. It may be precisely this kind of differentiation that Alexander (2002) objects to: after all, Caribbeans have a distinct cultural heritage and South Asians are just as, if not more, subject to racism. However, it is especially important to analyse diverse expressions of belonging and exclusion, and consider how they articulate with patterns of association and social interaction. Such association and interaction is social, and inseparable from the content of minority culture and religious beliefs, and from racist constructions of otherness. Most Caribbean interviewees in the PSI study said they felt they had much in common with British people, in cultural habits, in their attitudes, aspirations and behaviours (Modood *et al.* 1994). When asked who they saw as British, most Caribbean respondents described themselves as British, referring to Britain as a birthplace, and to a sense of belonging yet one which is contingent in so far as it meets racism and constructions of Britishness as white. Most second generation interviewees took their Britishness for granted, but saw colour exclusion as an obstacle to being accepted as British. In contrast second generation Asians felt Britishness was more contingent on giving up their culture (ibid.). The evidence here suggests the importance of the interlinking of cultural beliefs and practices on the one hand and patterns of social contact and interaction on the other. The PSI evidence reveals the differing positioning of Asian and Caribbean ethnicities in Britain. The evidence is indicative of a mutuality of cultural and religious beliefs, patterns of exclusion, and linked patterns of social contact and interaction. Together these processes shape and reshape ethnic boundaries.

7.4 Context and the meshing of cultural beliefs and social relations

Having explored some processes relating to ethnicity and perceptions of belonging and difference in 'open' contexts I turn now to some research in which context itself is defined, methodologically, as an object of analysis. Below I consider two studies by Wallman (1986) and Back (1996). Both authors develop analyses of particular social milieux, in developing grounded analyses of the making of difference, of ethnicities and of racism. As such their work helps illuminate links between cultural outlooks and social relationships and patterns of interaction within bounded, neighbourhood, contexts. Both studies go some way towards meeting the objective as identified by Solomos and Back (1996): to develop a framework in which racism can be analysed at the level of proximate lived contexts and in relation to wider public discourses on 'race' and ethnicity.

In an important study, Wallman (1986) argued that perceptions of ethnic difference relate to the nature of social networks. She researched two urban boroughs in London and found that differences in the recognition and strength of ethnic boundaries were related to the nature of social networks in the two locales. In one, networks were open and heterogeneous, encouraging diverse patterns of contact crossing ethnic boundaries, whereas in the other, networks were strongly overlapping, where neighbours were also work colleagues, friends and so on. In the former, the more diffuse nature of networks meant that it was easier for individuals to cross ethnic boundaries: since friendship, neighbourhood and work groups did not overlap extensively, individuals had only one boundary at a time to negotiate. Additionally, the resources held in such networks were more loosely distributed. In the latter more racist locale, because networks were strongly reinforcing, boundary processes were stronger, and network resources were concentrated within ethnic groups. Wallman thus provides a theorisation of the link between the 'associational' and the evaluational (ibid.). The salience of 'race'/ethnicity as a dimension of difference occurs within an asymmetrical structure and draws on wider cultural constructions of racialised difference and hierarchy. In the one, overtly racist, borough, this construction was mobilised as a set of racist assumptions and attributions. However, it held relatively limited salience in the other context. Wallman's research offers an empirically grounded argument about how different social contexts, theorised in terms of networks and patterns of social interaction, lend a varied salience to racialised constructions of difference.

In a study influenced by Wallman and holding some parallels to it, Back (1996) conducted a qualitative study of the making of ethnicities and racism, in two working-class estates in London in the late 1980s. In his study he shows the different articulations of racism – and anti-racism – across different contexts. The study offers insights into the mutuality of material and social relational factors and dispositions regarding race and difference.

His ethnography was based in two council estates in a South London borough, separated by about one mile, in an area once based on heavy engineering and which had subsequently seen cycles of severe economic decline, and significant immigrant settlement. In the 1960s housing authority decisions in the design and settlement of the new housing estates set the context for distinct cultural dynamics within the estates. In Riverview Estate housing policy was based on selection (through assessment of people's ability to pay rents) and there was an overt effort to engineer a community mentality, through the built environment amongst other things. Although not exclusively, the estate was predominantly ethnically white. In contrast the mass housing made available at Southgate Estate meant a more ethnically mixed population was established from the start.

Back explores perceptions of difference, and linked processes of inclusion and marginalisation, across the two estates. The period in the run up to the research had been one of significant economic decline, and Back explores how this was experienced by members of the different estates, and how their fortunes, and misfortunes, were perceived. Often misfortunes were perceived as having their origins in the immediate experiences of the neighbourhoods. Understandings of what had happened within the Riverview neighbourhoods came to be strongly racialised. Riverview had contained a group of black people from early on in the estate's life, and they had come to be deemed 'like us' by white majority residents. A later policy in the 1980s of allocating housing on the basis of need made estate residents feel themselves to be put in adverse circumstances by the newcomers, most especially given perceptions of unfairness in allocation procedures. Back explores the ways in which discourses, currencies of talk and logic shared by neighbours and prevalent in the estate were important in shaping and reinforcing people's perceptions of their felt misfortunes, perceptions which contained racist presumptions (Back 1996).

The racist constructions are not straightforward. Amongst young people racism was widely seen as inappropriate, and there was an assertion of commonality in 'our' estate expressed by white youth, but this was in a context, Back argues, where 'race' still mattered. So, for example, young white men on the Riverview Estate might see black men as different to themselves by virtue of their ethnicity, either in a negative way, or through a respect afforded to young black men shaped by conceptions of admirable black masculinities. The young white men were overtly racist towards young Vietnamese men who were relative newcomers to the estate. Back (1996) argues that in this context the inclusion of young black men by young white men was a contingent form of inclusion. Racism was partly rejected, but only so far as non-racism was part of an inclusive localism, and this inclusiveness was 'extended' to black youngsters but not to Asian residents.

In contrast, in Southgate Estate, Back argues that there was a significant and extensive anti-racist understanding. A more generally inclusive 'our area' neighbourhood discourse tended to dominate here, and Back argues that this discourse facilitated inter-ethnic contact and communication. Indeed he suggests that patterns of interaction and friendship here produced 'mixed ethnicities', and a tendency of young white people to deny their whiteness as relevant. Here rather than a contingent belonging afforded to minority groups, 'race' and ethnicity seemed to hold altogether less relevance (Back 1996).

Back (1996) seeks to illuminate an interweaving of three dimensions of social life: of discursive constructions (the beliefs and understandings people draw on and develop in seeking to explain their circumstances), of 'material' contexts (loss of economic livelihoods, the built environment, perceptions of inequality) and of patterns of interaction and association across 'boundaries'. In so doing he offers insights into contextual specificity and the social embeddedness of diverse cultural dispositions, locating 'difference' and its variable salience.[16]

The studies of Wallman and Back provide insights into how discursive or cultural constructions of 'race' and ethnicity are mobilised. These constructions may draw on generalised racist discourses and ideologies of the British nation as white. But equally, overt constructions of ethnicity and diversity may draw on other discourses, of 'tolerance' and multiculturalism, or of anti-racism and social transformation. What is of particular interest is how these generalised understandings, and claims, may or may not be mobilised in particular contexts. It is not enough to theorise claims of difference, whether racist constructions or claims to recognition, at the level of general discourse or generalised cultural constructions. Rather, to understand the purchase of generalised discourses we need to understand how they come to be mobilised across diverse milieux. Wallman's and Back's studies help reveal the mutual making of cultural constructions and the specific social milieux and social relationships through which people experience and understand the world. It is on this basis that certain discourses or general cultural stories or understandings get mobilised and drawn upon.

7.5 Conclusion

The concept of cultural difference is at the heart of recent debates and analyses of ethnicity and racism. Some writers have expressed a concern that this detracts from analysis of the shared experience of racism of different minority groups. This is an important political point. However, I have argued that the notion of a shared position of racialised otherness is too broad-brush to achieve sociological purchase on diverse experiences, subjectivities and social positions. A stress by many on the processes of cultural othering and the interest in imagined communities of difference has left relatively under-researched the question of how such 'imaginings' link to social relations and patterns of association and interaction. These social contexts remain relatively under-researched, yet crucial to a sufficient theorisation of ethnicity and its social and cultural reproduction and reshaping.

People and groupings are positioned across a highly differentiated social space. Minority groups are likely to come up against majoritarian normalising assumptions, a pattern illustrated through CAVA and PSI data. So, for example, many of the CAVA respondents cited expressed their sense of belonging in relation to kin, community and patterns of association, but also revealed a contingency to their sense of belonging linked to perceived discriminations. Thus as well as being sometimes subject to overt racist attitudes members of minority groups may feel themselves to be positioned 'against the grain' of majority assumptions. These implicit processes work towards the 'systematising' of cultural othering and devaluation. However, to understand and analyse diverse social experience and perceptions within the broader asymmetry it is crucial to understand how people are positioned, and the proximate contexts, social relations and networks in which they are embedded. This argument was developed through analyses of the links between social contexts and perceptions of belonging, difference and identification.

Taking a sufficiently differentiated conception of structural diversity we can again see coherence between position and disposition, and can productively explore the links between these two facets of social experience. In such an understanding we can see that perceptions of self and belonging, and the contours of solidarity, are as much social as they are cultural. In the next chapter on class and socio-economic hierarchy, I further explore people's perceptions and the ways these link to social location. And again, this gives us new insights into social inequality.

8 Difference, hierarchy and perceptions of social justice

8.1 Introduction

Do material inequalities no longer generate criticism or anger? Are people newly acquiescent in the face of structural injustices, or have material inequalities of class been eclipsed by concerns about other 'cultural' inequalities and claims for status recognition? Some argue that the recent erosion of class-based claims and politics is bound up with changes in the ways in which people understand and interpret society and its inequalities. In this argument people have become less aware of social process, and more individualised, and responsibilised, believing themselves to be the locus of their social fortunes and misfortunes (cf. Beck 1992; Rose 1999). Issues of social justice in respect of class are seemingly in retreat (Phillips 1999). Given the continued hold that social origins have on social destinations, the apparent demise of social explanation is deemed by some to be all the more deleterious, as people internalise and constantly struggle with the 'injuries of class' (after Sennett and Cobb 1973).

Certainly the processes underpinning the reproduction of social inequality are to a large degree hidden from view. However, this 'hidden hand' is an aspect of complexity and extant social processes, and not a specific outcome of late modern society. What we require is a more sufficient theorisation of the milieux through which, and processes by which, people reproduce inequalities even whilst, at the same time, generally disapproving of the extent of such inequality. In this chapter I focus on socio-economic inequalities and how they are perceived, exploring aspects of distributive justice and recent debates about class. I again focus on the gap, in recent analyses, between perceptions and dispositions at the level of the individual, and accounts of the general social structure. This analytic gap blocks understanding of social dynamics in the reproduction, and reshaping, of material social inequalities. In line with the arguments developed in relation to life course differentiation, ethnicity and gender, we need to reconceptualise social structural differentiation to achieve better analytic purchase on people's diverse social positioning, and their perspectives upon it.

Within research on social hierarchy, social milieux are very important yet under-researched dimensions of inequality and its reproduction. I will consider recent writing on redistribution and recognition by Nancy Fraser and Axel Honneth and argue that a sociologically grounded understanding of social position and perceived injustice requires a full specification of when and how extant conditions are subject to justice evaluations and experienced as unjust. Drawing on Runciman I will argue that whilst a matter for empirical investigation, reference groups and social comparison processes are crucial to conceptualising experiences of injustice and linked patterns of action, or inaction. It is crucial to better understand how people see their social position and link this to our knowledge of social structural inequalities. Without an analysis of social position it is unsurprising that we end up with models of disjuncture between the subjective and the objective, between perceptions and outlooks on the one hand and the structure of social relations on the other. In section 8.3 I review general data on perceptions of income inequalities and general inclinations which are more egalitarian than extant patterns of income distribution. I also discuss some empirical evidence on the ways in which social positioning entails diverse frames of reference. In section 8.4 I explore recent developments in debates about social class. Various writers here have presumed that people's social position should provide them with a class identification. Since in practice many people do not readily identify in class terms, some writers have interpolated an ideological gap, or pattern of resistance, at the level of individuals. However, we can better understand people's self-identification with a more nuanced understanding of their frames of reference. What is crucial is not just pointing to evidence of diverse frames of reference and subjectivities, but conceptualising the pattern of such diversity. To do so is to develop a more inclusive theory of the meshing of subjective views and perceptions and extant social relations. Consequently we can develop a more robust understanding of social inequality and its reproduction.

8.2 Redistribution, recognition and reference groups

A frequently rendered observation within sociological commentary is that the latter part of the twentieth century onwards manifested an eclipse of class-based identities and claims, and class politics, and the rise in importance of status-based identities and claims: around gender, 'race', disability and sexuality in particular. The alleged decline of class (e.g. Pakulski and Waters 1996; Phillips 1999) is generally seen not as an end of class-based inequality, but rather as an ending to class-based solidarities and politics. Many see this as a paradox: that the politics of class was eroded at a time when social inequalities and divisions were becoming as stark as they had been in many decades. In light of these currents many writers seek to ensure an adequate treatment of class-related inequalities in part through seeking to conceptualise the articulation and intersection of class and status-related aspects of inequality (e.g. Anthias 1998, 2001; Fraser 1995). Two highly influential figures are Nancy Fraser and Axel Honneth. Both write from a political philosophy perspective but they explicitly disavow disciplinary divisions and offer a social theory perspective as much as a philosophical one. They develop important and interesting insights and arguments (e.g. Fraser 1995; Fraser and Honneth 2003; Honneth 1995) and it is of interest here to engage with aspects of their debate.

Both authors seek to develop an adequate analytic perspective on the articulation of recognition and redistribution processes, to more fully discern the dynamics of contemporary capitalism. In the following I give not an overview of their latest debate (Fraser and Honneth 2003) but make some observations of relevance to my concerns with social location and subjectivities, the latter with a particular focus on perceptions of fairness.

For Fraser and Honneth recognition and redistribution processes are both relevant to theorising different kinds of inequality which might at first sight be read off as one or the other. For example, gender and 'race' inequalities are clearly in part composed of injustices of recognition where people are differentially treated as a direct result of (presumed) status attributes, and injustices of distribution, where gender and 'race' entail systematic inequalities in employment and income chances. One of the points of dispute between Fraser and Honneth is whether recognition as a cultural process and redistribution as an economic process should be construed as having different dynamics, or as comprising a unitary dynamic. Honneth takes the latter position and believes that all inequalities, including class inequalities, can be best understood in terms of culturally based moral misrecognition and disrespect.

I argue that, in a key domain, Honneth's perspective is more helpful than that of Fraser, in so far as he argues that redistributive processes are inseparable from cultural processes (see also Irwin and Bottero 2000). However, I will argue that in another interesting domain Fraser's argument is more helpful than that of Honneth, in her insistence that the recognition analytic seems to be a narrow basis for assessing the experience and articulation of felt injustice. Honneth has argued that in the past, sociological analyses have been inappropriately focused on analysts' notions of where people's interests lie – as supposedly given by objective inequalities. These interests, Honneth argues, are rarely analysed as elements of the 'everyday web of moral feelings'. He argues that the moral experience of misrecognition and linked feelings of indignation are under-researched and yet should be the starting point for theorising social conflict (Honneth 1995).

In *Redistribution and Recognition*, Honneth argues that an adequate theory of recognition should be at the heart of how we analyse contemporary society (Fraser and Honneth 2003). Whereas Fraser argues for a perspectival dualism in which we treat redistribution and recognition processes and claims as having distinct dynamics, Honneth argues that we should see both through the same analytic lens. He argues that we should see redistribution claims in cultural terms – as a specific type of recognition claim. Drawing on historians such as E.P. Thompson, Honneth maintains we should understand discontent and resistance to distributive injustice not just in relation to material deprivations but also (indeed primarily) in the misrecognition of ways of life and achievements. Distributive injustice should be properly conceived as a particular instance of a more general case – of misrecognition: '[s]ubjects perceive institutional procedures as unjust when they see aspects of their personality being disrespected which they believe have a right to recognition' (Honneth 2003: 132). Recognition, Honneth argues, is crucial to social well being. He criticises Fraser for seeing historical newness in the nature of recent recognition claims, arguing:

> [T]he conceptual framework of recognition is of central importance today not because it expresses the objectives of a new type of social movement, but because it has proven to be the appropriate tool for categorially unlocking social experiences of injustice as a whole.
>
> (Honneth 2003: 133)

And so, he says:

> It therefore seems more plausible to me that experiences of injustice be conceived along a continuum of forms of withheld recognition – of disrespect – whose differences are determined by which qualities or capacities those affected take to be unjustifiably unrecognized or not respected.
>
> (Honneth 2003: 135–6)

Honneth develops an historical account of the making of subjectivities linked to historically emergent social 'standards', of love, equality, and achievement. His account of misrecognition/ disrespect is measured against deviations from these standards. However, it is still an extremely aggregated and somewhat generalised picture that is developed. So, although Honneth argues that we need to eluicidate the 'moral order of society as a structure of graduated relations of recognition' (pp. 136–7) there is a question mark over the social grounding of such experiences. Honneth offers only extremely generalised comments in this respect:

> [F]orms of reciprocal recognition are always already institionalised in every social reality, whose internal deficits or asymmetries are indeed what can first touch off a kind of 'struggle for recognition'. What is therefore required first of all is an attempt to explicate the moral order of society as a fragile structure of graduated relations of recognition; only then can it be shown in a second step that this recognition order can touch off social conflicts on various levels, which as a rule refer to the moral experience of what is taken to be unfounded disrespect.
>
> (Honneth 2003: 136–7)

This image of the social order as an asymmetrical moral order is a powerful one, and Honneth develops a valuable framework for seeking to illuminate the grounds of recognition claims. However, there are questions arising which are in need of a more extended sociological treatment than Honneth accords to them. In particular why, and when, are the consequences of asymmetrical arrangements experienced as unjust, as political not personal traumas, and as changeable? Additionally Honneth seems to risk inappropriately delimiting perceived injustices to the 'withdrawal of recognition'. We need, instead, to broaden the base for theorising felt injustice, and for thinking about how people relate to asymmetries of power, reward and acknowledgement.

First, we can usefully ask, with Fraser (2003), what other contexts and experiences generate felt injustice? Fraser argues that no single moral expectation underlies social discontent, which is very often not a matter of denied recognition, but may arise from a wide variety of sources, including resentment of unearned privilege, aversion to arbitrary power, indignation at disparities of wealth, or perceived discrepancies between contribution and reward. Indeed all manner of sources of felt unfairness

> are not best interpreted as violations of personal identity. To insist on construing them as such is to shift the focus away from society and onto the self, implanting an excessively personalised sense of injury.
>
> (Fraser 2003: 204)

Honneth's discussion of misrecognition does seem to engender a very individualised subject. Fraser rightly challenges Honneth for not sufficiently addressing the social conditions which shape experiences of suffering, and of felt injustice, and she points to various important themes here. She indicates the need for a theory of the social grounding of aspects of felt unfairness. The sociological task remains important, and somewhat neglected: to more adequately specify under what conditions certain affairs are perceived as socially made, as unjust and as changeable. When there is a sense of felt injustice, when, how and why does this translate into social action? For example, does it generate a personal or a political response, fatalism, individual reaction, group action?

In short the Fraser-Honneth debate entails a rather limited engagement with the social grounding of experiences of disrespect and unfairness, and the translation of such experiences into particular responses and patterns of social action. There is a risk that perceptions and judgements about unfairness, and linked patterns of action, hold a rather individualised provenance in the work of Honneth (1995, 2003). We need a grounded sociological understanding of such perceptions and evaluations. Without this we remain short of any sufficient explanation of social process. I will argue that such an understanding requires engagement with diverse social milieux, for example patterns of association, networks and reference groups, that is the proximate contexts in which people engage in their most meaningful social relationships, and which play an important role in shaping their outlooks and the interpretation of their experiences. Reference group theory is a rather neglected but potentially extremely productive avenue for social research here (cf. Walby 2001).

Runciman's (1966) theory of reference groups and perceptions of distributive justice offers insights into felt unfairness as a socially grounded and sometimes non-intuitive outcome of social arrangements in a structure which is not 'flat' but hierarchical and differentiated. Social comparison is a crucial part of human social experience and motivation. Such comparisons are not made in random fashion but in a structured way, and reference groups play a key part in understanding people's assessment of their position. We cannot however assume that being on the disadvantaged side of an asymmetry will necessarily create a sense of injustice. Runciman's main concern is with the relationship between inequality and grievance. Runciman starts with, as he says, a familiar truism – that attitudes, aspirations and grievances depend on the framework of reference in which they are conceived. His contribution lies in part on helping elucidate the structure in which differential expectations and references are shaped. People do not make social comparison across large social distances, but tend to assess their own position with reference to people in fairly similar situations, and 'reference groups tend to be closely circumscribed at all levels of society except under some abnormal stimulus' (ibid.: 195). For Runciman, the link between felt injustice and circumstance is an empirical question:

> Most people's lives are governed more by the resentment of narrow inequalities, the cultivation of modest ambitions and the preservation of small differentials than by attitudes to public policy or the social structure as such. Inequalities which are scarcely visible and difficult to remedy will have very little influence on the day-to-day emotions of any but those whose political consciousness is unusally militant or sensitive; and envy is a difficult emotion to sustain across a broad social distance if gratification is nowhere within view . . . There is no single reaction to a condition of subordination which cannot be documented for some society at some period, from the degraded passivity of a subject race to the incendiary fury of a rioting jacquerie. There is some generalization appropriate to every one of these relationships between relative deprivation and inequality, but there is none which makes any particular relationship the obvious one.
>
> (ibid.: 285)

There are a number of issues we can usefully elaborate upon here in considering the link between the pattern of inequality and how this pattern is experienced and acted upon. Runciman argues that attitudes to inequality do not hold a direct relationship with people's objective positions within the social hierarchy. Felt deprivation links to opportunity in a non-linear way.

That is, someone who is poor does not necessarily see her or himself as disadvantaged, and nor a rich person necessarily see him or herself as advantaged. Runciman uses diverse evidence to show the importance of frames of reference to perceptions of fairness and felt satisfaction or dissatisfaction. One such example comes from a study called 'The American Soldier' (Stouffer *et al.* 1949, cited Runciman 1966). Within this study there is discussion of differing levels of satisfaction with promotion opportunities amongst the American Military Police and the Air Corps. The former held poor promotion opportunities in contrast to excellent opportunities in the latter, yet levels of satisfaction with such opportunities were higher where they were much more restricted. Why? In the Military Police where few men were promoted most could compare themselves with others in a similar position and not be dissatisfied. The few who *had* been promoted were satisfied. In the Air Corps in contrast, those who were not promoted would be relatively dissatisfied, comparing themselves with the large number of promotees, whilst the latter would feel they had done relatively less well, given the commonness of the achievement. Runciman gives this as just one example of a swathe of evidence on the importance of reference groups in shaping people's perceptions of 'how they are doing' (Runciman 1966). Through his own survey of workers conducted in 1962, Runciman looks at perceptions of deprivation and how these link to manual and non-manual workers' positions in the social hierarchy. So, for example, he finds that high-income working-class men are least likely to name people better off than them, whilst medium-income middle-class men are most likely to name people better off than themselves, and develops a picture of class-based reference groups and their link to felt deprivation.

This emphasis on the social bases of grievance is an important complement to recent discussions of the moral bases of recognitional and redistributive justice. It is clear that we must embed evidence of felt injustice, and its absence, in a sufficiently robust theorisation of social differentiation and social structure. Typically people make comparisons with those in a similar social position, and this is likely to encourage a more localised (in social comparison terms) sense of unfairness than one which takes the whole social structure as its object. This is an important counterweight to arguments that assume people adjudge their position against 'the whole' or, if they fail to do so, are somehow ideologically blindfolded. We can also see through Runciman a convincing account of the link between heightened or frustrated expectations and social action, particularly conflict. Things may not be perceived or evaluated in justice terms, if they are seen as immutable. Or they may be seen as unjust yet, in being construed as immutable, be no spur to social action. Runciman elaborates also on how an injustice may be experienced, or felt, yet the impossibility of changing things would impede social action: 'We must beware confusing acquiescence with contentment: the impossibility of remedy can inhibit action without inhibiting the sense of grievance' (Runciman 1966: 26).

That is, things may be experienced as unjust yet not acted on for a variety of reasons. This was an experience related by the women textile workers interviewed by Glucksmann, who described their experiences as wives in the 1930s and 1940s with all the privations and unequal relations with their husbands, which the women saw as unjust, although they felt nothing would be gained in challenging the situation (Glucksmann 2000). In contrast, where social arrangements are revealed, or newly perceived, as changeable there may be a sea change in attitudes and linked social movements. In general people's expectations remain fairly stable but shifts in the general context (most markedly evident perhaps in the case of war) alter people's referents and their ideas of what is desirable and what is possible (Runciman 1966).

Runciman's theory highlights the central importance of social position and social comparison processes to perceptions of injustice and linked modes of action, and inaction. This 'layer' of analysis is under-researched, indeed insufficiently recognised, in recent accounts of social inequality and class. I noted such a pattern in Chapter 6, where arguments of responsibilisation were shown to overstate the importance of 'normal' political reflection on the social structure, by social actors, and to read its absence as evidence of ideological distortion. In the following section I consider attitudinal patterns as revealed when people are invited to reflect upon the social structure as a whole. In section 8.4 I will look at why it is that people do not routinely make evaluations of the structure as a whole, and how milieux and reference groups should be more central to theorising subjective experience of social inequality. If we better understand how people see their own social position we can gain insights into the reproduction of inequality.

8.3 General perceptions of income inequalities

Although the party political *zeitgeist* over recent decades might lead one to doubt it, 'the public' of attitudinal surveys appears to be generally in favour of curbing current levels of income inequality. Attitudinal data reveals a fairly general level of opposition to inequalities deemed excessive with surveys showing that majorities see the current income gap, in Britain and elsewhere, as too large (Bromley 2003; Gijsberts 2002; Alwin *et al.* 1996; Kelley and Evans 1993). Approximately four-fifths of respondents to the BSAS believed the gap between high and low incomes to be excessive. This attitude is common across much of the population with high and consistent 'opposition' registered across all social classes and diverse income groups.

The International Social Survey Programme (ISSP), referred to in Chapter 5, is an international collaboration to allow cross-national comparisons of attitudes across a range of domains. In Britain ISSP modules of questions are asked as a component of the BSAS. As part of this there is a battery of questions on aspects of distributive justice. Respondents have been asked about the earnings that people in various occupations should be paid, and the earnings that people in these occupations are actually paid. The occupations identified are: unskilled worker in a factory, skilled worker in a factory, doctor in a general practice, cabinet minister in the UK government and chairman of a large national corporation. Typically when asked about earnings levels for different occupations – what people think members do earn, and additionally, what they should earn – British survey respondents revealed a presumed ratio of 1:12 between the lowest- and highest-paid occupations named, and a preferred ratio of 1:6 (Bromley 2003).

In respect of what preferences might follow on from these general attitudes, Bromley notes that in the British case there is quite high support for progressive taxation, at 76 per cent in 1999. (The question asked was: *Do you think that people with high incomes should pay a larger share of their income in taxes than those with low incomes, the same share, or a smaller share?* Seventy-six per cent responded 'a larger share' or 'a much larger share'.) However, there is less broad-based support for redistribution. Since the late 1990s, a comparatively low 39 per cent of respondents consistently have agreed that '*Government should redistribute from rich to poor*' (ibid.). Bromley discerns a puzzle in these markedly different percentages and speculates that there may be a distaste for the word redistribution. It seems very possible the questions are construed rather differently. It may be that when asked a question about progressive taxation it is seen by respondents as a progressively scaled contribution to a general fund, and when asked about redistribution this is seen as being about a direct transfer of wealth and more directly a penalty on the rich to help the poor. These questions are not necessarily tapping the same thing, indeed the difference in public opinion suggests that they are not. Nevertheless it remains strongly the case that the majority express attitudes which oppose unlimited inequality and they express attitudes which favour progressive taxation.

According to some views the picture of extant inequality which people have, and their views on distributive justice, are not wholly independent. Rather extant inequalities shape perceptions of 'what should be'. Within the literature there is fairly extensive consideration given to Homans' argument that 'the rule of distributive justice is a statement of what ought to be and what people say ought to be is determined in the long run and with some lag, by what they find in fact to be the case' (Homans 1974, cited Gijsberts 2002: 270; also see Alwin *et al.* 1992).

For Gijsberts there has been insufficient research into this issue of how the 'is' shapes the 'ought' (see also Liebig and Wegener 2000). In her study she explores ISSP data on perceptions of justice in western capitalist societies and post-transformation state socialist countries. She maintains her evidence is indicative of the structuring influence of extant patterns of inequality on people's perceptions of the legitimacy of such inequality. She argues that the more inequality people perceive the more they think legitimate. The data is examined across the period 1987 to 1992 to examine shifts in perceptions before and after the collapse of the state socialist regimes. She notes a very significant increase in perceived actual inequality in Hungary and Poland and an increase in the amount of inequality which was perceived as legitimate within these countries. However, we can note that the latter increase was much more muted than the former. Perceptions of legitimacy were nothing like as marked as the perceived actual growth (Gijsberts 2002). Although the new ratio put these countries into a similar 'is : ought' ratio as western countries, one might reasonably presume that the same objective gap might engender very different perceptions of its legitimacy or illegitimacy, due to preceding norms in state socialist societies regarding inequality, and given the dramatic and relatively chaotic ushering in of new social formations in transformation societies.

Gijsberts posits 'what is' shapes 'what ought'. This has plausibility but it is a tricky issue to disentangle methodologically as well as substantively. For example, it is important to ask whether, in answering survey questions, people require some reference point in responding to questions about legitimacy. Even if this is a reference point they have supplied themselves, through responding to actual income distribution questions, it offers a frame of reference in which to locate their views on legitimacy. Therefore we would expect an association between perceptions of 'what is' and 'what ought to be' by default of the need to relate the latter to some frame of reference. Furthermore, we do not have information about the salience of questions to respondents, nor then about the extent to which views are relevant to social behaviours. People may have an abstracted view of overall inequalities but we have no sense of the salience of the issues as people see them. People may not routinely think about the issues on which they are questioned, until they become posited as topics for evaluation by a researcher. Passionate and indifferent alike will provide data which receives equal weighting. Survey data provides us with an important and interesting general picture; however, it is one which remains general, and does not tap into the salience to people of social inequalities.

Differential location within a structure will itself impact upon dispositions and attitudes. It does so not simply because people may be self-interested (this is far too simplistic anyway) but because the issues we are dealing with are not made through uniform atomised processes. Social positioning itself alters people's frame of reference (e.g. Gijsberts 2002; Kelley and Evans 1995). Imagine a solid rugby ball-shaped piece of glass: differing positions within yield a different perspective on, and perception of, the whole.

Some writers seek a measure of inequality which captures relative deprivation and felt discontent better than measures of 'objective' inequality (Pedersen 2004; Podder 1996). Clearly very inegalitarian societies can have low relative deprivation and conversely more egalitarian societies high felt deprivation. Reference group theory seeks to embed felt discontent within processes of social comparison. In his critical appraisal of the uses and abuses of inequality measures, including the appropriate specification of the Gini coefficient, Pedersen argues the value of seeking to incorporate a theory of social comparison within the measure of inequality. For Pedersen we can only treat as a measure of relative deprivation one which reckons with reference groups:

> [I]t follows from the very nature of a relativistic conception of inequality that it can only be meaningfully applied at a certain level of aggregation – corresponding to the boundaries of the presumed reference population. Issues of aggregation and disaggregation from whatever is considered to be the appropriate boundaries of the reference population(s) becomes highly problematic.
>
> (Pedersen 2004: 33)

In short, perceptions of inequality may be bounded, for example contingent on what is deemed an appropriate reference group. Social comparison is an under-researched process in contemporary sociology, and so too is the linked question of how people 'choose' reference groups (Pedersen 2004; Bygren 2004).

Pedersen makes a distinction between relative deprivation and reference group theory as a basis for theorising 'externally directed complaints and grievances' (p. 40) and a concept of relative deprivation which is relevant to social evaluations, which he says also entails more latent psychic and psycho-social consequences, such as internalised feelings of failure, an absence of self-esteem and self-respect and so on (Pedersen 2004). However, I would contend that these are different facets of the same set of issues. It is an important sociological question as to how psychological positionings interact with social ones, and how apolitical interpretations of circumstances translate into political ones.

A recent qualitative study of inequalities and reference groups brings some greater detail at the level of individual experience and reflection (Lam 2004). It also offers some evidence on diverse (political and apolitical) interpretations of very similar circumstances, here in relation to gender inequalities. Lam interviewed a number of young women in Hong Kong, all of whom were single, middle-class and educated women in their twenties. She draws on Runciman's theory of reference groups and explores her interviewees' perceptions of gender inequalities and the ways in which such perceptions translate into acquiescence or resentment. She seeks to better understand the gap between diverse social locations and principles of justice used by her respondents. What, she asks, are the links between people's milieux, their perceptions of inequality and their ideas about justice (ibid.)? The study offers interesting insights and is a welcome and rare example of recent analysis drawing on reference group theory. Lam argues that where respondents perceived gender difference in terms of role differentiation they were less likely to see difference in terms of inequality.

Lam divides her respondents into three groups, dependent on their attitudes to gender inequalities, attitudes characterised by endorsement, accommodation or resistance. The group characterised by endorsement generally felt that they did not experience gender inequality. When they were pressed to talk in more concrete terms about personal experiences, they would cite examples of gender discrimination. However, they would particularise such treatment and see it as 'just a fact of life' (ibid.: 11). In contrast, opponents of gender inequality (the resistance position) explicitly made links between their own experiences and their sense of pervasive, society-wide, gender inequalities. The largest group, the accommodators, offered a rather more mixed set of responses revealing 'ambivalent emotions and evaluations regarding their sex roles and situations' (ibid.: 18). Lam argues that this group used mixed principles of justice in their evaluations of gender inequalities. They saw unequal treatment as unfair only if they saw women and men as appropriate reference groups for one another. Lam argues that her respondents used a principle of equality when challenging what they saw as double standards for women and men, and a principle of differentiation in assessing different gender roles. Inequality, Lam seems to be saying, is often justified through the principle of differentiation, as for example when one of her respondents says gender inequality is:

> Fair. It's fair because both sexes experience advantages and disadvantages . . . it's natural that males have to earn more money, to have better careers . . . That's fair enough! Men also suffer . . . women have the opportunity to quit working . . . [They have] almost the same [suffering].
>
> (Lam 2004: 19)

Lam says of the accommodating respondents:

> Holding double principles of differentiation and equality obscures the perceptions of gender inequality. Their pragmatic responses sensitize us to the crucial interplay between principles of justice and various locations in perceiving gender inequalities.
>
> (Lam 2004: 20)

For Lam, differentiation is a principle of justice although we could argue that the 'principle of differentiation' is simply a statement that people do not explicitly evaluate the situation as one of inequality. Where people believe that social differentiation is natural or appropriate, and that there is some balance between contribution and reward, the order may well be seen as fair. Indeed it may rarely be subjected to this kind of justice evaluation if it is deemed 'the way things are', a given. Clearly then social differentiation is important to theorising people's diverse attitudes and frames of reference in evaluating the legitimacy, or otherwise, of inequalities, but whether or not people even perceive social asymmetries as aspects of inequality cannot be taken for granted. Unlike social scientists the interviewees were not making connections between proximate differences and aggregate level inequalities.

What is particularly interesting is Lam's point that women only saw gender arrangements as unfair where they took men as an appropriate reference point: and this was something many did not do when it came to assessing gender differentiated roles. Comparison processes are crucial to perceived injustices. We need to better understand whom people take as their points of comparison in making evaluations about their circumstances.

In the next section I explore the ways in which some recent claims about class have become stranded in a gap between analytic categories and empirical evidence. A crucial component of an adequate reconstruction is a more sophisticated understanding of social comparison processes.

8.4 Inequality inside, or inside inequality?

8.4.1 Theorising milieu: the example of class

The issue of whether or not people 'see' and evaluate social structure and their place within it is a core theme in debates about class. A recurrent theme has been the question of why people seemingly acquiesce to the extent they do in an unequal and unjust social hierarchy. This question has found a new poignancy in recent decades with the growth of social inequalities across the British population. Some writers have argued that class can no longer be considered a key aspect of people's social identifications, and yet class inequalities and processes are seen by analysts to be still very important, possibly increasingly so. How it is that class referents appear weaker; and why has class seemingly been eclipsed in popular consciousness? Phillips suggested that:

> Contemporary culture has become astonishingly fatalistic about economic inequalities, regarding them either as undesirable but inevitable, or even as positively fair.
>
> (Phillips 1999: 34)

Various writers have sought to understand processes shaping this apparent historical tendency away from a 'class reading' of social inequality. For Savage the remaking of individualisation

> allows the creation of a society that routinely reproduces social inequality at the same time as deflecting the attention . . . so making the issue of social inequality largely 'invisible' and somehow 'uninteresting'.
>
> (Savage 2000: 159)

In Chapter 6 we saw other writers addressing the same question (e.g. Furlong and Cartmel 1997; Arnot 2002). A linked argument is that the rise of market ideologies and a new individualism extant in society, along with linked government policies, amount to a pattern of 'responsibilisation' (Rose 1999;

Reay 1998c; Arnot 2002; Walkerdine *et al.* 2001). In the absence of class-based explanations of social inequality in popular and political discourse, the argument runs, the working classes are no longer entitled to a sense of unfairness. In this way class is individualised, increasingly hidden from view. Many authors, then, argue that class processes are no less significant than in the past, but emphasise their hidden nature. In respect of our question about perceptions of fairness then, this would mean that people are relatively acquiescent in the face of unfairness because the nature of the unfair distribution of resources is hidden. Much recent writing here is a variation on the same theme.

The question about the 'surprising' absence of class in popular discourse is repeated in research into social identities. A puzzle which has beset class theory and been strongly articulated in recent years has been the ongoing recognition of the importance of class-related inequalities and their reproduction, even exacerbation, over recent decades, and the accompanying evidence that, whilst people see Britain as a class society, they do not typically articulate a class identity for themselves.

Several writers have been influenced by Bourdieu in developing a culturalist perspective on class inequalities and classed subjectivities. A key theme here is the move away from a model of class as a structure, theoretically distinguishable from individual action, to a more dynamic processual account in which structural position and individual action are indivisible.

> The relationship between the social agent and the world is not that between a subject (or a consciousness) and an object but a relationship of 'ontological complicity' – or 'mutual possession' . . . between habitus, as the socially constituted principle of perception and appreciation, and the world which determines it.
>
> (Wacquant 1992: 20)

In his extended review of of Bourdieu's approach, Wacquant refers to 'cohesion without concept', a unity between subjective and objective in which 'consciousness is nothing other than the dialectic of milieu and action' (ibid.: 21).

Drawing in particular on Bourdieu's concept of habitus a number of theorists have explored 'inequality inside', that is how people 'carry' inequality as part of their outlook, part of how they know the world. Differing positions and access to differing levels of resources, material and cultural, differing perceptions of self-worth and entitlement, combine to re-affirm boundaries and the reproduction of inequalities. Additionally a desire to 'fit in', mix and associate with social similars feeds into such a process. Class is about diverse dispositions, and dispossessions, as those with fewer resources are marginalised culturally and morally as well as economically (e.g. Skeggs 1997; Reay 1998a; Sayer 2000; Ball 2003; Walkerdine *et al.* 2001). Class then is construed not as a description of structural position, at least not primarily, but as a set of dispositions and practices. In this way class and inequality operates 'through' people and is best construed as an internal disposition as much as a social position. Various writers have argued that individuals dis-identify with class membership in seeking to distance themselves from the 'injuries of class' (e.g. Sayer 2002; Skeggs 1997). For Sayer, the fact that people tend to not identify as members of a class is a form of criticism of a system in which moral worth is attached to class position. In refusing to classify themselves people are delivering a moral indictment of the class system (Sayer 2002). Writing in this area helps to illuminate the reproduction of social inequalities as well as developing a framework for articulating the cohesion of structure and action. However, it is notable that there is a discrepancy between researchers' categories (of class) and assumptions of its relevance and interviewees' own perceptions. This discrepancy is interpreted in terms of resistance (and parallels interpretations of later life discussed in Chapter 6). An alternative view, elaborated below, is that the rejection by people of class labels should be read less as a moral indictment of the class structure as a whole, a refusal of its injustice, but rather more generally, in terms of the non-salience of class categories for people's immediate, lived experience. Again, what we see is a coherence of social location and perception, not disjuncture. From this viewpoint, and as argued by Savage (2000) and Bottero (2004), it might be said that to achieve 'cohesion without concept' (after Wacquant 1992), a melding of disposition and position, would require analysts to drop, or at least significantly delimit, the category of class.

Savage and his colleagues argue that, when asked if they feel themselves to belong to a social class, most people express a significant degree of ambivalence. In their research project on social networks and leisure (Savage *et al.* 2001) interviewees were asked for their views about Britain as a classless society, and whether they saw themselves as members of a social class. Typically people were ambivalent and the authors argue that in general people do not clearly identify with a particular social class. When asked if they would describe themselves as belonging to a class some typical responses were:

> 'No. I don't think I would really but, er, you know. No.'
> 'I'd just say ordinary' (Savage 2000: 111).
>
> 'No, I just think I am me, and this is how I am, take me or leave me, you know' (Savage *et al.* 2001: 882).

Where people did identify with a class it was often the case that they would qualify such statements. It was rare that they articulated an unambiguous sense of class identification. Further, where they do refer to themselves in class terms it is typically to articulate differentiation from others above and below, rather than to express belonging. For Savage, people see Britain as a class-ridden society, but do not readily themselves identify with a social class, since they see themselves rather as 'individuals'. Savage argues that people often identified as middling, or ordinary, desiring to be seen as themselves rather than as 'social ciphers':

> [T]he need to 'perform' individual identity can be related to class aware frameworks which celebrate the advantages of being free from power networks and hierarchical structures.
>
> (Savage 2000: 118)

This might be an unduly individualistic account of people's ethics. In insisting on their individuality, their refusal of generalising categories, people are not *necessarily* seeing themselves as free from power networks. Clearly people are not unaware of the fact they are placed within an unequal society. As Savage himself states:

> [P]eople seem keen to invoke a distinction between their personal lives – in which class is rarely seen as a salient issue – and the world 'out there', the world of politics, the economy, the media, and so forth. Here class is often regarded as having a more important presence. Identities are relational constructs, in which individuals develop a sense of their own selves by comparing themselves with 'meaningful' others.
>
> (Savage 2000: 117)

Savage indicates the importance of milieux, and relations to others, as important to people's sense of themselves, and their self-description in terms of ordinariness rather than in class terms.

Bottero (2004) develops the same themes but argues that full recognition of the importance of patterns of social association and interaction means that we should move more decisively beyond class categories to reach a more inclusive theorisation of social hierarchy and inequality. In such a theorisation 'class' needs to be located as a particular claim or 'vision' of the nature of hierarchy. The argument here is that a variegated structure is experienced and translated in action first and foremost at this proximate level of social relations. Class may be seen as a category of relevance for describing the social hierarchy, but subjectivities are shaped and expressed in specific contexts and patterns of association, and are not direct reflections on the structure as a whole. It is unsurprising that people do not self-identify in class terms, Bottero argues, because social interaction is strongly constrained and shaped by people's position within the social hierarchy (Bottero 2004). Rather than construe social inequality in terms of class, and resolve the riddle of why people do not identify themselves in class terms, if we acknowledge that routine social interactions, preferences for mixing with 'people like us' and linked patterns of association, then there is no reason we would expect people to see themselves as members of a class.

> The people we are closest to tend to come from a very similar social location to our own, and it appears that our choices are governed both by contiguity and by the social comfort that comes from associating with 'people like us' . . . Since hierarchy is embedded in the most intimate social relationships, and 'social location' and 'culture' are united in the structured nature of everyday social practices, hierarchical practices emerge as 'second nature', unremarkable and ordinary.
>
> (Bottero 2004: 989)

Patterns of association which are predominantly with social similars means that despite being situated in a hierarchical structure people do not routinely reflect upon that structure. For Bottero, analysis of social hierarchy, and not class *per se*, is the more appropriate general focus for research in socio-economic inequalities.

Rather than ask why, and why now, people do not much identify in class terms, the more pertinent question for Bottero and others is why it is in particular contexts that class discourse and organisation acquire importance (Bottero 2004; Therborn 2002; Cannadine 2000). It is against routine processes of hierarchical reproduction, which work against holistic justice evaluations, that we should locate the specificity of class claims when they are made. For Cannadine:

> [C]lass is best understood as being what culture does to inequality and social structure: investing the many anonymous individuals and unfathomable collectivities in society with shape and significance, by moulding our perceptions of the unequal social world we live in. As with landscape, this is partly a matter of the social structure itself, which does change and evolve in terms of numbers, occupation, wealth and location. But this is also a matter of politics and perceptions, rhetoric and language, feeling and sentiment. And just as the meaning of landscape is often contested, so the meaning of social structure is disputed, not so much in terms of language, as in terms of the different models of it that are employed by different people at different times for different purposes.
>
> (Cannadine 2000: 188)

How does this relate to our discussion about perceptions of fairness? It implies that people do not routinely experience social inequalities as unfair or illegitimate. Inequality *may* go unquestioned. It may be that attributions of moral worth are internalised or engender social suffering but this may occur without the general social order necessarily being subject to most people's justice evaluations. In everyday lives people make relational comparisons but do so within a limited range and also in diverse contexts whose contours are often experienced as givens.

The chapter opened with a question as to whether people are newly acquiescent in the face of structural inequalities. The analysis here suggests that resistance to such inequalities is a political act which draws on and makes claims about the nature of such inequality. However, standard social processes tend not to orient people to reflect on the social structure as a whole. Consequently we do not need to see people as newly filled with an individualising ideology, nor see people as celebrating their own individualism in asserting distance from the class structure, nor see them as offering a critique of the immorality of the class structure. An alternative explanation of the absence of expected protest requires no such *deus ex machina* concepts but operates with a different model of social structural differentiation. This model takes much fuller account of how people orient themselves to proximate contexts of interaction, association and social comparison. In the critique of class and identification it is when we dispense with generalising class categories and examine people's position of relative advantage and disadvantage within a continuous hierarchy that we can see more clearly a coherence of disposition and position, of subjective and objective.

In the next section I consider further two themes alluded to already. One is the issue of how individual decisions and actions can serve to reproduce social inequalities without this necessarily being a desired outcome. The second relates to the distinction between the proximate social contexts which provide the immediate setting for people's lived experiences and outlooks, and the broader social order, to which people do at times orient themselves but not necessarily in their daily lives and sense of self. Nevertheless, attitudes here have important implications for policy interventions.

8.4.2 *Social positioning and the reproduction of inequalities*

Much recent research with its interest in cultural patterns tends to focus in particular on overt values and beliefs but it is crucial to recognise how routinised expectations and linked patterns of behaviour themselves contribute to reproducing a social order in which there are very significant continuities in the ordering of inequality. These continuities relate both to the general structure of relative advantage and disadvantage, and to continuities over generations in people's positioning within this structure.

I will consider some recent research into schooling and the reproduction of social inequalities through the example of parental decisions and preferences around their children's schooling. Writers here in particular emphasise the classed nature of social practices, and are interested in the ways in which inequalities are 'encoded', an implicit and ineradicable part of people's self and disposition (e.g. Reay 1998a, b and c; Ball 2003; Walkerdine *et al.* 2001). For example, Reay argues that in home–school interactions it is a sense of confidence and of self-entitlement which marks out middle-class parents in contrast to working-class parents whose competencies and confidence are undermined in systematic ways (Reay 1998a; and cf. Ball 2003). We can see an alignment of subjectivities and social position. Following the writers being reviewed, I use the terminology of class in the discussion below, but in light of the preceding discussion I see it as a shorthand for unequal social positions within a continuous hierarchy.

Reay has conducted research into processes shaping the reproduction of inequalities through education, with particular reference to class varying relations to schooling, and higher education (Reay 1998a, b). In her 1998 study, Reay conducted interviews with parents of children in two schools in inner London, one predominantly ethnically white and middle-class, the other multi-ethnic and predominantly working-class. Reay documents the extent to which working-class and middle-class parents were committed to their children's education, spending large amounts of time, energy and money in supporting their children's schooling. In particular she argues that class reproduction, through schooling, is largely underpinned through the practical and emotional labour of mothers (Reay 1998a). Significant class differentiation occurred through the kinds of support available to children and modes of parent–school interaction, amongst other things. The women interviewed were all quite heavily involved in their children's education, and sought to support their children, but the differing contexts and resources available to them meant that working-class mothers were positioned in such a way that their efficacy was undermined, in contrast to the middle-class mothers. For example, in respect of parents' relations with teachers, Reay highlights the ways in which middle-class mothers acted on their concerns and ensured they were recognised and taken on board by schools. Working-class mothers may have expressed similar concerns but were less likely to make demands of school staff or to seek changes. They had fewer material and cultural resources, lower educational qualifications, less knowledge about the system, and so on. So whilst they held similar concerns they were less equipped to act on their concerns, and lacked middle-class mothers' sense of entitlement. Consequently 'Middle class children's activities, and mothers' work in support of them, constituted a systematic laying down of educational and cultural advantage; a sedimentation of privilege' (Reay 1998b: 201).

Reay, Ball and other educational writers have been exercised by the ways in which the expansion of school choice may contribute to and exacerbate social inequalities. Changes here have been dubbed a move to a 'parentocracy' (Brown 1997). Ball explores the ways in which middle-class choices, preferences and dispositions are articulated in respect of school choice, particularly over the appropriateness of comprehensive schooling for their children (Ball 2003). He argues that belonging is important in understanding the preferences of parents for their children, but also as part of the process through which boundaries are maintained and associated class divisions reproduced:

> [D]ifferentiation is enacted as much through belonging, through a recognition of mutuality, fit and identification, as it is through distinctions.
>
> (Ball 2003: 176)

Using data available through various qualitative research projects Ball explores the perceptions and values of middle-class parents in respect of school choice and educational preferences. He explores the ways in which middle-class parents seek to ensure the best for their children, including their desire for their children to fit in to the educational and general ethos and environment of a school, and to be stretched intellectually. He talks then about how parents want their children to go to the right kind of school for them, where they would be with others 'like us' (p. 60). This desire for social similarity Ball interprets very clearly as being expressed in class terms, and as entailing an othering, a differentiation from people 'not like us'. As well as emphasising the reproduction of boundaries *between* schools through the operation of school choice and linked middle-class strategising, Ball stresses the importance of boundaries within schools, and middle-class parents' preferences for streaming, as a vehicle for attaining educational goals but also for insulating or protecting children from 'corrupting', that is working-class, influences (Ball 2003).

Ball's analysis echoes Savage and Reay's arguments about the importance to people of mixing with 'people like us', particularly in parents seeking a school where they feel their child will 'fit in'. In situating their choices Ball points to the importance of locale and context; and conversations at the school gate in reinforcing 'what people like us' want. Clearly this is one factor amongst many in shaping schooling decisions and actions, issues which cut deep into the psyche of many parents. Ball, too, seeks to understand the lack of salience of class categories in people's sense of themselves, and the processes by which class-related inequalities get reproduced. His interpretation is that 'class happens' through practices and dispositions: 'an activation of resources and social identities' (p. 176). The aggregate of individual choices serves to re-create and reproduce social divisions, divisions which may be exacerbating in the current context of market-oriented policies.

In this context we might ask when, how and why do people relate their decisions and actions to their perceptions of the wider society in which they live? Do perceptions of social justice, for example, play a role? Ball is interested in the ethos, the principles middle-class parents evoke when making educational choices for their children. Some try to seek positional advantage, with a view to maximising future returns on their children's education; some identify with the comprehensive ideal, the importance of social diversity and the value of a decent education. Many of Ball's quotes show parents seeking to do the best for their children. For Ball this motivation often means that socially progressive principles are held contingently, as parents put their children first, and orient to practical issues, ahead of abstract principles. Ball sees a tension for many between doing the best for their children and reconciling this (or not) with a vision of the social good. Ball does seem unsure about the motives of many middle-class parents, it is as if they cannot truly hold onto progressive principles, or the fact they do so contingently shows such principles to be weakly held, not really principles at all. After all, he says, 'Some parents were frank enough to indicate that their principles might not have operated in the same way in a different locality' (p. 123).

In this way we might use the evidence as a parallel to Savage's comment that 'the brute realities of social inequality . . . are constantly effaced by a middle class, individualized culture that fails to register the social implications of its routine actions' (Savage 2000: 159). Ball offers a similar analysis, emphasising the ethical dilemmas faced by parents but also the commitment by some 'to achieve maximal positional advantage for their child' (Ball 2003: 115). Whilst no doubt many parents embrace choice in an educational market and the opportunity to maximise their children's educational credentials, many of Ball's respondents were not at all celebrating 'the advantages of being free from power networks' (referred to by Savage and cited earlier). We should qualify arguments of a middle-class individualism. Middle-class interviewees were clearly seeking a good education for their children but doing so, as Ball shows, with some awareness of the divisiveness of class-stratified schooling. Further it remains the case that many parents did not express their desire for a good education for their children in class-exclusive terms. The desire of middle-class parents to ensure that *their* children were not held back by other 'types' of child is expressed by parents not in class terms, but in terms of educational aspiration. That the latter so easily slides into a seemingly implied reference to class says as much about flaws in the educational system and the correspondence between educational success and position in the social economic hierarchy, as it does about a middle-class desire for exclusiveness. The contradiction identified by Ball between being a good parent and a bad citizen should be located as much with government and policy-makers as with 'classed' practices. A good parent wants a *good* education for their children. A bad citizen wants a good education for *their* children (exclusively). In a more progressive context a desire for a good education for one's own children would square with a desire for a good education for all children. A truly well resourced and effectively structured school system would make good parenting and good citizenship much more compatible than they often are at present.

In this section I have described some examples of research showing the ways in which diverse orientations, expectations and resources contribute to reproducing social inequalities. For Ball issues of justice and fairness do obtain, but more at a level of 'abstract principle' and as a loose guide to action rather than providing any tighter prescription, since practical concerns and the needs of loved ones come first, and may supersede general principles regarding the social good. In this division we can see a parallel with that discussed earlier, between relatively tightly bound criteria of social belonging and notions of society 'out there'. However, as our discussion has shown, people clearly also have principled understandings of, and attitudes towards, general social arrangements. The task for social intervention must be to design frameworks through which there can be an expansion of social belonging, and through which private choices are consistent with the expansion of the public good.

8.5 Conclusion

How do people see their position on society? How do they perceive their lot, and when is this an issue for them, and how does it shape their experience, and propensity to act to change it? Researchers have moved on from presuming that interests are given by different social positions, and stress the importance of better accessing people's perceptions of self and society. In part this shift occurred as a response to the gap between descriptions of people's social position, and predictions about how they would perceive and act upon it. However, paradoxically analysts still often arrive at a position where actors' perceptions do not align with analysts' categories. Consequently it is deduced that a gap exists between individual-level apprehensions of social inequalities and objective structures of inequality. Particular concepts are then invoked to rescue analysis which on the face of it is contradicted by empirical evidence. So, for example, theorists insist there is a new culture of the individual which prevents people from seeing the true functioning of the social system. Here the gap between subjective and objective is filled by cultural ideological processes, of responsibilisation for example. For others, the retreat of social explanations of individual fortunes means that individual denial of class identification reveals moral resistance, an implicit critique of a class structure. For some writers this is why people deny class membership and yet live classed lives. However, all this fails to register and analyse sufficiently the diverse social contexts in which people perceive and evaluate the social world. Once again a gap between researchers' analytic categories and social actors' perceptions is interpreted as an aspect of the social system, a disjuncture between the subjective and objective, rather than as a problem of explanation. A more adequate analysis of inequality and perceptions of fairness and of class requires a much more robust theorisation of how people are embedded in diverse milieux, and what they see as salient, or not, in their own social experiences. A more resourceful explanation would not cut across social actors' understandings, but rather accommodate them, take them as a particular lens on aspects of the social structure, and locate them within a renewed conception of that structure.

The working of social processes means that most people do not routinely reflect on the overall social structure as part of their everyday practice, unless they are taking a particular, politicised, stance on social arrangements. Nevertheless, people are aware of injustice and inequalities, and aggregate attitudinal data on income inequalities shows that people disapprove, in general, of the extent of social inequality. The qualitative evidence from the example of parental decisions around children's schooling shows that their desires to do the right thing for their own children are often contextualised as part of a desire for a better comprehensive education system. Whilst people may not routinely take a politicised stance on issues of inequality, indeed may not even reflect on the issues unless specifically required to do so, it is incumbent on forward-thinking politicians and policy-makers to develop the mechanisms through which abstractly held desires for a better, more just, society can be translated into progressive social change.

9 Conclusion

In sociology there has been a renewed interest in normative and cultural processes and yet, paradoxically, current concepts and methodological preferences pull away from a social understanding of such processes. This generates a particular dilemma of explanation, given the importance of current social changes. This book has developed a new conceptual perspective and elaborated it through analysis of a series of substantive social domains relating to family, work, care, the life course, ethnicity, class and perceptions of fairness. The perspective offers a new way of slicing into aspects of the social world and contributes to a renewal of *social* explanation.

Within sociological theory and research, the cultural turn has been influential and many seek a more detailed and nuanced understanding of the texture of social life. Many writers across diverse areas have recently stressed the key importance of norms, values and agency in the reshaping of social life. For some this is a self-conscious move away from earlier structuralist theories which allowed little conceptual space for individual autonomy and agency. The renewed interest in norms and cultural process is well placed, given that they are at the heart of human experience and social arrangements. However, there are a number of difficulties in how we best conceptualise these issues. Qualitative research into people's experiences, perceptions and constructions of diverse social worlds has shed new light on aspects of the social fabric, but there are real difficulties in understanding the links between belief and action at the micro level, and general social processes. In quantitative research, such as attitudinal survey analysis, the normative and the social often appear to comprise two planes of analysis, and again it is difficult to reveal connections between them in any detailed way. Norms and values often appear 'free floating'. They are not adequately linked to social relations and contexts.

The difficulty connecting subjective evaluations and social structural relations is not simply a consequence of the methodological issues indicated above. Rather, the separation of norms and social arrangements is reproduced within influential theories. For example, within theories of individualisation there is an argument that volition, choice and agency are partly 'disembedded' from their social contexts. Individuals are seen to operate within institutional constraints but these are at a layer removed and individuals' values and choices are under-theorised. Within debates about diversity and difference there is a tendency to stress cultural process but again there is a risk that this becomes free-floating of social contexts, as there is relatively limited research on the articulation of normative and social process. The difficulties are echoed elsewhere in sociological explanation. Whilst many mainstream sociological researchers would still stress structure, and especially constraint, as a central feature of social life, we are short of tools for describing the nature of this 'structure'. This is a serious problem. The separation of norms and values on the one hand and extant social relations on the other obstructs our ability to develop a more adequate understanding of social change and social diversity.

The alternative perspective developed in this book draws on a number of concepts. At its heart is a consideration of the links between social relationality, difference and interconnection on the one hand and norms, values and identifications on the other. The perspective locates agency, values, choices and routinised practices as inseparable from changing social relations. Shifts in general contexts of reproductive decision-making and of gendered identifications and divisions were explored in Chapters 3 and 4. Chapter 5 explored more closely the shaping of diverse dispositions and identifications relating to gender, work and care, and the latter part of the book took social context and social positioning as a focus for rethinking the articulation of subjectivities and wider social processes. In the following I draw out some of the main issues.

Family life and organisation underwent significant transformations in the last third of the twentieth century. Difficulties explaining current family demographic changes are in part due to the analytic separation of norms and social relations. For example it is commonly asserted that new aspirations for independence, especially amongst women, entail a 'freeing' of agency from social structural processes. It is particularly informative to reflect on historical change. Evidence on the first fertility decline at the end of the nineteenth century reveals the coherence of radically new kinds of choices and behaviours which might at first glance parallel those being made today. No longer bound by older social constraints people were seemingly more autonomous from structural process. However, the crucial issue is to locate and contextualise new kinds of motivation, choice and behaviour. To do so helps reveal the contours of social structural change. The period from the 1870s to the 1930s reveals a pattern of significant social change, with the dramatic historical decline in fertility, changes in generational and gendered positions and an entrenchment of a breadwinner mode of social organisation. Many factors contributed to the first fertility decline and it is a complex issue of explanation. However, a crucial component of the decline was the shifting social position of children and adults, and linked changes in the organisation of interdependence, of exchange and support across the generations. Changing gendered relations also fed into fertility decline. We see a context in which the reshaping of social relations was bound up with radically new kinds of motivation and choice. It was a clear demonstration of the force of agency and yet it would be meaningless to separate out such agency and choice from the social structural context of which it was a part.

We see also in the earlier period a meshing of change in the relative positioning of different groups (children and parents, women and men) and normative shifts in assumptions about their proper role and social positioning. We can see how, in a context of significant social and economic restructuring, norms fed into altered social relations, a key example being constructions of proper masculine and feminine identities. The early part of the twentieth century saw a hardening of gendered divisions of labour, and of separate home and labour market spheres. Women and men acquired a new positioning in conjunction with the entrenchment of particular assumptions about their proper social roles. There is evidence of a shift in social identifications, and a willingness by people to accept social arrangements if not as natural, certainly as a fact of social life. In this way we can see an example of the reshaping of social positions, of gendered difference and interdependence, and a reshaping of normative constructions and assumptions.

The historical perspective holds important lessons for today. We do not see a retreat of structural process in social change, as is often assumed. People respond to the new contexts in which they find themselves, and the link between perceptions, actions and the wider social structural context itself remains very strong. The first fertility decline of the latter third of the nineteenth century provides a fascinating point of comparison with the changes in family demography occurring in the last third of the twentieth century. Some writers have argued that these recent changes are bound up with a pattern of individualisation and a linked expansion in people's autonomy from structural constraint and cultural mores. Whilst many people do have new spaces in which to act and new levels of autonomy, it is a mistake to interpret this as a 'retreat' of social structural forces and a concomitant freeing of individual agency. Rather we need a more nuanced understanding of structure, not just in terms of choice and constraint, but in terms of altered contours and contexts in which people make sense of their lives, and in which some courses of action are much more likely to be 'chosen' than others. Patterns of deferral in ages at parenthood and increasing rates of childlessness are not an outcome of individualisation but are linked to the reshaping of the ties that bind social groups and the linked repositioning of groups. Change in women's position particularly has been linked to expanded educational and employment commitments and rising aspirations for independence and a measure of autonomy. As in the case of the first fertility decline we can interpret new kinds of motivation and choice, and the absence of choice, as an integral part of the changing social and economic context.

The repositioning of women in the latter part of the twentieth century has been one of the most significant and remarked upon dimensions of recent social change. In relation to employment and the family we see important continuities of inequality and new departures, including new patterns of diversity and class-related inequalities. There has been an erosion of the breadwinner pattern of social reproduction as women's paid work becomes more important in the economy as a whole and in household-level employment arrangements. We can see the importance here of normative change and its link to changes in the social positioning of women and men. For example, both gendered claims and market-related claims have, in the context of industrial and economic restructuring, repositioned women and men and reshaped gender as a dimension of difference in the economy. We can see shifts in normative and evaluative dispositions at the level of the individual, which link to these general changes. In Chapter 5 I took as a focus work, care and commitment at a particularly interesting point in the family life course, and focused on the experiences and dispositions of parents of young children, since it is amongst this group that women have most significantly altered their employment participation patterns over recent decades. This is a particularly useful focus too for exploring recent arguments of an expanding importance of values in shaping people's (especially women's) decisions and actions around the care of young children. Within preference theory and elsewhere there is an emphasis on values as now more autonomous from structure and thus more significant to understanding people's decisions and behaviours. Again, however, we are without explanation of the nature of such values and decisions, and we have no sense of how they are socially grounded. The analyses of Chapter 5 revealed clear evidence of continuities across people's social position and their dispositions. There is no evidence of a chronic gap between dispositions and social structure. In general, women and men have altered their social locations and linked identities. Emergent dispositions are consistent with changes in the general social context, and accord with how people are positioned. For example, across a growing proportion of the population of women with young children, paid work has become more normalised and routinised than in the past. We can understand significant shifts in patterns of behaviour and linked dispositions as an integral part of a reconfiguring of contexts of social action. In short we see a mutuality of the subjective and objective even in a context of significant change.

The meshing of subjective experiences and social structural processes must not be taken as meaning that change is without problems. The difficulties of reconciling paid work and family commitments are heightened in the current context, and whilst women and men both carry the costs and stresses, it is women who most acutely experience the difficulties here, given the specificities of their social positioning.

Through analysing developments in gender, work and family in periods of social change I highlighted how problems of explanation occur and how these often stem from a presumed or implicit analytic gap between normative processes and the social order. The perspective developed in the book allows us to conceptualise and analyse the mutuality between norms and social relations. In consequence it allows not just a new lens, but new analytic purchase, on social change in family organisation and in gender relations which is all too often read as chaotic.

In seeking to understand contemporary social life in a context of change many theorists have made an analytic leap between structure and agency, and between general social arrangements and individual dispositions and subjectivities. Part of the problem here lies in the attempt to make too direct a link between the social structure (as seen by the analyst) and individual level perceptions of and reactions to that structure. Such points of comparison generate a gap, where for example it is asserted that individuals fail to see patterns of oppression which disadvantage them, or they offer resistance where they do see oppression. This diagnosis is an outcome of an analysis in which people's perceptions and orientations are seen to be out of line with their social position. Part of the problem is that the latter is read in light of the analyst's overview of the system as a whole. However, in their routine actions people are practitioners rather than theorists and, as such, their dispositions and actions are best interpreted as being linked to diverse social positions. This layer of analysis, of people's social position as experienced and interpreted by those people, is something of a missing dimension of explanation.

Chapters 5 to 8 continued the analysis of the mutuality of subjective experience and wider social relations through incorporating micro level empirical evidence. Chapter 5, as just indicated, furthered the analysis of changes in women's social position and identifications and dispositions. In the subsequent chapters I developed in more depth the focus on social context, and the meshing of individual perceptions and dispositions on the one hand and social arrangements on the other. The domains explored in the latter part of the book included life course transitions, aspects of ethnicity, and perceptions of class and social inequalities. The focus on social contexts and social positioning is not simply a case of bringing in a layer of analysis which is insufficiently addressed in the literature. It is partly this, but also consideration of social context at this 'meso' level requires us to rethink social processes more widely. The adequate analysis of social position and experience allows us to tackle riddles of explanation and offer a more resourceful understanding of social diversity.

Within studies on the life course, within research into ethnicity and research on class and inequality, there are many examples of analytic separation of subjective experience and evaluations on the one hand and social arrangements on the other. There is a tendency to make a presumption of too direct a link between people's perceptions and outlooks and their position within a general structure, with the latter insufficiently grounded in an empirical understanding of how people themselves see their position. Such an analysis is not simply a 'missing component' or part of the jigsaw which will complete the picture. Analysis of how people perceive their own position can be part of a reinvigorated conceptualisation of the social structural arrangements of which they are a part. It can help reveal how diverse contexts are composed, and how they articulate with the whole.

The issue of how position and disposition link is not simply a case of using standard socio-economic 'coordinates' (of class, ethnicity, life course, gender) to map social position. Rather than make assumptions about how these presumed dimensions of difference have immediate relevance and purchase and shape people's experience and outlooks, we need to locate difference, and analyse when, where and how it is relevant.

For example, within studies of later life we witness a separating out of subjective experience and social arrangements. Writers have used metaphors which tend to position older people 'at the edges' of society. Later life identities, where they are used as evidence, are then often read against theoretical assumptions about the positioning of older people as 'other'. There is a risk that behaviour in an older person is read quite differently from the same behaviour in a younger person, and that presumptions about the difference of later life become reified in conceptual frameworks. It is imperative that we locate, rather than assume, social difference if we are to better understand the experience of those in later life, and analyse processes shaping inequalities over the life course. Studies of youth have been less likely to consider youth as a group but to focus on intra-cohort inequalities, especially in the context of recently changing transitions from youth to adult status. Again, however, writers diagnose a gap between subjective and objective, and presume it to be filled with new ideologies of individualisation and responsibilisation. This is a feature too of some recent arguments about social class and its demise as a significant dimension of identity and solidarity. More productively we can build on alternative insights into subjectivities which reveal them to be closely and strongly linked to the social location in which people find themselves. For example, their positioning in relation to others, how they perceive their position, and when, why and how they compare their position to that of others are core components in a theorisation of social context. We can read the experience and identifications of young adults, as of older people, as very much consistent with their social positioning. The improved specification and analysis of social positioning and context contributes to breaking with the sterile structure agency division and allows much greater insight into social diversity and change in the shape of life course trajectories and inequalities.

The evidence on youth and later life points to the significance of social location and an ability to better conceptualise social diversity. In the discussion of ethnicity and belonging, and of class and perceptions of inequality and fairness, I focused in more detail on aspects of social context as revealed through empirical data. Again we can clearly see an alignment between disposition and position in the domains explored here. This consistency requires analysis of the nature of social diversity, and the nature of social contexts under examination. Much debate on class and ethnicity has focused on the cultural making and embedding of difference but this has not been matched by analysis of the ways in which cultural constructions mesh with social contexts. In discussion of ethnicity and belonging I explored social contexts through rather different kinds of empirical evidence. I explored perceptions of belonging and identification as these related to social positioning, networks and patterns of association, with reference to diverse primary and secondary data and evidence. The data helps reveal the articulation of beliefs and social circumstances, the latter examined with reference primarily to patterns of association and interaction. This kind of account moves us away from presumptions of racialised difference to a more nuanced contextual analysis of when different understandings and constructions of ethnicity, difference and social belonging hold purchase.

If recent decades have seen a growing interest in aspects of cultural diversity and recognition politics, they have also seen a decline in the importance of class-based claims and politics, at least as expressed in the language of class. Across a range of surveys and qualitative research people are found not to self-identify in terms of class, and sociologists have asked why, when class-related inequalities are so important in shaping diverse life chances, class should have quite limited relevance as an aspect of people's expressed identifications. The presumed discrepancy between social position and disposition is again frequently read as an ideological gap, or as a celebration of individual freedom, or pattern of moral resistance. In each case a gap is identified between subjective experience and objective social location. However, analysis of social positioning which more fully takes on board evidence on how people see their own position, and against whom they compare it, allows a different interpretation. In this reinterpretation there is a coherence between subjective experiences of diverse social positions and the highly differentiated objective social order. An improved understanding of such consistency would allow a step change in analysis of the reproduction of social inequalities.

Evidence on perceptions of social inequality reveals ways in which evaluative judgements are made in relation to perceptions of what exists, and are thus themselves partly shaped by people's social position. However, whilst we can map people's position against standard indicators we will have a poor sense of their experience, perceptions and evaluations unless we know how they perceive their position and against what they adjudge it. Crucial to understanding social action in this domain is a more adequate concept of how, when and why people perceive their situation as unjust and act upon this perception.

The book has put relationality, norms and social contexts at the heart of analysis, and at the heart of a renewed concept of social process. In so doing it has developed new resources for understanding change and diversity. It is hoped that such resources may contribute to a broader renewal of social explanation.

Notes

1 Baldwin describes how social solidarity is as much an outcome of struggle between opposing groups as it is a product of agreement. He examines how welfare developments often emerged from cross-class alliances where perceptions of shared interest were contingent, emerging in historically particular circumstances (Baldwin 1990).
2 Zelizer is referring to the American experience but her argument is widely presumed to hold salience for understanding the British cultural positioning of children, and Zelizer herself refers extensively to British experience.
3 The Total Period Fertility Rate (TPFR) is the aggregate of age-specific birth rates across all fertile ages in the reference year and can be interpreted as the average number of children a woman would have if she experienced the age-specific fertility rates of that year throughout her childbearing life.
4 The fertility replacement rate is 2.1.
5 Interestingly, in Sweden, where declining fertility rates witnessed a recovery from the latter part of the 1980s, the evidence suggests this was largely due to a 'catching up' by older women, commencing families and spacing children closer to one another (Springfeldt 1991).
6 We are grateful to the ESRC for funding the work of the ESRC Research Group for the Study of Care, Values and the Future of Welfare, which is based at the University of Leeds (award M564281001) See http://www.leeds.ac.uk/cava for more information.
7 The link between dispositions and circumstance is not straightforward. It may be that if people do not feel particularly strongly about something then their response may be based on their practical experience. However, this does not mean that we should treat such data as mere artefact. We might reflect also that much social action, even in a context of aggregate social change, may be fairly routinised or pragmatic, rather than necessarily value-driven.
8 The International Social Survey Programme (ISSP) is an international collaboration in which survey questions are asked across different countries to allow for comparison, and batteries of questions are included on a rolling basis in the British Social Attitudes Survey. The gender role attitudes are part of the ISSP.
9 Unless otherwise stated BSAS analysis is done by the author on original data made available by the National Centre for Social Research.
10 Women were asked whether a married woman should work if she has children under school age, and given these options: Ought to work if she's fit, it's up to her, should only work if she needs the money, ought to stay at home.
11 In the 2002 BSAS women were asked: Do you think that women should work outside the home full time, part time or not at all under these circumstances? – when there is a child under school age.

12 Pro maternal care is used as a shorthand to denote an attitude that care should be provided by mothers full time excepting during school hours for primary school aged children.

13 The Life as a Parent research was a small follow-on (pilot) project, conducted by the present author designed to generate data to complement the qualitative research done as the core of the CAVA research project. One purpose here was to generate quantifiable data on attitudes (comparable to BSAS data) and explore this in relation to both circumstances and more in-depth and diverse data on perceptions and values. The research comprised 102 interviews with parents of children aged 4 to 7 and attending schools in specific locales across Leeds. Schools were used as a point of access to parents. Wards and target schools were chosen to provide diversity along a range of socio-economic indicators. Three locales were chosen, two of which correspond to CAVA locales in the Leeds area (Duncan 2000a, b). In terms of social inequality the overall sample was 'middle ranging' – it encompassed a range of unequal situations, but not those in the most disadvantaged areas where unemployment rates are extremely high, since I wanted to select circumstances in which there was a realistic possibility of work for most residents, and some genuine scope for making choices and decisions in respect of employment participation. See Irwin 2004 for more detail.

14 The analysis in the text presents responses to open-ended questions amongst respondents favouring the part time 'solution' to the vignette. Some illustrative responses amongst those who favoured the full time 'solution' are follows:

> 'If she really wants the job it is something important to her. Being a mother is not all that she is. She can still strike up a healthy balance of work and family even if she is working full time';
>
> 'Because it's what she wants to do. She has a childminder to cover the hours and would be able to afford the childminder';
>
> 'Because she wants the job and if she gets it she can turn it down. It's a time in her life to start a career for the future'.

15 Sniderman and Carmines analyse data from surveys which question people in quite innovative ways on their attitudes to blacks and whites. One could question whether inviting respondents to discuss their attitudes to 'blacks' and 'whites' reifies stereotyping assumptions about the validity of grouping people on the basis of skin colour. However, some interesting attitudinal questions are asked in the survey. For example, the 'excuse experiment' questions provide a 'socially acceptable' reason for offering negative attitudes towards black people or white people, and found little evidence of what might be called underground racism amongst those consistently positive in their general attitudes 'towards blacks'. The point here is not to doubt the significance of under-reported racist attitudes, but to question the notion that there has been no change.

16 Amin (2002) draws on a similar argument of the meshing of cultural beliefs and social contexts, in making policy recommendations. He is critical of recent rhetoric around community cohesion and idealistic notions of shared community and argues that in 'communities without community' it would be of value to develop sites in which interactions and negotiations across ethnic divides are routinised, and that 'the gains of interaction need to be worked out in local sites of everyday encounter' (Amin 2002: 969) and through contexts which would encourage meaningful dialogue.

References

Abrams, P. (1982) *Historical Sociology*, Somerset: Open Books.

Afshar, H. and Maynard, M. (eds) (1994) *The Dynamics of 'Race' and Gender. Some feminist interventions*, London: Taylor & Francis Ltd.

Alexander, C. (2002) 'Beyond Black: re-thinking the colour/culture divide', *Ethnic and Racial Studies* 25, 4: 552–71.

Alwin, D.F., Braun, M. and Scott, J. (1992) 'The separation of work and the family: attitudes towards women's labour-force participation in Germany, Great Britain and the United States', *European Sociological Review* 8, 1: 13–37.

Amin, A. (2002) 'Ethnicity and the multicultural city: living with diversity', *Environment and Planning A* 34: 959–80.

Anderson, B. (1983) *Imagined Communities*, London: Verso.

Anderson, M. (1998) 'Highly restricted fertility: very small families in the British fertility decline', *Population Studies* 52: 177–99.

Anderson, M. (1985) 'The emergence of the modern life cycle in Britain', *Social History* 10, 1: 69–87.

Anthias, F. (2001) 'The material and the symbolic in theorizing social stratification: issues of gender, ethnicity and class', *British Journal of Sociology* 52, 3: 367–90.

Anthias, F. (1998) 'Rethinking social divisions: some notes towards a theoretical framework', *Sociological Review* 46, 3: 505–35.

Arber, S. and Ginn, J. (1995) 'The mirage of gender equality: occupational success in the labour market and within marriage', *British Journal of Sociology* 46, 1: 21–43.

Arber, S. and Ginn, J. (1991) *Gender and Later Life. A sociological analysis of resources and constraints*, London: Sage.

Aries, P. (1980) 'Two successive motivations for the declining birth rate in the West', *Population and Development Review* 6: 645–50.

Armitage, B. and Babb, P. (1996) 'Population review: (4) trends in fertility', *Population Trends* 84: 7–13, London: ONS.

Arnot, M. (2002) *Reproducing Gender? Essays on educational theory and feminist politics*, London: RoutledgeFalmer.

Arnot, M., David, M. and Weiner, G. (1999) *Closing the Gender Gap. Post war education and social change*, Cambridge: Polity Press.

Back, L. (1996) *New Ethnicities and Urban Culture. Racisms and multiculture in young lives*, London: UCL Press.

Baldwin, P. (1990) *The Politics of Social Solidarity. Class bases of the European welfare state 1875–1975*, Cambridge: Cambridge University Press.

Ball, S.J. (2003) *Class Strategies and the Education Market. The middle classes and social advantage*, London: RoutledgeFalmer.

Ball, S.J., Maguire, M. and Macrae, S. (2000) *Choices, Pathways and Transitions Post-16. New youth, new economies in the global city*, London: RoutledgeFalmer.

Banks, J.A. (1954) *Prosperity and Parenthood. A study of family planning among the Victorian middle class*, London: Routledge and Kegan Paul.

Bardasi, E. and Jenkins, S. (2002) *Income in later life: Work history matters*, Bristol: Policy Press, in association with the Joseph Rowntree Foundation.

Barnes, H., Parry, J. and Lakey, J. (2002) *Forging a New Future: The experiences and expectations of people leaving paid work over 50*, Bristol: Policy Press / JRF.

Baudelot, C. (2000) 'The future remains open', in Jenson, J., Laufer, J. and Maruani, M. (eds) *The Gendering of Inequalities: Women, men and work*, Aldershot: Ashgate.

Bauman, Z. (2002) 'Individually, together', Foreword to Beck, U. and Beck-Gernsheim, E., *Individualization. Institutionalized individualism and its social and political consequences*, London: Sage.

Bauman, Z. (1995) *Life in Fragments. Essays in postmodern morality*, Oxford: Blackwell.

Beck, U. (1992) *Risk Society. Towards a new modernity*, London: Sage.

Beck, U. and Beck-Gernsheim, E. (2002) *Individualization. Institutionalized individualism and its social and political consequences*, London: Sage.

Becker, G. (1991) *Treatise on the Family*, Cambridge, MA: Harvard University Press.

Beechey, V. and Perkins, T. (1987) *A Matter of Hours: Women, part-time work and the labour market*, Cambridge: Polity Press.

Bernhardt, E.M. (1993) 'Fertility and employment', *European Sociological Review* 9, 1: 25–42.

Berrington, A. (2004) 'Perpetual postponers? Women's, men's and couples' fertility intentions and subsequent fertility behaviour', *Population Trends* 117: 9–19.

Biggs, S. (1997) 'Choosing not to be old? Masks, bodies and identity management in later life', *Ageing and Society* 17: 553–70.

Biggs, S. (1993) *Understanding Ageing*, Buckingham: Open University Press.

Blackburn, R.M., Browne, J., Brooks, B. and Jarman, J. (2002) 'Explaining gender segregation', *British Journal of Sociology* 53, 4: 513–36.

Block, F. (1990) *Postindustrial Possibilities: A critique of economic discourse*, Berkeley: University of California Press.

Bonoli, G., George, V. and Taylor-Gooby, P. (2000) *European Welfare Futures. Towards a theory of retrenchment*, Cambridge: Polity Press.

Bottero, W. (2004) 'Class identities and the identity of class', *Sociology* 38, 5: 979–97.

Bottero, W. (2000) 'Gender and the labour market at the turn of the century: complexity, ambiguity and change', *Work, Employment and Society* 14, 4: 781–91.

Bottero, W. and Irwin, S. (2003) Locating difference: class, 'race' and gender and the shaping of social inequalities', *Sociological Review* 51, 4: 463–83.

Bourdieu, P. and Wacquant, L. (1992) *An Invitation to Reflexive Sociology*, Cambridge: Polity Press.

Bradley, H. (1996) *Fractured Identities: Changing patterns of inequality*, Cambridge: Polity Press.

Brah, A. (1992) 'Difference, diversity and differentiation', in Donald, J. and Rattansi, A. (eds) *'Race', Culture and Difference*, London: Sage.

Brannen, J. and Nilsen, A. (2002) 'Young people's time perspectives. From youth to adulthood', *Sociology* 36, 3: 513–37.

Braybon, G. and Summerfield, P. (1987) *Out of the Cage. Women's experiences in two world wars*, London: Pandora.

Bromley, C. (2003) 'Has Britain become immune to inequality?', in Park, A., Curtice, J., Thomson, K., Jarvis, L. and Bromley, C. (eds) *British Social Attitudes. The 20th Report. Continuity and change over two decades*, London: Sage and National Centre for Social Research.

Brookes, B. (1986) 'Women and reproduction c. 1860–1919', in Lewis, J. (ed.) *Labour and Love. Women's experience of home and family 1850–1940*, Oxford: Basil Blackwell.

Brown, P. (1997) 'The "third wave": education and the ideology of parentocracy', in Halsey, A.H., Lauder, H., Brown, P. and Stuart Wells, A. (eds) *Education. Culture, economy, society*, Oxford: Oxford University Press.

Brubaker, R. (2002) 'Ethnicity without groups', *European Journal of Sociology*, 43, 2: 163–89.

Bruegel, I. (2000) 'The restructuring of the family wage system, wage relations and gender', in Clarke, L., Gijsel, P. and Janssen, J. (eds) *The Dynamics of Wage Relations in the New Europe*, London and Dordrecht: Kluwer Academic Publishers.

Bruegel, I. (1999) 'Globalization, feminization and pay inequalities in London and the UK', in Gregory, J., Sales, R. and Hegewisch, A. (eds) *Women, Work and Inequality. The challenge of equal pay in a deregulated labour market*, Basingstoke: Macmillan.

Bruegel, I. (1996) 'Whose myths are they anyway?: a comment', *British Journal of Sociology* 47, 1: 175–7.

Bruegel, I. and Perrons, D. (1998) 'Deregulation and women's employment: the diverse experiences of women in Britain', *Feminist Economics* 4, 1: 103–25.

Burkitt, I. (1998) 'Sexuality and gender identity: from a discursive to a relational analysis', *Sociological Review* 46, 3: 483–504.

Butler, J. (1990) *Gender Trouble. Feminism and the subversion of identity*, London: Routledge.

Bygren, M. (2004) 'Pay reference standards and pay satisfaction: what do workers evaluate their pay against?', *Social Science Research* 33: 206–24.

Bynner, J. *et al.* (2002) 'The changing situation of young people', in Bynner, J., Elias, P., McKnight, A., Pan, H. and Pierre, G. (eds) *Young People's Changing Routes to Independence*, York: Joseph Rowntree Foundation.

Bynner, J. and Pan, H. (2002) 'Changes in pathways to employment and adult life?', in Bynner, J., Elias, P., McKnight, A., Pan, H. and Pierre, G. (eds) *Young People's Changing Routes to Independence*, York: Joseph Rowntree Foundation.

Caldwell, J. (1980) 'Mass education as a determinant of the timing of fertility decline', *Population and Development Review* 6, 2: 225–55.

Campbell, A. (1999) *Childfree and Sterilised. Women's decisions and medical responses*, London: Cassell.

Cannadine, D. (2000) *Class in Britain*, London: Penguin.

Castells, M. (1996) *The Rise of the Network Society*, Oxford: Blackwell.

Cliquet, R. (1991) *The Second Demographic Transition: Fact or fiction?*, Strasbourg: Council of Europe, Population Studies No. 23.

Coleman, D.A. (1998) *Reproduction and Survival in an Unknown World: What drives today's industrial populations, and to what future?*, Netherlands

Interdisciplinary Demographic Institute Hofstee Lecture Series 5, The Hague: NIDI.

Coleman, D. (1996) 'New patterns and trends in European fertility: international and sub-national comparisons', in Coleman, D. (ed.) *Europe's Population in the 1990s*, Oxford: Oxford University Press.

Creighton, C. (1999) 'The rise and decline of the "male breadwinner family" in Britain', *Cambridge Journal of Economics* 23, 5: 519–41.

Crompton, R. (2002) 'Employment, flexible working and the family', *British Journal of Sociology* 53, 4: 537–58.

Crompton, R. (ed.) (1999) *Restructuring Gender Relations and Employment. The decline of the male breadwinner*, Oxford: Oxford University Press.

Crompton, R. and Harris, F. (1998) 'Explaining women's employment patterns: "orientations to work" revisited', *British Journal of Sociology* 49, 1: 118–36.

Crompton, R., Brockmann, M. and Wiggins, R.D. (2003) 'A woman's place . . . employment and family life for men and women', in Park, A. *et al.* (eds) *British Social Attitudes. The 20th Report*, National Centre for Social Research, London: Sage.

Dale, A. and Holdsworth, C. (1998) 'Why don't minority ethnic women in Britain work part-time?', in O'Reilly, J. and Fagan, C. (eds) *Part-time Prospects. An international comparison of part-time work in Europe, North America and the Pacific Rim*, London: Routledge.

Dale, A., Shaheen, N., Kalra, V. and Fieldhouse, E. (2002) 'Routes into education and employment for young Pakistani and Bangladeshi women in the UK', *Ethnic and Racial Studies* 25, 6: 942–68.

Davidoff, L., Doolittle, M., Fink, J. and Holden, K. (1999) *The Family Story. Blood, contract and intimacy 1830–1960*, London: Longman.

Davin, A. (1978) 'Imperialism and motherhood', *History Workshop Journal* 5: 9–65.

Dex, S. (1988) *Women's Attitudes Towards Work*, Basingstoke: Macmillan.

Dex, S. and Joshi, H. (1999) 'Careers and motherhood: policies for compatibility', *Cambridge Journal of Economics* 23, 641–59.

Di Maggio, P. (1990) 'Cultural aspects of economic action and organization', in Friedland, R. and Robertson, A.F. (eds) *Beyond the Marketplace. Rethinking economy and society*, New York: Aldine de Gruyter.

Dilnot, A., Disney, R., Johnson, P. and Whitehouse, E. (1994) *Pensions Policy in the UK*, London: Institute for Fiscal Studies.

Dowd, J. (1984) 'The old person as stranger', in Marshall, V.W. (ed.) *Later Life. The social psychology of aging*, London: Sage.

Drew, E., Emerek, R. and Mahon, E. (1998) 'Introduction', in Drew, E., Emerek, R. and Mahon, E. (eds) *Women, Work and the Family in Europe*, London: Routledge.

Duncan, S. (2005) 'Mothering, class and rationality', *Sociological Review* 53, 2: 50–76.

Duncan, S. (2000a) *Localities Paper 2: Choosing case study areas for strand 3 research – localities and neighbourhoods*, CAVA Workshop Paper 17A (ERSC Research Group for the Study of Care, Values and the Future of Welfare, University of Leeds, http://www.leeds.ac.uk/cava/papers/workshoppapers.htm).

Duncan, S. (2000b) *Localities Paper 3: Variations in parenting and partnering at the local level*, CAVA Workshop Paper 17B (ERSC Research Group for the Study of Care, Values and the Future of Welfare, University of Leeds, http://www.leeds.ac.uk/cava/papers/workshoppapers.htm).

Duncan, S. (1994) 'Theorising differences in patriarchy', *Environment and Planning A* 26, 8: 1177–94.

Duncan, S. and Edwards, R. (1999) *Lone Mothers, Paid Work and Gendered Moral Rationalities*, Basingstoke: Macmillan.

Duncan, S., Edwards, R., Reynolds, T. and Alldred, P. (2003) 'Motherhood, paid work and partnering: values and theories', *Work, Employment and Society* 17, 2, 309–30.

Dyer, R. (1997) *White*, London: Routledge.

Egerton, M. and Savage, M. (2000) 'Age stratification and class formation: a longitudinal study of the social mobility of young men and women, 1971–1991', *Work, Employment and Society* 14, 1: 23–49.

Elder, G.H. (1974) *Children of the Great Depression: Social change and life experiences*, Chicago: University of Chicago Press.

Elias, N. (1985) *The Loneliness of the Dying*, Oxford: Basil Blackwell.

Elias, P. and Pierre, G. (2002) 'Pathways, earnings and well-being', in Bynner, J., Elias, P., McKnight, A., Pan, H. and Pierre, G. (eds) *Young People's Changing Routes to Independence*, York: Joseph Rowntree Foundation.

Ellison, N. (2003) 'Changing the mix: pensions, privatization and the problem of equality in old age', Paper for ESPAnet conference, Copenhagen Nov 2003, http://www.sfi.dk/graphics/ESPAnet/papers/nellison.pdf (accessed November 2003).

Ellwood, D. (1998) 'Dynamic policy making: an insider's account of reforming US welfare', in Leisering, L. and Walker, R. (eds) *The Dynamics of Modern Society*, Bristol: Policy Press.

Epstein, C.F. (1988) *Deceptive Distinctions: Sex, gender and the social order*, London/New Haven: Yale University Press.

Esping-Andersen, G. (1990) *The Three Worlds of Welfare Capitalism*, Cambridge: Polity Press.

Evandrou, M. and Falkingham, J. (2000) 'Looking back to look forward: lessons from four birth cohorts for ageing in the 21st century', *Populations Trends* 99: 27–36, London: ONS.

Fagan, C. (2001) 'Time, money and the gender order: work orientations and working time preferences in Britain', *Gender, Work and Organization* 8, 3: 239–66.

Fagan, C. and O'Reilly, J. (eds) (1998a) *Part-Time Prospects. An international comparison of part-time work in Europe, North America and the Pacific Rim*, London: Routledge.

Fagan, C. and O'Reilly, J. (1998b) 'Conceptualising part-time work: the value of an integrated comparative perspective' in O'Reilly, J. and Fagan, C. (eds) *Part-time Prospects. An international comparison of part-time work in Europe, North America and the Pacific Rim*, London: Routledge.

Falkingham, J. and Hills, J. (eds) (1995) *The Dynamic of Welfare. The welfare state and the life cycle*, London: Prentice Hall/Harvester Wheatsheaf.

Featherstone, M. and Hepworth, M. (1991) 'The mask of ageing and the postmodern life course', in Featherstone, M., Hepworth, M. and Turner, B. (eds) *The Body. Social process and cultural theory*, London: Sage.

Featherstone, M. and Wernick, A. (eds) (1995) *Images of Aging. Cultural representations of later life*, London: Routledge.

Finch, J. and Mason, J. (1993) *Negotiating Family Responsibilities*, London: Tavistock Routledge.

Foster, P., Gomm, R. and Hammersley, M. (1996) *Constructing Educational*

Inequality: An assessment of research on school processes, London: Falmer Press.

Frankenberg, R. (2000) 'White women, race matters', in Back, L. and Solomos, J. (eds) *Theories of Race and Racism*, London: Routledge.

Fraser, N. (1995) 'From redistribution to recognition? Dilemmas of justice in a "post socialist" age', *New Left Review* 212: 68–93.

Fraser, N. and Honneth, A. (2003) *Redistribution or Recognition? A political–philosophical exchange*, London: Verso.

Friedland, R. and Robertson, A.F. (1990) 'Beyond the marketplace', in Friedland, R. and Robertson, A.F. (eds) *Beyond the Marketplace. Rethinking economy and society*, New York: Aldine de Gruyter.

Friedman, M. (2000) 'Autonomy, social disruption and women', in Mackenzie, C. and Stoljar, N. (eds) *Relational Autonomy. Feminist perspectives on autonomy, agency and the social self*, Oxford: Oxford University Press.

Friedman, S.S. (1995) 'Beyond white and other: relationality and narratives of race in feminist discourse', *Signs* 21, 1: 1–49.

Furlong, A. (1998) 'Youth and social class: change and continuity', *British Journal of Sociology of Education* 19, 4: 591–7.

Furlong, A. and Cartmel, F. (1997) *Young People and Social Change. Individualization and risk in late modernity*, Buckingham: Open University Press.

Gardiner, G. (1996) *Gender, Care and Economics*, Basingstoke: Macmillan.

Gijsberts, M. (2002) 'The legitimation of income inequality in state-socialist and market societies', *Acta Sociologica* 45: 269–85.

Gillespie, R. (1999) 'Voluntary childlessness in the UK', *Reproductive Health Matters* 7, 13: 43–53.

Gillies, V., Holland, J. and Ribbens McCarthy, J. (2003) 'Past/present/future: time and the meaning of change in the "family"', in Allan, G. and Jones, G. (eds) *Social Relations and the Life Course*, Basingstoke: Palgrave Macmillan.

Gilligan, C. (1993) *In a Different Voice. Psychological theory and women's development*, Cambridge, MA, Harvard University Press.

Gillis, J.R., Tilly, L.A. and Levine, D. (eds) (1992) *The European Experience of Declining Fertility 1850–1970*, Oxford: Blackwell.

Ginn, J., Street, D. and Arber, S. (eds) (2001) *Women, Work and Pensions. International issues and prospects*, Buckingham: Open University Press.

Ginn, J. *et al.* (1996) 'Feminist fallacies: a reply to Hakim on women's employment', *British Journal of Sociology* 47, 1: 167–74.

Gittins, D. (1982) *Fair Sex. Family size and structure, 1900–39*, London: Hutchinson.

Glover, J. and Arber, S. (1995) 'Polarization in mothers' employment', *Gender, Work and Organization* 2, 4: 165–79.

Glucksmann, M. (2000) *Cottons and Casuals. The gendered organisation of labour in time and space*, Durham: sociologypress.

Glucksmann, M. (1990) *Women Assemble. Women workers and the new industries in inter-war Britain*, London: Routledge.

Goodman, A., Johnson, P. and Webb, S. (1997) *Inequality in the UK*, Oxford: Oxford University Press.

Hakim, C. (2000) *Work-lifestyle Choices in the 21st Century. Preference theory*, Oxford: Oxford University Press.

Hakim, C. (1996) *Key Issues in Women's Work. Female heterogeneity and the polarisation of women's employment*, London: Athlone Press.

Hall, S. (2000) 'Conclusion: the multicultural question', in Hesse, B. (ed.) *Un/settled Multiculturalisms: Diasporas, entanglements, transruptions*, London: Zed Books.

Handwerker, W.P. (1986) 'Culture and reproduction: exploring micro/macro linkages', in Handwerker (ed.) *Culture and Reproduction. An anthropological critique of demographic transition theory*, Boulder and London: Westview Press.

Hardy, M.A. and Waite, M. (1997) 'Doing time: reconciling biography with history in the study of social change', in Hardy, M.A. (ed.) *Studying Ageing and Social Change. Conceptual and methodological issues*, London: Sage.

Harris, J. (1993) *Private Lives, Public Spirit. Britain 1870–1914*, London: Penguin.

Harrop, A. and Moss, P. (1995) 'Trends in parental employment', *Work, Employment and Society* 9, 3: 421–44.

Haskey, J. (1996) 'The proportion of married couples who divorce: past patterns and current prospects', *Population Trends* 83: 25–36, London: ONS.

Hattery, A. (2001) *Women, Work and Family. Balancing and weaving.* Thousand Oaks and London: Sage.

Hendrick, H. (1997) *Children, Childhood and English Society 1880–1990*, Cambridge: Cambridge University Press.

Hendrick, H. (1990) 'Constructions and reconstructions of British childhood: an interpretative survey, 1800–present', in James, A. and Prout, A. (eds) *Constructing and Reconstructing Childhood: Contemporary issues in the sociological study of childhood*, London: Falmer.

Hesse, B. (2000) 'Introduction: unsettled multiculturalisms', in Hesse, B. (ed.) *Un/settled Multiculturalisms: Diasporas, entanglements, transruptions*, London: Zed Books.

Hibbett, A. and Meager, N. (2003) 'Key indicators of women's position in Britain', *Labour Market Trends*, October: 503–11.

Himmelweit, S. (2002) 'Economic theory, norms and the care gap, or: why do economists become parents?', in Carling, A., Duncan, S. and Edwards, R. (eds) *Analysing Families. Morality and rationality in policy and practice*, London: Routledge.

Hobcraft, J. (2003) 'Continuity and change in pathways to young adult disadvantage: results from a British birth cohort', CASE Paper 66, London: London School of Economics, Centre for Analysis of Social Exclusion.

Hobcraft, J. (1996) 'Fertility in England and Wales: a fifty year perspective', *Population Studies* 50: 485–524.

Hobsbawm, E. (1994) *Age of Extremes 1914–1991. The short 20th century*, London: Michael Joseph.

Hobsbawm, E. (1987) *The Age of Empire 1875–1914*, London: Weidenfeld and Nicolson.

Hobsbawm, E. (1969) *Industry and Empire*, Harmondsworth: Penguin.

Hockey, J. and James, A. (1993) *Growing Up and Growing Old. Ageing and dependency in the life course*, London: Sage.

Holdsworth, C. and Dale, A. (1997) 'Ethnic differences in women's employment', *Work, Employment and Society* 11: 435–57.

Honeyman, K. (2000) *Women, Gender and Industrialisation in England 1700–1870*, Basingstoke: Macmillan.

Honneth, A. (1995) *The Struggle for Recognition. The moral grammar of social conflicts*, Oxford: Polity Press.

Hopkins, E. (1994) *Childhood Transformed. Working class children in nineteenth century England*, Manchester: Manchester University Press.

Humphries, J. and Rubery, J. (1992) 'The legacy for women's employment: integration, differentiation and polarization', in Michie, J. (ed.) *The Economic Legacy 1979–1992*, London: Academic Press.

Hurd, L.C. (1999) '"We're not old!" Older women's negotiations of aging and oldness', *Journal of Aging Studies* 13, 4: 419–39.

Irwin, S. (2004) 'Attitudes, care and commitment. Pattern and process', *Sociological Research Online* 9, 3 http://www.socresonline.org.uk/9/3/irwin.html

Irwin, S. (1999a) 'Resourcing the family: gendered claims and obligations and issues of explanation', in Silva, E.B. and Smart, C.C. (eds) *The New Family?*, London: Sage.

Irwin, S. (1999b) 'Later life, inequality and sociological theory', *Ageing and Society* 19: 691–715.

Irwin, S. (1998) 'Age, generation and inequality: a reply to the reply', *British Journal of Sociology* 49, 2: 305–10.

Irwin, S. (1996) 'Age related distributive justice and claims on resources', *British Journal of Sociology* 47, 1: 68–92.

Irwin, S. (1995) *Rights of Passage. Social change and the transition from youth to adulthood*, London: UCL Press.

Irwin, S. and Bottero, W. (2000) 'Market returns? Gender and theories of change in employment relations', *British Journal of Sociology* 51, 2: 261–80.

Irwin, S. and Williams, F. (2002) 'Understanding social values and social change: the case of care, family and intimacy', Paper presented to the ESPRN Conference on Social Values, Social Policies, 29–31 August 2002, University of Tilburg, the Netherlands.

James, A. and Prout, A. (1990) *Constructing and Reconstructing Childhood: Contemporary issues in the sociological study of childhood*, London: Falmer.

Jarvis, L., Hinds, K., Bryson, C. and Park, A. (2000) *Women's Social Attitudes: 1983 to 1998*. A report prepared for the Women's Unit, Cabinet Office, National Centre for Social Research.

Jenkins, R. (1997) *Rethinking Ethnicity. Arguments and explorations*, London: Sage.

Jenkins, R. (1996) *Social Identity*, London: Routledge.

Jenson, J. (1986) 'Gender and reproduction: or, babies and the state', *Studies in Political Economy* 20: 9–46.

Jones, G. (2002) *The Youth Divide. Diverging paths to adulthood*, York: Joseph Rowntree Foundation.

Jones, G. and Wallace, C. (1992) *Youth, Family and Citizenship*, Milton Keynes: Open University Press.

Jones, H. (2000) *Women in British Public Life, 1914–50. Gender, power and social policy*, Harlow: Pearson Education.

Joshi, H. and Hinde, P.R.A. (1993) 'Employment after childbearing in post-war Britain: cohort study evidence on contrasts within and across generations', *European Sociological Review* 9, 3: 203–27.

Kaufman, G. and Elder, G.H. (2002) 'Revisiting age identity. A research note', *Journal of Aging Studies* 16: 169–76.

Kelley, J. and Evans, M.D.R. (1995) 'Class and class conflict in six western nations', *American Sociological Review* 60, 2: 157–78.

Kelley, J. and Evans, M.D.R. (1993) 'The legitimation of inequality: occupational earnings in nine nations', *American Journal of Sociology* 99, 1: 75–125.

Kiernan, K., Land, H. and Lewis, J. (1998) *Lone Motherhood in Twentieth Century Britain. From footnote to front page*. Oxford: Clarendon Press.

Kohli, M. (1986) 'The world we forgot: a historical review of the life course', in Marshall, V.W. (ed.) *Later Life. The social psychology of aging*, London: Sage.

Kohli, M. and Rein, M. (1991) 'The changing balance of work and retirement', in Kohli, M., Rein, M., Guillemard, A.-M. and van Gunsteren, H. (eds) *Time for Retirement. Comparative studies in early exit*, Cambridge: Cambridge University Press.

Lam, M. (2004) 'The perception of inequalities: a gender case study', *Sociology* 38, 1: 5–23.

Land, H. (1980) 'The family wage', *Feminist Review* 6, 55–78.

Leisering, L. and Walker, R. (1998) 'Making the future: from dynamics to policy agendas', in Leisering, L. and Walker, R. (eds) *The Dynamics of Modern Society*, Bristol: Policy Press.

Lesthaeghe, R. (1998) 'On theory development: applications to the study of family formation', *Population and Development Review* 24, 1: 1–14.

Lesthaeghe, R. (1995) 'The second demographic transition in Western countries: an interpretation', in Oppenheim Mason, K. and Jensen, A.-M. (eds) *Gender and Family Change in Industrialized Countries*, Oxford: Clarendon Press.

Lesthaeghe, R. and Surkyn, J. (1988) 'Cultural dynamics and economic theories of fertility change', *Population and Development Review* 14, 1: 1–45.

Levine, D. (1987) *Reproducing Families. The political economy of English population history*, Cambridge: Cambridge University Press.

Lewis, J. (2002) 'Individualisation, assumptions about the existence of an adult worker model and the shift towards contractualism', in Carling, A., Duncan, S. and Edwards, R. (eds) *Analysing Families. Morality and rationality in policy and practice*, London: Routledge.

Lewis, J. (1991) 'Models of equality for women: the case of state support for children in twentieth century Britain', in Bock, G. and Thane, P. (eds) *Maternity and Gender Policies. Women and the rise of the European welfare states, 1880s–1950s*, London: Routledge.

Lewis, J. (1986) 'The working-class wife and mother in state intervention', in Lewis, J. (ed.) *Labour and Love. Women's experience of home and family 1850–1940*, Oxford: Blackwell.

Lewis, J. (1980) *The Politics of Motherhood. Child and maternal welfare in England, 1900–1939*, London: Croom Helm.

Liebig, S. and Wegener, B. (2000) 'Is the "inner wall" here to stay? Justice ideologies in unified Germany', *Social Justice Research* 13, 2: 177–95 (International Social Justice Project, Arbeitsbericht nr. 62).

McAllister, F. and Clarke, L. (1998) *Choosing Childlessness*, London: Family Policy Studies Centre.

McClelland, K. (2000) 'England's greatness, the working man', in Hall, C., McClelland, K. and Rendal, J. (eds) *Defining the Victorian Nation. Class, race, gender and the Reform Act of 1867*, Cambridge: Cambridge University Press.

Machin, S. and Waldfogel, J. (1994) 'The decline of the male breadwinner. Changing shares of husbands' and wives' earnings in family income', STICERD discussion paper WSP/103, LSE, London.

MacInnes, J. (1998) 'Analysing patriarchy, capitalism and women's employment in Europe', *Innovation* 11, 2: 227–48.

McKie, L., Bowlby, S. and Gregory, S. (2001) 'Gender, caring and employment', *Journal of Social Policy* 30, 2: 233–58.

Mackinnon, A. (1997) *Love and Freedom. Professional women and the reshaping of personal life*, Cambridge: Cambridge University Press.

McRae, S. (2003) 'Constraints and choices in mothers' employment careers: a consideration of Hakim's preference theory', *British Journal of Sociology* 54, 3: 317–38.

McRae, S. (1999a) 'Introduction: family and household change in Britain', in McRae, S. (ed.) *Changing Britain. Families and households in the 1990s*, Oxford: Oxford University Press.

McRae, S. (ed.) (1999b) *Changing Britain. Families and households in the 1990s*, Oxford: Oxford University Press.

Marks, G. and Houston, D.M. (2002) 'Attitudes towards work and motherhood held by working and non-working mothers', *Work, Employment and Society* 16, 3: 523–36.

Marshall, V. (1986) 'A sociological perspective on aging and dying', in Marshall, V.W. (ed.) *Later Life. The social psychology of aging*, London: Sage.

Martin, J. and Roberts, C. (1984) *Women and Employment. A lifetime perspective*, London: HMSO.

Mason, J. (2004) 'Managing kinship over long distances: the significance of "the visit"', *Social Policy and Society* 3, 4: 421–9.

Mason, J. (2002) 'Qualitative interviewing: asking, listening and interpreting', in May, T. (ed.) *Qualitative Research in Action*, London: Sage.

Mason, J. (2000) 'Researching morality', CAVA Working Paper 14, http://www.leeds.ac.uk/cava/papers

Maynard, M. (1994) '"Race", gender and the concept of difference in feminist thought', in Afshar, H. and Maynard, M. (eds) *The Dynamics of 'Race' and Gender. Some feminist interventions*, London: Taylor & Francis.

Mellor, P.A. and Shilling, C. (1993) 'Modernity, self identity and the sequestration of death', *Sociology* 27, 3: 411–31.

Midwinter, E. (1997) *Pensioned Off. Retirement and income examined*, Buckingham: Open University Press.

Minichiello, V., Browne, J. and Kendig, H. (2000) 'Perceptions and conseqences of ageism: views of older people', *Ageing and Society* 20: 253–78.

Modood, T., Beishon, S. and Virdee, S. (1994) *Changing Ethnic Identitites*, London: Policy Studies Institute

Modood, T., Berthoud, R., Lakey, J., Nazroo, J., Smith, P., Virdee, S. and Beishon, S. (1997) *Ethnic Minorities in Britain. Diversity and disadvantage*, London: Policy Studies Institute.

Morell, C.M. (1994) *Unwomanly Conduct. The challenges of intentional childlessness*, London: Routledge.

Murphy, M. (1993) 'The contraceptive pill and women's employment as factors in fertility change in Britain 1963–1980: a challenge to the conventional view', *Population Studies* 47: 221–43.

Murphy, M. and Berrington, A. (1993) 'Household change in the 1980s: a review', *Population Trends* 73: 18–26, London: ONS.

Nilsen, A. and Brannen, J. (2002) 'Theorising the individual-structure dynamic', in Brannen, J., Lewis, S., Nilsen, A. and Smithson, J. (eds) *Young Europeans, Work and Family. Futures in transition*, London: Routledge.

ONS (Office for National Statistics) (2004) 'Focus on older people: labour market', National Statistics Online, http://www.statistics.gov.uk/CCI/nugget.asp?ID=878

ONS (Office for National Statistics) (2002a) *Social Trends*, no. 32, London: Stationery Office.

ONS (Office for National Statistics) (2002b) 'Report: live births in England and Wales, 2001: area of residence', *Population Trends* 108: 89–90.

ONS (Office for National Statistics) (1997a) *British Birth Statistics*, Series FM1 no. 26, London: Stationery Office.

ONS (Office for National Statistics) (1997b) *Living in Britain. Results from the General Household Survey*, London: HMSO.

Oppenheimer, V.K. (1994) 'Women's rising employment and the future of the family in industrial societies', *Population and Development Review* 20, 2: 293–342.

O'Reilly, J. and Spee, C. (1998) 'The future regulation of work and welfare: time for a revised social and gender contract?', *European Journal of Industrial Relations* 4, 3: 259–81.

Pakulski, J. and Waters, M. (1996) *The Death of Class*, London: Sage.

Pearce, D., Cantisani, G. and Laihonen, A. (1999) 'Changes in fertility and family sizes in Europe', *Population Trends* 95: 33–40, London: ONS.

Peattie, L. and Rein, M. (1983) *Women's Claims. A study in political economy*, Oxford: Oxford University Press.

Pedersen, A.W. (2004) 'Inequality as relative deprivation. A sociological approach to inequality measurement', *Acta Sociologica* 47, 1: 31–49.

Pedersen, S. (1993) *Family, Dependence and the Origins of the Welfare State. Britain and France 1914–1945*, Cambridge: Cambridge University Press.

Pedersen, S. (1989) 'The failure of feminism in the making of the British welfare state', *Radical History Review* 43: 86–110.

Pfau-Effinger, B. (1998) 'Culture or structure as explanations for differences in part-time work in Germany, Finland and the Netherlands?', in O'Reilly, J. and Fagan, C. (eds) *Part-time Prospects. An international comparison of part-time work in Europe, North America and the Pacific Rim*, London: Routledge.

Pfau-Effinger, B. (1994) 'The gender contract and part-time paid work by women – Finland and Germany compared', *Environment and Planning A* 26, 9: 1355–76.

Phillips, A. (1999) *Which Inequalities Matter?*, Oxford: Polity Press.

Phillipson, C. (1998) *Reconstructing Old Age. New agendas in social theory and practice*, London: Sage.

Podder, N. (1996) 'Relative deprivation, envy and economic inequality', *Kyklos* 49, 3: 353–76.

Priestley, M. (2000) 'Adults only: disability, social policy and the life course', *Journal of Social Policy* 29, 3: 421–39.

Reay, D. (1998a) *Class Work. Mothers' involvement in their children's primary schooling*, London: UCL Press.

Reay, D. (1998b) 'Engendering social reproduction: mothers in the educational marketplace', *British Journal of Sociology of Education* 19, 2: 195–215.

Reay, D. (1998c) 'Rethinking social class: qualitative perspectives on class and gender', *Sociology* 32, 2: 259–75.

Riley, M.W., Kahn, R.L. and Foner, A. (eds) (1994a) *Age and Structural Lag. Society's failure to provide meaningful opportunities in work, family, and leisure*, New York: Wiley-Interscience.

Riley, M. W., Kahn, R.L. and Foner, A. (1994b) 'Introduction: the mismatch between people and structures', in Riley, M.W., Kahn, R.L. and Foner, A. (eds) *Age and Structural Lag. Society's failure to provide meaningful opportunities in work, family and leisure*, New York: John Wiley and Sons.

Roberts, E. (1995) *Women and Families. An oral history, 1940–1970*, Oxford: Blackwell.

Roberts, E. (1986) 'Women's strategies, 1890–1940' in Lewis, J. (ed.) *Labour and Love. Women's experience of home and family 1850–1940*, Oxford: Blackwell.

Roberts, E. (1984) *A Woman's Place. An oral history of working-class women 1890–1940*, Oxford: Blackwell.

Roberts, K. (1968) 'The entry into employment: an approach towards a general theory', *Sociological Review* 16, 1: 165–84.

Roberts, K., Clarke, S.C. and Wallace, C. (1994) 'Flexibility and individualisation: a comparison of transitions into employment in England and Germany', *Sociology* 28, 1: 31–54.

Rose, N. (1999) *Powers of Freedom. Reframing political thought*, Cambridge: Cambridge University Press.

Rose, S. (1992) *Limited Livelihoods. Gender and class in nineteenth century England*, London: Routledge.

Roseneil, S. (1995) 'The coming of age of feminist sociology: some issues of practice and theory for the next twenty years', *British Journal of Sociology* 46, 2: 191–205.

Ross, E. (1993) *Love and Toil. Motherhood in outcast London 1870–1918*, Oxford: Oxford University Press.

Rubery, J. (1997) 'Wages and the labour market', *British Journal of Industrial Relations* 35, 3: 337–66.

Rubery, J. (1996) 'The labour market outlook and the outlook for labour market analysis', in Crompton, R., Gallie, D. and Purcell, K. (eds) *Changing Forms of Employment. Organisations, skills and gender*, London: Routledge.

Rubery, J., Smith, M. and Fagan, C. (1999) *Women's Employment in Europe. Trends and prospects*, London: Routledge.

Runciman, W.G. (1966) *Relative Deprivation and Social Justice. A study of attitudes to social inequality in twentieth-century England*, London: Routledge and Kegan Paul.

Savage, M. (2000) *Class Analysis and Social Transformation*, Buckingham: Open University Press.

Savage, M., Bagnall, G. and Longhurst, B. (2001) 'Ordinary, ambivalent and defensive: class identities in the northwest of England', *Sociology* 35, 4: 875–92.

Sayer, A. (2004) 'Moral economy', Department of Sociology, Lancaster University, at http://www.comp.lancs.ac.uk/sociology/papers.sayer-moral-economy.pdf (accessed June 2004).

Sayer, A. (2002) 'What are you worth? Why class is an embarrassing subject', *Sociological Research Online* 7, 3, http://www.socresonline.org.uk/7/3/sayer.html

Scott, J., Alwin, D.F. and Brown, M. (1996) 'Changing sex-role attitudes', *Sociology* 30, 3: 471–92.

Scott, J., Braun, M. and Alwin, D. (1998) 'Partner, parent, worker: family and gender roles', in Jowell, R. *et al.* (eds) *British and European Social Attitudes. The 15th Report*, Aldershot: SCPR/Ashgate.

Seccombe, W. (1993) *Weathering the Storm. Working-class families from the industrial revolution to the fertility decline*, London: Verso.

Sennett, R. and Cobb, J. (1973) *The Hidden Injuries of Class*, New York: Vintage Books.

Siim, B. (2000) *Gender and Citizenship. Politics and agency in France, Britain and Denmark*, Cambridge: Cambridge University Press.

Siltanen, J. (1994) *Locating Gender*, London: UCL Press.

Silva, E. and Smart, C.C. (eds) (1999) *The New Family?*, London: Sage.

Skeggs, B. (1997) *Formations of Class and Gender. Becoming respectable*, London: Sage.

Smallwood, S. (2002) 'New estimates of trends in births by birth order in England and Wales', *Population Trends* 108: 32–48, London: ONS.

Smallwood, S. and Jefferies, J. (2003) 'Family building intentions in England and Wales: trends, outcomes and interpretations', *Population Trends* 112: 15–28, London: ONS.

Smart, C. (1997) 'Wishful thinking or harmful tinkering? Sociological reflections on family policy', *Journal of Social Policy* 26, 3: 301–21.

Smart, C. and Shipman, R. (2004) 'Visions in monochrome: families, marriage and the individualisation thesis', *British Journal of Sociology* 55, 4: 491–509.

Smart, C., Neale, B. and Wade, A. (2001) *The Changing Experience of Childhood: Families and divorce*, Cambridge: Polity Press.

Smith, K. (2002) 'Some critical observations on the use of the concept of "ethnicity" in Modood *et al.*, Ethnic minorities in Britain', *Sociology* 36, 2: 399–417.

Smith, M., Fagan, C. and Rubery, J. (1998) 'Where and why is part-time work growing in Europe?', in O'Reilly, J. and Fagan, C. (eds) *Part-time Prospects. An international comparison of part-time work in Europe, North America and the Pacific Rim*, London: Routledge.

Sniderman, P.M. and Carmines, E.G. (1997) *Reaching Beyond Race*, Cambridge, MA/London: Harvard University Press.

Solomos, J. and Back, L. (1996) *Racism and Society*, Basingstoke: Macmillan.

Springfeldt, P. (1991) 'Sweden', in Rallu, J.-L. and Blum, A. (eds) *European Population. Volume 1: Country analysis*, Montrouge, France: John Libby Eurotext, for the European Population Conference.

Stephens, W.B. (1998) *Education in Britain 1750–1914*, Basingstoke: Macmillan.

Strohmeier, K.P. and Kuijsten, A. (1997) 'Family life and family policies in Europe: an introduction', in Kaufmann, F.-X., Kuijsten, A., Schulze, H.-J. and Strohmeier, K.P. (eds) *Family Life and Family Policies in Europe. Volume 1: Structures and trends in the 1980s*, Oxford: Clarendon Press.

Szreter, S. (1996) *Fertility, Class and Gender in Britain, 1860–1940*, Cambridge: Cambridge University Press.

Taylor, B. (1983) *Eve and the New Jerusalem. Socialism and feminism in the nineteenth century*, London: Virago Press.

Thair, T. and Risdon, A. (1999) 'Women in the labour market: results from the spring Labour Force Survey', *Labour Market Trends* 107, 3: 103–28.

Thane, P. (2002) *Old Age in English History. Past experience, present issues*, Oxford: Oxford University Press.

Thane, P. (1999) 'Population politics in post-war British culture', in Conekin, B., Mort, F. and Waters, C. (eds) *Moments of Modernity. Reconstructing Britain 1945–64*, London: Rivers Oram Press.

Thane, P. (1991) 'Visions of gender in the making of the British welfare state: the case of women in the British Labour Party and social policy, 1906–1945', in Bock,

G. and Thane, P. (eds) *Maternity and Gender Policies. Women and the rise of the European welfare states, 1880s–1950s*, London: Routledge.

Therborn, G. (2002) 'Class perspectives: shrink or widen?', *Acta Sociologica* 45: 221–5.

Thompson, E.P. (1991) *The Making of the English Working Class*, London: Penguin.

Thompson, J. (1980) 'The age at which childbearing starts – a longitudinal study', *Population Trends* 21: 10–13, London: ONS.

Thomson, K. (1995) 'Working mothers: choice or circumstance?', in Jowell, R. *et al. British Social Attitudes: The 12th Report*, London: Sage/NCSR.

Tilly, L.A. and Scott, J.W. (1989) *Women, Work and Family*, London: Routledge.

Tomlinson, J. (2003) 'How are women's decisions about transitions in and out of part-time work affected by their work/life balance and changing policy and employment contexts?' unpublished thesis, University of Leeds.

Turner, B. (1998) 'Ageing and generational conflicts: a reply to Sarah Irwin', *British Journal of Sociology* 49, 2: 299–304.

Turner, B. (1995) 'Aging and identity: some reflections on the somatization of the self', in Featherstone, M. and Wernick, A. (eds) *Images of Aging. Cultural representations of later life*, London: Routledge.

Turner, B. (1989) 'Ageing, politics and sociological theory', *British Journal of Sociology* 40, 4: 588–606.

Twomey, B. (2002) 'Women in the labour market: results from the spring 2001 Labour Force Survey', *Labour Market Trends* 110, 3: 109–27.

Van de Kaa, D.J. (1996) 'Anchored narratives: the story and findings of half a century of research into the determinants of fertility', *Population Studies* 50: 389–432.

Van Krieken, R. (1997) 'Sociology and the reproductive self: demographic transitions and modernity', *Sociology* 31, 3: 445–71.

Vincent, J.A. (1995) *Inequality and Old Age*, London: UCL Press.

Wacquant, L.D. (1992) 'Towards a social praxeology: the structure and logic of Bourdieu's sociology', in Bourdieu, P. and Wacquant, L.D. *An Invitation to Reflexive Sociology*, Oxford: Polity Press

Walby, S. (2001) 'From community to coalition. The politics of recognition as the handmaiden of the politics of equality in an era of globalization', *Theory, Culture and Society* 18, 2–3: 113–35.

Walby, S. (1997) *Gender Transformations*, London: Routledge

Walby, S. (1992) 'Post-post-modernism? Theorising social complexity', in Barrett, M. and Phillips, A. (eds) *Destabilizing Theory. Contemporary feminist debates*, Oxford: Polity Press.

Walby, S. (1986) *Patriarchy at Work. Patriarchy and capitalist relations in employment*, Oxford: Polity Press.

Walkerdine, V., Lucey, H. and Melody, J. (2001) *Growing up Girl: Psycho-social explorations of gender and class*, Basingstoke: Palgrave.

Wallman, S. (1986) 'Ethnicity and the boundary process in context', in Rex, J. and Mason, D. (eds) *Theories of Race and Ethnic Relations*, Cambridge: Cambridge University Press.

Ward, C., Dale, A. and Joshi, H. (1996) 'Combining employment with childcare: an escape from dependence?', *Journal of Social Policy* 25, 2: 223–47.

Warren, T. (2001) 'Divergent female part-time employment in Britain and Denmark and the implications for gender equity', *Sociological Review* 49, 4: 223–47.

Warren, T. (2000) 'Diverse breadwinner models: a couple-based analysis of gendered working time in Britain and Denmark', *Journal of European Social Policy* 10, 4: 349–71.

Webb, S. (1993) 'Women's incomes: past, present and prospects', *Fiscal Studies* 14, 4: 14–36.

Wendell, S. (1996) *The Rejected Body: Feminist philosophical reflections on disability*, London: Routledge.

Williams, F. (2004) *Rethinking Families*, London: Calouste Gulbenkian Foundation.

Williams, F. (2001) 'Changing families – changing values?', Paper given to the National Family and Parenting Institute at the Launch of Parents' Week, October 2001, http://www.leeds.ac.uk/cava/papers/changingfamilies.htm

Williams, F. (1999) 'Good-enough principles for welfare', *Journal of Social Policy* 28, 4: 667–87.

Williams, R. (1961) *The Long Revolution*, London: Chatto and Windus.

Willmott, H. (2000) 'Death. So what? Sociology, sequestration and emancipation', *Sociological Review* 48, 4: 649–65.

Wray, S. (2003) 'Women growing older: agency, ethnicity and culture', *Sociology* 37, 3: 511–28.

Wright Mills, C. (1959) *The Power Elite*, Oxford: Oxford University Press.

Young, I.M. (1997a) 'Difference as a resource for democratic communication', in Bohman, J. and Rehg, W. (eds) *Deliberative Democracy. Essays on reason and politics*, Cambridge, MA: MIT Press.

Young, I.M. (1997b) *Intersecting Voices: Dilemmas of gender, political philosophy and policy*, Princeton: Princeton University Press.

Young, I. (1990) *Justice and the Politics of Difference*, Princeton: Princeton University Press.

Zaidi, A., Rake, K. and Falkingham, J. (2001) *Income Mobility in Later Life*, SAGE Discussion Paper No. 3, London School of Economics.

Zelizer, V. (1985) *Pricing the Priceless Child*, Princeton: Princeton University Press.

Index